WHERE SILENCE SPEAKS

WHERE
SILENCE
SPEAKS

Feminism,
Social
Theory,
and
Religion

VICTORIA LEE ERICKSON

Fortress Press   *Minneapolis*

WHERE SILENCE SPEAKS
FEMINISM, SOCIAL THEORY, AND RELIGION

Scripture quotations unless otherwise noted are from the Revised Standard Version of the Bible, copyright © 1946, 1952, and 1971 by the Division of Christian Education of the National Council of Churches. Used with permission.

Cover design: Judy Swanson

Library of Congress Cataloging-in-Publication Data

Erickson, Victoria Lee, 1955–
    Where silence speaks : feminism, social theory, and religion / Victoria Lee Erickson.
        p.   cm.
    Includes bibliographical references and index.
    ISBN 0-8006-2635-4 (alk. paper) : $
    1. Religion and sociology.   2. Feminism—Religious aspects.
3. Durkheim, Emile, 1858–1917.   4. Weber, Max, 1864–1920.
I. Title.
BL60.E75   1993
306.6'082—dc20   92–26577
                                                                      CIP

The paper used in this publication meets the minimum requirements of American National Standard for Information Sciences—Permanence of Paper for Printed Library Materials, ANSI Z329.48–1984. ∞™

Manufactured in the U.S.A.   AF 1–2635

97   96   95   94   93   1   2   3   4   5   6   7   8   9   10

*Dedicated to my colleague Dale T. Irvin.
In memory of Otto H. Peterson, my grandfather,
who knew the sacred and resisted.*

For Germany the criticism of religion *is in the main complete, and the criticism of religion is the premise of all criticism.* . . . *The immediate* task of philosophy, *which is at the service of history, once the* holy form *of human estrangement has been unmasked, is to unmask self-estrangement in its* unholy forms. *Thus the criticism of heaven turns into the criticism of the earth.* . . . *Luther, we grant, overcame the bondage of* piety *by replacing it by the bondage of* conviction. . . . *It was no longer the case of the layman's struggle against the* priest outside himself *but of his struggle against* . . . *his* priestly nature.

—Karl Marx and Frederick Engels, *On Religion*

Do not trust in these deceptive words: "This is the temple of the Lord, the temple of the Lord, the temple of the Lord." For if you truly amend your ways and your doings, if you truly act justly one with another, if you do not oppress the alien, the orphan, and the widow, or shed innocent blood in this place, and if you do not go after other gods to your own hurt, then I will dwell with you in this place. . . . *For in the day I brought your ancestors out of the land of Egypt, I did not speak to them or command them concerning burnt offerings and sacrifices. But this command I gave them, "Obey my voice and I will be your God, and you shall be my people; and walk only in the way I command you so that it may be well with you.* . . . *Yet, they did not listen to me, or pay attention, but they stiffened their necks. They did worse than their ancestors did.*

—Jeremiah 7:4-6, 22, 26

CONTENTS

CONTENTS

Part Two
MEN, BEASTS, CATTLE, AND SEEDS: MAX WEBER

Part Three
SPEAKING IN THE DARK AND HEARING THE VOICES

CONTENTS

PREFACE

Religion has long been recognized as a significant source of personal and collective power, or disempowerment, one that cannot be neglected. Pursuing sources of power and disempowerment, this book advances a feminist critique of and dialogue with classical social theory of religion and its dichotomizing of social life into the sacred and the profane. My feminist rereading of classic texts locates an implicit gender bias in the development of social theories of religion themselves. The search for a deeper understanding of gender inequality, as a base for a feminist social theory of religion, has led to engaging the silences within the classic texts. These silences are about gender and power.

The primary goal of feminist research is to understand how gender figures in relationships of power between people. Some feminists have also sought to understand how "gender" itself arises in the first place. Feminist theorists need to hold a clearer theoretical and practical understanding of how religion participates in the creation of gendered identity and then how it produces the violent forces that threaten to destroy, and often do destroy, women's spiritual, moral, and physical lives.

Feminist practitioners, biblical scholars, theologians, ethicists, and philosophers of religion have contributed significantly to our understanding of the dynamics of gendered religious life. They include Carol Christ (1987), Mary Daly (1968, 1978), Elisabeth Schüssler Fiorenza (1983, 1984), Jacquelyn Grant (1989), Beverly Harrison (1983, 1986), Ada María Isasi-Díaz (1987, 1993); Rosemary Radford Ruether (1983,

1985); Starhawk (1979, 1982); Luisah Teish (1985); and Phyllis Trible (1978, 1984). These feminist scholars desire to liberate and empower women, to discover, create, re-create, and reclaim women's experiences. They frequently discuss religion's exclusion of women and its propensity for seeing women as unclean or profane. Their work finds that women are not really "profane," and so various feminist scholars and thinkers have explored the "sacredness" of women's lives: the possibilities of "woman church," the return to goddess worship, and the potential of magic. Research like Trible's *Texts of Terror* (1984), which stays within and accepts the integrity of the "profane" sphere and wrestles with it on its own terms, without attempting to sacralize it, is becoming less rare. Trible's work also demonstrates the kind of labor required in order to hear into the silences of a gendered world. More typically, feminist research accepts the "profane" reality as such and celebrates it as "pagan" or argues for it as "really sacred" (see, e.g., Christ 1987, Teish 1985).

Feminist researchers would agree that contributions can still be made, particularly by sociology, to feminist analyses of the role of religion in social production of gendered power-domination relationships. For example, we still do not understand sufficiently what it means to "sacralize women's experience," to call women "sacred," to name certain activities as women's "sacred rituals." Just what is a feminist sociological understanding of "the sacred" and of "religion"?

Yet for sociology and social theory of religion to contribute to feminist analyses, they must follow the other disciplines and reexamine their own basic tools. Social theorists must be willing to name the gender biases within their own discipline that hinder the development of a feminist sociology of religion. I believe that in the sociology of religion no tool is more critical, no bias more important than the gendered concept of "sacred" and "profane" life. Feminist social scientists such as Gilkes (1985, 1986) and Jay (1981, 1992) have already contributed to this area.

Attempts to understand dichotomized life certainly precede modern feminism. It is obvious that the sociology of religion as a discipline is profoundly indebted to the sociological observations and theories of Emile Durkheim and Max Weber (see Randall Collins's review 1982). But not so obvious are their implicit theories of gender. Feminist researchers should not be altogether surprised by systematic gender bias and methodological gender blindness. We come to expect them (e.g., see Harding 1987). Unexplored gender bias is dangerous. It allows the use of definitions and assumptions that keep our theories anchored in patriarchal thinking.

The purpose of exegeting bias is not simply to critique but also to initiate dialogue, that is, to clear space within the disciplines for deepened observations and analyses of social life. It is surprising how much space can be cleared for reinterpreting and reconstructing of social realities.

It would make sense, then, that a feminist theory of religion would seek an intimate understanding of the discipline's use of gender-biased concepts, such as sacred/profane and religion/magic, that serve as foundational supports. Unfortunately, a comprehensive treatment of the sociology and theory of religion cannot be undertaken here. Instead I will narrow my focus to the above-named key conceptual units as found in Durkheim's and Weber's and a few other theorists' work on religion. My choice of Durkheim and Weber is motivated by the fact that Durkheim's theoretical observations need to be more widely examined by feminists because they are often silently and opaquely lodged in contemporary feminist discourse on religion; and Weber's work on religion can be used by feminists to understand gender-blind theories of social life.

This rereading does not attempt to rescue either theorist. Despite its very close reading, it is not a defense of Durkheim's structural functionalism or sociological idealism, but an acknowledgment, following Godlove (1986), that Durkheim's considerations are so significantly far-reaching that they are hard to put off. Likewise, this rereading of Weber is an attempt to stand on the shoulders of a giant in order to understand the Western crisis in masculinity and to catch a glimpse of the magical way of life that offended as well as enchanted Weber.

The sacred/profane dichotomy serves a multitude of exclusionary purposes. Not only does it help to justify misogyny, it also protects other oppressions, such as racism and homophobia. This text thus owes a great debt to the resistance to white, middle-class feminist theory by black, Latin, and Native American feminist, womanist, and *mujerista* scholarship (see Patricia Collins's review [1990] of black feminist theory; although she finds empirical studies of black women's religiosity, she names no black feminist theory of religion). Challenged also by resistant and gay-affirming scholarship, I began this study open to discovering possible connections among race, religion, and homophobia (and was subsequently pleased to discover Eve Kosofsky Sedgwick's *Epistemology of the Closet* [1990], which will make a stellar, but indirect, contribution to religious studies through its critique of language and literature). In general, I find sexism, heterosexism, and racism to be so intimately intertwined with religion that to examine them separately is to frustrate the larger liberation project.

As my colleagues remind me, however, the question remains: Why begin constructing a feminist social theory of religion with a book on Durkheim and Weber? Why them? I have spent many years engaged with women in the church, feminist theology, and feminist social theory. This interdisciplinary and multileveled engagement has started me on a journey I have called "back to the basics."

My colleagues on the Great Journey have challenged and teased out of me my social constructionist perspective. They have invited me to a clearer definition of those spaces in social life where gender is constructed. Defending these positions required that I look for resources in addition to those developed within feminist social theory itself, a field that has remained relatively uninterested in religion. Given that socially constructed gender relationships condition not only women's lives but men's as well, I found that feminism's historically rightful focus on women had not yet produced a sufficiently broad understanding of the gendered lives of men. It seemed obvious to me that this lack of data directly affected what feminists could say about the role of religion in gendered power.

From my ethnomethodological perspective I returned to the classics with an understanding that "people know more about their lives than researchers think they do." I began this rereading by asking: Is there something that Durkheim and Weber wrote about their lives, religion, and masculine identity (and therefore of feminine identity) that feminists have not yet explored in their work?

Furthermore, I was pursued by a nagging desire to begin to unravel the multiple feminist uses of "the sacred and the profane." Since feminist thought has not fallen out of nowhere, I began a search for the origins of sociological understandings of these concepts. Thus these two questions—(1) where can I find rich descriptive material that would lend itself to expanded theorizing on the social construction of gendered identity as it relates to religion? and (2) where are the primary sources for our sociological understanding of the sacred in social life?—led me to reread Durkheim and Weber, two theorists who defined and authored the modern, Euro-American discourse on religion. Prolific writers, these sociologists produced extensive libraries that are not yet exhausted of their resources.

Although Durkheim and Weber have been classified, respectively, as conservative and liberal thinkers, there is a radical quality about their work that arises from their desire to make the world a better place. For the most part, they attempted these improvements without God and without Woman. Their radical colleague Karl Marx did the same. None of these men, however, dispensed with "the sacred"; it remained an operative tool in the building of theory and social life. This observation might lead us to ask: What socially produced systems of accountability created these affirmations and exclusions? Is it possible to discover the social mechanisms that link gender and "the sacred"?

This book, then, did not grow out of criticism only. It approaches Durkheim and Weber as friends, colleagues in the struggle for human dignity. It agrees with Rose Laub Coser (1989) in questioning whether feminist and women's theory is any better than profeminist and men's theory. Even so, in this text I do not critique feminist theory in the same way I critique the masculine thinking found in the classics; that project belongs to another book. Moreover, I promote dialogue with Durkheim and Weber in addition to critique. They are men who sought a just and moral life for their age or era and gave their lives to these efforts; they have much to offer to feminist concerns for justice. The fact that Durkheim and Weber were profoundly focused on particular concerns that do not adequately address contemporary feminist liberation questions shapes the conversation I have tried to create across this century of sociological inquiry.

The conversation occasioned here challenges me to work harder at inclusivity, to work at dismantling our racial, ethnic, class, and heterosexual biases within the context of feminism. Efforts such as these are made all the more difficult when the question arose for me: Is feminism currently an inclusive enough context in which to address these concerns?

To make this book a discussion, it needs the reader's active critique. It can then become one in a collectivity of voices creating inclusive and sociable communities. It will be sociable accountabilities between gendered persons that enable people to grasp the everyday, grace-filled community that Durkheim and Weber, in their own brokenheartedness, tried to leave behind but never could. Perhaps when people learn to live together justly we will learn how to live without "gender."

Victoria Lee Erickson

ACKNOWLEDGMENTS

The most difficult part of writing this book has been containing the size of the acknowledgments; there are many more people who contributed to my work than there is space to name. My Master of Divinity students at Union Theological Seminary and Doctor of Ministry students at New York Theological Seminary have heard and read various sections of this text. Their reflections and willingness to debate ideas have been most helpful. I wish specifically to thank Irene Monroe, Moses Knott, Douglas Donley, Renee Hill, Vivian Brown, Lisa Hill, and Melissa Aase, who stretched me in areas all too well known to them.

My companions along the way shared more of the burden than I had anticipated would need sharing. For high-quality child care I am grateful to Tammy Erickson, Doreen Irvin, Patricia Hazeltine, and Sonia Ramirez. These friends provided spiritual encouragement, as did Cynthia Stuen, Bill Weisenbach, Mary Solberg, Kathleen Talvacchia, Julie Duncan, and Agenta Enermalm-Ogawa. My colleagues Ada María Isasi-Díaz, Janet Walton, Joan Speaks, Susan Farrell, Angela Bauer, Linda Pershing, Russell Davis, Minka Sprague, Susan Davies, Angela Askew, and Pam Darling have shared not only much needed critique but encouragement and, most importantly, a feminist soulfulness that empowered the Great Search. I am deeply grateful to the many people who refereed and responded to articles, lectures, chapters, and papers at the AAR, ASA, ASR, SSSR, and RRA meetings. I would like especially to thank Larry Rasmussen, Eleanor Scott Meyers, Edward Lehman, Jr., Dan Spencer, and Cindy Slominski.

This text has been read in its entirety by several wise and dedicated persons who might wish, when they see this final product, that more of their wisdom had been incorporated. This book would not have been completed without Roslyn Wallach Bologh's gift of endless hours of reading and critique that have shaped these pages in significant ways. Her willingness to catch the spirit of the project and reread Durkheim with me is evidence of the feminist collegiality she tirelessly advocates. Her own work on Max Weber widened my approach to his sociology of religion. Stanley Aronowitz, Beverly Harrison, William Kornblum, and T. Richard Snyder read and critiqued the manuscript, and their feminist, profeminist, and global liberationist perspectives have provided valuable reflections and have greatly contributed to the outline of my next book. I want to thank Lindsy Churchill for believing in this project at the first and crucial moment. A great debt is owed to Seth Kasten of the Burke Library. Also, there are people who have not read a word of this book, but who understand the soul's need for laughter: Dick Norris, Christopher Morse, and Garland Walker.

The heartbeat of this text can be heard by listening through the lives of other people. The memory of the many women who nurtured me in the kitchens of Lutheran churches in Minnesota pushed me to understand what caused the differences between kitchen spirituality and the theology found in the sanctuary. Coparenting my sons Douglas Steven and Andrew Thomas Irvin-Erickson has taught me to listen well to their own struggles in becoming sociable people; by the age of five both boys began to document for me the sources of masculine identity as found in religion and ritual life. Their lives have reinforced the ethnomethodological principle that the theory of everyday life is found in the practice of everyday life.

Contained in this text is a great hope for the future of communities of faith. The progressive praxis of this hope found a home in the United Church of Christ, where its flames were fanned by the leadership of Bill and Helen Weber and Bill and Suzie Briggs. It also found a home with Fortress Press. My colleague Kosuke Koyama and I have talked about what it will take to turn our intellectual ships into nipa huts, and to turn our work into sounds created out of the accountabilities produced in everyday life. A significant part of what it takes is a good editor like J. Michael West. I am also greatly indebted to Ann M. Potthoff and Nancy Benvenga for excellent copyediting and design work. Artist Judy Swanson caught the soul of this project in delightful ways. When God and the angels crafted this story they sprinkled it with humor. But then they are good at crafting stories. My life with Dale Irvin, which produces books out of a shared computer and familyhood out of a small apartment in Manhattan, is filled with cosmic drama. However, God, the angels, good editors, and friends are not responsible for my deficiencies—all errors are mine alone.

Finally, I am grateful to the following publishers for permissions to quote from their works:

The poem by Joy Harjo is from *Secrets from the Center of the World* by Joy Harjo and Stephen Strom (Tucson: The University of Arizona Press, 1989). Used by permission of the publisher.

The poems by Reynaldo Clemena Ileto are from *Pasyon and Revolution: Popular Movements in the Philippines, 1840–1910* (Quezon City: Ateneo de Manila University Press, 1979). Used by permission of the publisher.

The excerpt from "Letter from the Elysian Fields" by Jane Kramer is from *The New Yorker*, March 2, 1987, and is used by permission of *The New Yorker*.

Excerpts from *Sociology of Religion* by Max Weber, English translation copyright © 1963 Beacon Press, are used by permission of the publisher.

Excerpts from *Economy and Society*, vols. 1 and 2, by Max Weber, trans. and ed. by G. Roth and C. Wittich, are copyright © 1978 by the Regents of the University of California. Used by permission of the University of California Press.

Excerpts from *General Economic History* by Max Weber, copyright © 1984 Transaction Publishers, are used by permission of the publisher.

Excerpts from *Suicide* by Max Weber, tr. John A. Spaulding and George Simpson (New York: The Free Press, 1951), are used by permission of Macmillan Publishing Co.

Excerpts from *The Elementary Forms of Religious Life* by Emile Durkheim, tr. Joseph Ward Swain (New York: The Free Press, 1965), are used by permission of The Free Press, a division of Macmillan, Inc.

Excerpts from *Moral Education* by Emile Durkheim, tr. E. K. Wilson and Herman Schnurer (New York: The Free Press, 1973), are used by permission of Macmillan Publishing Co.

Excerpts from *The Division of Labor in Society* by Emile Durkheim, with an introduction by Lewis A. Coser, tr. W. D. Halls (New York: The Free Press, 1984), are used by permission of Macmillan Publishing Co.

Excerpts from *On Morality and Society* by Emile Durkheim, ed. Robert N. Bellah (Chicago: The University of Chicago Press, 1973), are used by permission of the publisher.

Part One

ON GENDER, VIOLENCE, AND RELIGION
Emile Durkheim

1

THE SEARCH

FOR ELEMENTARY

FORMS

*Once women wove blankets
to warm their children
out of love
and, out of love and
fierce desire of
their own hearts,
they made them beautiful.*

*Their art did not hang
on museum walls
but covered bodies
of sleeping children.
(Where is your Rembrandt?
the men asked us.)
She was a Navaho
and the white man killed her.*

Kathleen Thompson poster

In a stimulating book, *Sociological Insight: An Introduction to Non-Obvious
Sociology* (1982, v), Randall Collins proclaims that "real knowledge
ought to be communicable. It should be possible to say it so that it is

understood. And there should be something to say, something which makes a difference once you know it, something you did not already know before." Collins proceeds to show how Emile Durkheim's sociology of religion uncovered something new and vital about religion, identity, and power. A feminist perspective points out something new about the effects of gender on sociological interpretation and theorizing. The hard part about Collins's challenge is that while there are no new things to be said about women's oppression, what is new is a theory that attempts to explain experiences voiced by feminists for a long time.

We know these experiences; they are all too common to the world of people who are gendered female. To name only three examples: not so long ago a female colleague was prevented from officiating as clergy at a community gathering by a male colleague who "did not believe in the ordination of women"; "Christians" are regularly heard discussing homeless people in terms denoting a lower social status, a status from which "they" can be "rescued"; and a lesbian mother's baby girl was refused baptism by the pastor of her church and by other local pastors as well. The baby's and mother's spiritual health was attended to by a feminist pastor who found, gathered at the baptism, a community of people joyfully willing to "raise the child in the faith." These story fragments represent types of social death facilitated by a holy violence that establishes quite clearly, on an individual and social level, who is profane. Although feminists have made great strides in understanding how religion produces the violent forces that threaten to destroy and often do destroy our spiritual, moral, and physical lives, we still have a long way to go. Yet a cup of cold water might appear from an unexpected source. Far from attempting to rescue Durkheimian sociology, I argue here that once his gender-blind theory is reexamined, theorists may find a resource in Emile Durkheim, who, a century ago, sought to understand the role of religion in social life, and in doing so documented the role and purpose of violence in religion.

Method

In *The Elementary Forms of Religious Life* (1965), Emile Durkheim (1858–1917) began his sociology of religion by explaining what religion is not. It is not about things "supernatural" (39), and it is not about things "divine" (44). Religion is a set of beliefs and rites that

> presuppose the classification of all the things real and ideal, of which men think, into classes or opposed groups, generally designated by two

distinct terms which are translated well enough by the words *profane* and *sacred* (*profane, sacré*). This division of the world into two domains, the one containing all that is sacred, the other all that is profane, is the distinctive trait of religious thought; the beliefs, myths, dogmas and legends are either representations or systems of representations which express the nature of sacred things, the virtues and powers which are attributed to them, or their relations with each other and with profane things. (1965, 52; emphasis original)

People in everyday life think about things real and ideal, and it is through religion (a set of beliefs and rites) that they categorize things they see (real and ideal) as sacred or profane. The real and ideal things contemplated include frequent references to birth and death. Religion, then, is a way of knowing and thinking about reality.

In Durkheim's ethnographic description of them, belief and rites systems function to address difference, knowledge, and meaning. Thus religion identifies, classifies, and establishes identity. Religion and identity may be "secular," as Robert Bellah points out in his "civil religion" thesis, which examines the religion of humanity and the cult of the individual (1975). Or, as Durkheim discusses it in *The Elementary Forms*, it may be a religion of "sacred" things—perhaps including gods and deities with their adoring or questioning adherents.

In either case, identity must be secured or made sacred. I have chosen to focus on the identity that is made sacred and is related to sacred beliefs and rites. I agree with Hans Mol (with whom Bellah would not disagree) that religion is the "sacralization of identity" and that "the mechanisms of sacralization consist of objectification, commitment, ritual, and myth . . . religion defines man and his space in the universe" (1976, ix–x, 2). Furthermore, in establishing this space, religion finds it necessary to control, or at least direct, all socially constructed identities (differentiations) in its effort to maintain social order. "Religion always appears to modify or stabilize differentiations it has been unable to prevent. More important, future differentiation appears to hinge on a base line identity and the guarantee of future identity" (Mol 1976, 3).

Mol examines sacralization patterns and finds that in order to sacralize identity a previous identity must be "de-sacralized." Sacralization is a "fluid process" that seeks to cover and protect its base identity: that is, the core of social knowledge, understanding, and agreement that secures its survival. Eventually, the process of sacralization stops and begins to "cement" identity's foundation so as to protect its creation from (1) the infinite adaptability of symbol systems, and

(2) a change in meaning or definition of reality. Sacralization "modifies, obstructs or (if necessary) legitimates change" (Mol 1976, 6).

Mol states that Durkheim did not examine the process of sacralization because for "Durkheim the sacred was completely separate, even antagonistic to the profane. It was something given" (Mol 1976, 6). What bothers Mol about Durkheim's model is that it cannot be used to explain "the emergence of sacredness in our time and for its objectifying separating characteristics once it has emerged" (Mol 1976, 6).

Mol has a good point. How do we understand the creations of new sacred identities that are not historically continuous with the past? Mol's larger concern is to explain how the sacred keeps reappearing, especially in modern reality, and manages to keep making distinctions between itself and what it is not. A detailed awareness of this process is missing in Durkheim. *The Elementary Forms* describes in detail what the sacred is; and, occasionally Durkheim also describes what must be excluded from entering identity in order for the sacred to be "sacred." On this point, I believe that there is more in Durkheim than Mol sees. Durkheim was definitely interested in modern sacred reality. The first page of *The Elementary Forms* states:

> Sociology raises other problems than history or ethnography. It does not seek to know the past forms of civilization with the sole end of knowing them and reconstructing them. But rather, like every other positive science, it has as its object the explanation of some actual reality which is near to us and which consequently is capable of affecting our ideas and our acts: this reality is man, and more precisely, the man of today, for there is nothing which we are more interested in knowing. (Durkheim 1965, 13)

There is something, then, in religious beliefs and rites and their separation of things into the sacred and the profane that Durkheim sees to be "near to us" and "capable of affecting our ideas and our acts." Durkheim maintained that the acts of exclusion found in the categorizing activity of beliefs and rites form a process of sacralization that has its ancient and modern manifestations.

Durkheim believed that we are able to understand the present by understanding the past. He employed the tools of history and ethnography in readdressing "the old problem of the origin of religion." This new look at religion realized that history and ethnography have not found origins, because in fact none exist. Durkheim formulated the question in a new way. "What we want to do is find a means of discerning the ever present causes upon which the most essential forms of religious thought and practice depend" (Durkheim 1965, 20). The study of religion was important to Durkheim because "religion has not confined itself to enriching the human intellect . . . it has contributed to forming the intellect itself. Men owe to it not only a good part of *the substance* of their knowledge, but also *the form* in which this knowledge has been elaborated" (Durkheim 1965, 21; emphasis added).

Durkheim examined the philosophical categories of thought that provide "the framework of intelligence," for example, "ideas of time, space, class, number, cause, substance, personality, etc.," and concluded, "They are born in religion and of religion; they are a product of religious thought" (Durkheim 1965, 22). Moreover, for Durkheim "religion is something eminently social." "Religious representations are collective representations that express collective realities; the rites are a manner of acting which take rise in the midst of assembled groups and which are destined to excite, maintain or recreate certain mental states in these groups" (Durkheim 1965, 22). Individuals do not produce religious thought by themselves, and religious thought is more than the sum of individual thoughts. It is thought collectively represented.

Understanding the social nature of knowledge allowed Durkheim to develop a new, social basis for the "old problem of knowledge." Not only did he seek to understand the individual's experience, as prior sociology of religion had done, but he sought to expand his inquiry to include the individual transcended, the collective, social, nature of experience. Feminists share with Durkheim a intense interest in the collective experience. At the same time, we underscore the importance of the personal. While not much is known about Durkheim's private life, I have found the surviving tidbits helpful. A son of an eight-generation rabbinical family, yet an atheist sociologist, Durkheim studied religion from the point of view of the questioning adherent who was a being transcended, a member of a collective at one with his society. *The Elementary Forms of Religious Life* was so successful that Protestant pastor Marc Boegner, onetime head of the French Protestant church and an ex-president of the World Council of Churches, wrote in his tribute to Durkheim: "One seemed to hear a believer testifying to what he believes to be essential to his faith, to that which he holds most dear" (Lukes 1972, 518).

The quality of the stories captured in *The Elementary Forms* is important to method and to theory. Durkheim's theory grew out of empirical research. It was important for him to know how many people thought in a particular way. It is this empirical and theoretical precision that I try to capture here.

Other readers have been more critical of Durkheim's sociology, focusing on what they consider to be a fundamental problem with his source of data. However, comprehensive reviews of Durkheim's critics conclude that his theory that "the origin of society and morality of knowledge is in religion" stands unaffected by unsuccessful attempts to locate the Australian tribes and their totems that informed his theorizing (Lukes 1972 and Morris 1987; affirmed by Seger 1957, LaCapra 1985, and Bellah 1973). What is important to them is distinguishing between the empirical basis and the theoretical significance of his work.

They do agree that ethnographic evidence is important. The place to look for it is not in Australia but in Durkheim's mind. The lack of evidence for the heterogeneity between the sacred and the profane that disturbs critics such as Belot (Lukes 1972, 511) does not at all bother Boegner, who sees, feels, and lives the Durkheimian paradigm. The more interesting question is not whether Durkheim can prove that the sacred and the profane are profoundly separated everywhere, but rather, what does he believe causes the separation, and does he explain how it is maintained? It is important to remember that the distinction between the sacred and the profane is found in thought that has material consequences.

The Durkheimian Project

Lukes suggests that the object of Durkheimian sociology was to "determine the conditions for conserving society [the Third Republic and its ideals]" (Lukes 1972, 139). He also finds that Durkheim believed that sociology must promote personal achievement and, at the same time, personal dependence upon society. Not surprisingly, Durkheim found that the conservation process required him to understand and to support a particular social and sexual division of labor that he analyzed as elemental to the keeping of social order. "Keeping order" is the sacred activity of society.

As a critic, Durkheim realized that if modern European, and particularly French, society was to survive secularization, it needed to construct a new moral order (Durkheim 1973b; Hughey 1983; Lukes 1972). Seeking to discover how the previous order was constructed, Durkheim developed the theory (for which he is best known) that in primitive society order was created and maintained by religion; and that in modern society order is kept by a division of labor historically rooted in religion (Durkheim 1984, 119, 231, and Coser's introduction xv–xviii; Morris 1987, 108). Durkheim's impact on American sociology, and particularly on the sociology of religion, has been profound. But not so obvious is his implicit theory of gender, which is built into his theory of religion.

Like Durkheim, feminists have also sought to understand the division of labor and have frequently examined primitive life in search of clues. Durkheim's profoundly thorough and thoughtfully descriptive material is useful to feminist theorizing in that many of his interests are also feminist interests; for example, the division of labor, the marriage relationship, and education (the public and private dichotomy). As Bellah (in Durkheim 1973b, xliv) suggests, Durkheim locates the origin of these social institutions in religion.

The Elementary Forms of Religious Life

The Elementary Forms of Religious Life (Durkheim 1965) is first and foremost a study of the sociology of knowledge. Durkheim wished to uncover the elementary forms of religious life in order to discover the genesis of thought. Religion, argued Durkheim, shaped the form of all past and future knowledge; therefore, if one could just "go underneath the symbol to the reality which it represents and which gives it its meaning," one would understand "human need" that produces thought (Durkheim 1965, 14). Durkheim's method relied on ethnological evidence to confirm just what in human life needed and produced particular religious forms. He argued that this human need was for strength, power, and knowledge, the full potential of which science eventually possessed. Durkheim also sought to know the causes for action. In order to plan a new direction for French life, Durkheim needed to know how action had hitherto been prompted.

Durkheim's sociology of religion will be examined here from his ethnological and sociological viewpoints. It is important to remember that Durkheim is looking through a profoundly Western, Judeo-Christian lens. In addition, what Durkheim "saw" when he examined social life is very important to a feminist critique that understands the methodological gender blindness of his era. This study will challenge Durkheim's claim that what he "saw" represented a "collective religious experience," and will show instead that the explicit recognition in

Durkheim's sociology of religion that "the sacred" is gendered masculine and "the profane" is gendered feminine carries with it an implicit understanding of violence against women. Therefore, it is possible to hypothesize that what produced "religion" was not a collective experience but a masculine one, and to argue that what Durkheim "saw" when he looked at religion was activity produced primarily to satisfy the needs of men.

2

THE
SACRED/PROFANE
DICHOTOMY

The priest answered David, "I have no ordinary bread at hand, only holy bread—provided that the young men have kept themselves from women." David answered the priest, "Indeed women have been kept from us always when I go on expedition; the vessels of the young men are holy even when it is a common journey; how much more today will their vessels be holy?" So the priest gave him the holy bread; for there was no bread there except the bread of the Presence.

—1 Sam. 21:4-6

Durkheim's search for elementary forms located the most profound distinction of human thought in the differentiation between the sacred and the profane. He wrote: "The traditional opposition of good and bad is nothing beside this; for the good and the bad are only two opposed species of the same class, namely morals . . . while the sacred and the profane have always everywhere been conceived by the human mind as two distinct classes, as two worlds between which there is nothing in common" (Durkheim 1965, 53–54).

For all practical purposes, the two worlds do not share time and space. "In the first place, the religious life and the profane life cannot coexist in the same place. If the former is to develop, a special spot must be placed at its disposition, from which the second is excluded. . . . Likewise, the religious and the profane life cannot coexist in the same unit of time" (Durkheim 1965, 346–47). If it is true that the sacred and the profane do not coexist, then it follows in Durkheim's obser-vations that the sacred and the profane do not share the content of the philosophical categories that make up the "framework of intelligence" (for an in-depth discussion of logic and the nature of intelligence in Durkheim see Jay 1981).

It is important to underscore the clarity with which the religious sees itself as associated with the sacred and not the profane. Religion is separate from the profane sphere and ritualistically maintains this separation. The religious-sacred belongs to one world, the profane to another. "Between the two worlds there is no common measure" (Durkheim 1965, 78). "Perhaps it is easier to see the profane as a residual term. Thus all that is not sacred is profane" (Pickering 1984, 137). Even so, an individual does not always exist in one or the other world. Durkheim was interested in boundary crossing and the occasions of movement between the worlds. For example, "[The] initiation is a long series of ceremonies with the object of introducing the young man into the religious life: for the first time, he leaves the purely profane world where he passed his first infancy, and enters into the world of sacred things. It is said that at this moment the young man dies, that the person he was ceases to exist, and that another is instantly sub-stituted for it. He is re-born under a new form" (Durkheim 1965, 54). The young man leaves the profane world, aided by rites and rituals that show him his "profane" self is now dead, and he is given a new life in sacred society. These ceremonies "are not understood in a merely symbolic sense, but are taken literally. Does this not prove that between the profane being which he was and the religious being which he becomes, there is a break in continuity?" (Durkheim 1965, 54).

Durkheim recognized a "break in continuity" when this profane being is transformed. This opposite identity is so absolutely established that the transformation itself initiates "antagonism" between the two worlds, which become not only "separate" but "even hostile and jealous rivals of each other" (Durkheim 1965, 55). In this opposition, the sacred represents rationality and mysteriousness, the profane represents ir-rationality and intelligibility (Durkheim 1965, 54; cf. 45). We can understand the irrationality of the profane, but the rationality of the sacred is a mystery.

The dualism is maintained by beliefs and rites that ensure that "the sacred thing is par excellence that which the profane should not touch, and cannot touch with impunity" (Durkheim 1965, 55). This dualism allows magic and religion, which are always found in great tension with each other, to be distinguished. "Magic takes a sort of professional pleasure in profaning holy things; in its rites it performs the contrary of the religious ceremony. On its side, religion, when it has not condemned and prohibited magic rites, has always looked upon them with disfavor" (Durkheim 1965, 58). Because his project was to research religion, he was not interested in pursuing magic, so he had to "stop at the point where magic commences" (Durkheim 1965, 59). He had only to draw a line of demarcation, and did so by summarizing that the difference between them is a social versus a personal one: religion has a defined group attached to it, a church (a church could also be a nationality, as in the case of the Hebrews [Durkheim 1965, 59]). However, "*there is no Church in magic.*" Magic, unlike religion, is a generalized matter, "diffused in large masses of the population" (Durkheim 1965, 60; emphasis original). Individuals "utilize" magic, but magic does not create for them a "moral community" (Durkheim 1965, 61). This opposition between the moral and the material is the opposition between religion and magic, between the social and the individual. The religious is the "majestic"; the magical is the common (see also Durkheim 1965, 79).

What facilitates the individual's separation from the masses so that religion, the church, can be formed? Durkheim analyzed this process and the social aspects of religion by examining what he believed to be the most elemental form of religious experience: totemism. Totemism, based on the clan, or gens, is a name or an emblem (Durkheim 1965, 131), a coat of arms of the clan (134). This emblem is a "collective label" of "religious character"; "in fact, it is in connection with it, that things are classified as sacred or profane. It is the very type of sacred thing" (Durkheim 1965, 139–40). In addition, "totemic images are not the only sacred things. . . . Before all others, are the beings of the totemic species and the members of the clan" (Durkheim 1965, 150).

The sacredness of the clan member is not materially inferior to that of the totem. "So each individual has a double nature: two beings coexist within him, a man and an animal [the totemic figure]" (Durkheim 1965, 157). On behalf of the modern thinker, Durkheim found the myths around this duality to be illogical. These myths are usually "represented to us under the form of violent and, as it were, surgical operations" (Durkheim 1965, 158). However inaccessible to the scientist, this mythic structure clearly allows believers to participate in the nature of the animal. Connected through the animal to the totem, "man has something sacred about him" (Durkheim 1965, 159). Sacredness is "diffused" but exists in a "privileged" sense in "blood and hair" (Durkheim 1965, 159). For example, "There is no religious ceremony where blood does not have some part to play . . . and this blood is so sacred a thing that women may not be present while it is flowing. . . . The blood lost by a young initiate during the very violent operations he must undergo has very particular virtues . . . no woman should approach it. . . . Hair has similar properties" (Durkheim 1965, 160).

Totems are of two kinds, collective or individual. Although different, they are inseparable (Durkheim 1965, 188). On the collective level the clan identifies with the totemic figure in a descent metaphor. The individual does not believe this literally. The totem is "a friend, a protector" (Durkheim 1965, 188). One distinguishes between the two kinds of totems by how they are bequested. "The collective totem is a part of the civil status of each individual; it is generally hereditary. . . . Sometimes the child has the totem of his mother; . . . sometimes of his father; . . . sometimes the one predominating in the locality where the mother conceived [that is, the totem of the fecundating agent]" (Durkheim 1965, 188).

In contrast, "the individual totem is acquired by a deliberate act" (Durkheim 1965, 188). Durkheim found that in North America the young native man, usually with the assistance of drugs, sees a vision and claims a patron. In Australia, and apparently almost everywhere else, a second person assists in the process: an old woman, an old man, or the father. "The grandmother or some other woman takes a little piece of umbilical cord to which the placenta is still attached and whirls it about violently. Meanwhile, the other old women propose different names. That one is adopted which happens to be pronounced just at the moment when the cord breaks" (Durkheim 1965, 190). Whereas in one group old women symbolically fling the young man from the womb, in another tribal group, old men, if they are the helpers, break off the young man's tooth and name the young man's totem according to the shape of the resulting blood clot. In both instances something is violently flung away or broken off. Another type of choice is the direct handing down of totem from father to son. Even if the society had by heredity given the son his mother's totem, after initiation he certainly does not retain it.

Durkheim discovered that on rare occasions there is another kind of totem, the sexual totem, that exists between the collective totem and the individual totem (Durkheim 1965, 191). It was a new development, found only in some regions of Australia.

> The totem of each sex protects it from harm. Men and women are profoundly separated by their sexual totem and each is required to respect it. Every violation of this interdiction gives rise to actual bloody battles between men and women. (Durkheim 1965, 193)

In some cases, Durkheim notes, tribes ritualize these battles as a precursor to the marriage rite (cf. Durkheim [1965], 193, footnote 62). Sexual totems such as these "result from men's representing the tribe as descended as a whole from one couple of mystical beings" (Durkheim 1965, 193).

To summarize, in the rare instances where Durkheim found sexual totems, they were found to include violent or pain-inducing actions of old women or old men who chose the totem for the young man; or, the totem selection resulted from a tribe inheriting its identity from a mythic heterosexual couple who apparently did not get along very well. So rare is the sexual totem that Durkheim drops the discussion of it and proceeds with discussing the other two types, the clan and individual totems (Durkheim 1965, 200). In no observed case did the individual totem exist without the clan totem. The clan totem may exist without the individual one, and in those cases the individual accepts the clan totem as his or her own. It was evident to Durkheim that the clan totem existed first and the individual totem originated from it (Durkheim 1965, 216). Apart from the women having their own sexual totem, Durkheim was not clear as to whether women, as profane beings, have their own totems or relate only to the sacred totem.

Durkheim analyzed maternal and paternal totems that are not clan totems but sexual totems and concluded that the maternal totem existed before the totem of the locality (the paternal totem). If the two coexist, the mother's totem plays the minor role:

> For to-day, the maternal totem has only an accessory and supplementary role; it is a second totem. . . . But, in order that it should be able to retain this secondary place, being employed along with the local totem, there must have been a time when it held a primary place in religious life. It is, in part, a fallen totem, but one recalling an epoch when the totemic organization of the Arunta was very different from what it is today. (Durkheim 1965, 211–12)

When Durkheim reached the most elemental form of religious life he sought the cause of this elemental form. He could not arrive at a cause without first discussing force:

> This is what the totem really consists in: it is only the material form under which the imagination represents this immaterial substance, this energy diffused through all sorts of heterogeneous things, which alone is the real object of the cult. . . . Thus, the universe, as totemism conceives it, is filled and animated by a certain number of forces . . . there are as many of them as there are clans in the tribe, and each of them is also found in certain categories of things, of which it is the essence and vital principle. (Durkheim 1965, 218)

Responding to the forces of the universe, then, is the essence of the totem. He wrote: "When we say that these principles are forces, we do not take the word in a metaphorical sense; they act like veritable forces. In one sense, they are even material forces which mechanically engender physical effects. . . . But in addition to this physical aspect, they also have a moral character" (Durkheim 1965, 218). Fear and respect of the forces facilitates the moral life of the clan. "So, while the totemic principle is a totemic force, it is also a moral power; so we shall see how it easily transforms itself into a divinity properly so-called" (Durkheim 1965, 219). This "ambiguity" between cosmic and moral is an attribute of all religions.

Finally, having discovered force at the bottom of totemic reality, Durkheim could generalize about the nature of religion. In the totemic principle, in the separating of the sacred and the profane, exists the "first form of the idea of force" (Durkheim 1965, 232; see also 233). For Durkheim, it was crucial that the history of science understand this process. Although the idea of force originated in religion, it was borrowed first by philosophy, and then by science (Durkheim 1965, 234; see also Takla and Pope 1985). Durkheim considered religious forces real forces.

Thinking along a social-psychological continuum, Durkheim then asked how the idea of the totemic principle and its forces is "constructed" and "out of what materials" (Durkheim 1965, 235). Obviously he found nothing intrinsic in the totemic figure itself (e.g., in a carrot or a kangaroo) that inspires force. "Thus the totem before all is a symbol, a material expression of something else. But of what?" (Durkheim 1965, 236).

The totem is not only a symbol of the clan and the member, it is also a symbol of "god." "God" and the society become one (Durkheim

1965, 236). The intensity of the collective mind creates moral ascendancy. Its representations are affirmed by all members collectively. The collective voice, which is stronger than the sum of individual voices, is a forceful one whose threat of violence maintains a submissive membership. "The very violence with which society reacts, by way of blame or material suppression, against every attempted dissidence, contributes to strengthening its empire by manifesting the common conviction through a burst of ardor" (Durkheim 1965, 238). Totemic society uses violence and so does its god. "Since it is in spiritual ways that social pressure exercises itself, it could not fail to give men the idea that outside themselves there exist one or several powers, at least in part, as outside themselves, for these address them to do violence to their most natural inclinations" (Durkheim 1965, 239).

Violence done to personal impulses is similar to material violence. Both are created from mental "energy" that through its very existence becomes the sign of moral authority (Durkheim 1965, 238). Since moral authority or social opinion is equated with the sacred, the god(s) are seen to give the adherent energy to face the world (Durkheim 1965, 240). Through rituals and worship, the adherent gathers strength also to organize and change the self and the world outside of the self. Durkheim found that collective rites produce passionate sensual intensity that can induce violent and unrestrained actions that then need to be directed at some object.

> Men see more and differently now than in normal times. Changes are not merely of shades and degrees; men become different. The passions moving them are of such an intensity that they cannot be satisfied except by violent and unrestrained actions, actions of superhuman heroism or of bloody barbarism. This is what explains the Crusades. (Durkheim 1965, 241)

Here I believe Durkheim connects violence done to the self with violence done to others. The forces that create "heroes and butchers" find moral grounding outside of the self; these forces come from the collective experiences of the group that legitimates them (Durkheim 1965, 242, cf. footnotes 9 and 11). The individual feels that "benevolent powers" are at his side in these conquests urging him on, giving him strength (Durkheim 1965, 243), and reaffirming his belief that he belongs to the sacred collective. So assured, he does what the collective demands of him. The process of sacralization is a powerful social tool in controlling individual actions. Whole nations and armies can be convinced through religious rituals that violence done to others in the name of the sacred is justified (cf. Durkheim 1965, 243, 250).

Durkheim's observation might help explain the connection between sacralization rituals and the massive support of Hitler's destruction of the Jews, widespread Christian support for slavery in the United States, and the previous ignoring of wife and child abuse. What Durkheim's theory cannot help explain is how some individuals come to resist collective sentiment: how, for example, many practicing Christians worked to save Jewish people as they did earlier to abolish slavery, or why some men did or do not use the sacred as an excuse to beat their families.

Durkheim has described well scenes that show the role of ritual in violence, such as when women are used by men to liven up their bleak hunting and gathering lives in midnight ceremonies producing "violent super-excitation":

> Towards ten or eleven o'clock, the Uluuru and Kingilli men arrived on the ground, sat down on the mound and commenced to sing. Everyone was evidently very excited. A little later in the evening, the Uluuru brought up their wives and gave them over to the Kingilli, who had intercourse with them. Then the recently initiated young men were brought and the whole ceremony was explained to them in detail, and until three o'clock in the morning singing went on without a pause. (Durkheim 1965, 248)

Collective sentiment is further defined by what it is not:

> So he could not escape the feeling that outside of him there are active causes from which he gets the characteristic attributes of his nature and which, as benevolent powers, assist him and assure him of a privileged fate. . . . Consequently, we get the impression that we are in relations with two distinct sorts of reality and that a sharply drawn line of demarcation separates them from each other: on the one hand is the world of profane things, on the other, that of sacred things. (Durkheim 1965, 242–43)

Profane reality is "dull and unexciting." When adherents gather together, in "concentrated groupings from their dispersed existences," their creative thought is sufficient to make life more exciting (the passions are excited, which in turn induces violence) and thus to alter reality. The concentration of individuals makes these rituals effective.

> Gathering the grains or herbs that were necessary for food, or hunting and fishing are not occupations to awaken very lively passions. . . . The

very fact of the concentration acts as an exceptionally powerful stimulant. . . . The human voice is not sufficient for the task; it is reinforced by artificial processes. . . . But while they express it, they also strengthen it. This effervescence often reaches such a point that it causes unheard-of actions. . . . The sexes unite contrarily to the rules governing relations. Men exchange wives with one another. Sometimes even incestuous unions, which in normal times are thought abominable and are severely punished, are now contracted openly and with impunity. If we add to all of this that the ceremonies generally take place at night in a darkness pierced here and there by the light of fires, we can easily imagine what effect such scenes ought to produce on the minds of those who participate. They produce such a violent super-excitation of the whole physical and mental life that it cannot be supported very long: the actor taking the principal part finally falls exhausted on the ground. (Durkheim 1965, 246–48)

Extracted from ordinary life, the individual finds moral power to exist in this state because this power, which is society, generates the powerful god on whom the adherent depends (Durkheim 1965, 257). Being both physical and moral, it has an ambiguousness that allows it to "dominate the two worlds." "It is this double nature which has enabled religion to be like the womb from which come all the leading germs of human civilization" (Durkheim 1965, 255).

The adherent is correct to believe "in the existence of a moral power upon which he depends and from which he receives all that is best in himself: this power exists, it is society" (Durkheim 1965, 257). Not only does the adherent depend on the collective religious force of the clan, but the individual's being is radically transformed. Religious thought is not of the ordinary. It grows not out of the material life of the profane, but out of the moral and material life created by the sacred:

How could such experiences as these, especially when they are repeated every day for weeks, fail to leave in him the conviction that there really exist two heterogeneous and mutually incomparable worlds? One is that where his daily life drags wearily along; but he cannot penetrate into the other world without at once entering into relations with extraordinary powers that excite him to the point of frenzy. This first is the profane world, the second, that of sacred things. . . . Therefore, the sacred character assumed by an object is not implied in the intrinsic properties of this latter: it is *added to them*. The world of religious things is not one particular aspect of empirical nature; *it is superimposed upon it*. (Durkheim 1965, 250, 261; emphasis original)

My feminist sociological suspicions have led me to ask: Who are these members of a sacred society that identifies itself with a god and thereby accepts divine violence and claims divine authority to violence? Who are these adherents who feel that relations with the ordinary are dull but relations with the sacred, which are superimposed upon empirical nature, are intoxicating? In Durkheim's scheme, "by definition, sacred beings are separated beings. What characterizes them is that there is a break of continuity between them and profane beings" (Durkheim 1965, 337–38). In my reading, the separated and sacred beings are men. And the majority of the profane beings are women:

> Sometimes the religious dignity which is inherent in each member of the clan on this account is not equal for all. Men possess it to a higher degree than women; in relation to them, women are like profane beings. Thus, every time that there is an assembly, either of the totemic groups or of the tribe, they have a separate camp, distinct from that of the women, and into which these latter may not enter: they are separated off. (Durkheim 1965, 161–62)

And again he noted a connection between the profane and the feminine, "[as] it frequently happens that certain animals are specially designated as the food of women; for this reason, they believe that they partake of a feminine nature and that they are consequently profane" (Durkheim 1965, 342). The remaining profane are animals and beings not belonging to the totemic species; children and those young men not deemed worthy of men's society (Durkheim 1965, 142).

Women and children are instructed never to learn the secret language of the cult or to see the secret instruments (Durkheim 1965, 342–44). "Not only are the sacred beings separated from profane, but also nothing should be confused with the religious life" (Durkheim 1965, 343). So essential is this separation that often complete nudity is required of boys before admission to sacred rites. Nudity apparently symbolizes the shedding of all profane things and establishes that the persons admitted to the rite were not the profane sex.

Durkheim concluded that "the religious life and the profane life cannot coexist in the same place . . . [and] time" (Durkheim 1965, 347). Fearing contamination (Durkheim 1965, 359), they are rigidly separated in order to protect the moral force of society. Durkheim discovered that for the religious believer:

> They feel that the real function of religion is not to make us think, to enrich our knowledge, nor to add to the conceptions which we owe to science others of another origin and another character, but rather it is to make us act, to aid us to live. The believer who has communicated

with his god is not merely a man who sees new truths of which the unbeliever is ignorant; he is a man who is *stronger*. He feels within him more force, either to endure the trials of existence, or to conquer them. It is as though he were raised above the miseries of the world, because he is raised above his condition as a mere man. (Durkheim 1965, 463–64; emphasis original)

However, the believer cannot claim a privileged understanding of the experience apart from the understanding produced in society. "It may be said that nearly all the great social institutions have been born in religion. . . . If religion has given birth to all that is essential in society, *it is because the idea of society is the soul of religion*. Religious forces are therefore human forces, moral forces" (Durkheim 1965, 466; emphasis added).

Durkheim found magic to be "born of religion" (1965, 405). He did not go further than establishing a "definite derivation between them." "We do not want to say that there was ever a time when religion existed without magic" (1965, 405, cf. note 26). Religious forces, unlike magic, are ideal forces. "Men alone have the faculty of conceiving the ideal, of adding something to the real" (Durkheim 1965, 469). But "where does this singular privilege come from?" asked Durkheim. He appears to have found its source in the intense collective life of believers who have excluded the magical—women, children, and other men not capable of existing in their collective.

The sacred adds something to the adherent's understanding of life. "In a word, above the real world where his profane life passes he has placed another which, in one sense, does not exist except in thought, but to which he attributes a higher sort of dignity than to the first. Thus from a double point of view it is an ideal world" (Durkheim 1965, 469–70). The ideal world "is a natural product of social life" (Durkheim 1965, 470). The ideal is not only natural, but it is also "the condition of his [man's] very existence. He could not be a social being, that is to say, he could not be a man, if he had not acquired it"; to be a man is to live in an ideal world, to "suppress certain elements and add others" (Durkheim 1965, 471). In *The Elementary Forms* to be a man requires the exclusion of women from social life. By sacralizing the masculine community and denigrating the feminine, men become social and women natural beings. Reread, Durkheim's work outlines the exclusion of women from the ideal world as a given activity of social life.

Because this idealization is a mental process, Durkheim could not say that religion is a product of historical material forces. However, he qualified his conceptual model, stating that religion is "essentially so-cial" and thereby responds to but does not "confine itself to" material realities (Durkheim 1965, 471). In order for this particular idealization, religion, to become a part of collective consciousness, *a particular consciousness had to be added to the collective consciousness,* causing a "disengage[ment of] a whole world of sentiments, ideas, and images which once born, obey laws all their own" (Durkheim 1965, 471). The creation of a sacred identity within a collective identity particularizes the sacred by allowing the individual to be identified as sacred, and simultaneously creates a new and particular individual consciousness that now relates directly to the sacred. Religion's collective consciousness requires an individual consciousness that does not remain connected to the community it has left but responds to the sacred collective. This sacralization process was not created without reason. For Durkheim, the function of the sacred is to generate power. Power is created by the force that maintains the division between the sacred and the profane and reaffirms collective opinion:

> The force isolating the sacred being and holding profane beings at a distance is not really in this being; it lives in the minds of believers. So they perceive it at the very moment when it is acting upon their wills, to inhibit certain movements or command others. . . . [This action] is readily perceptible here because everything is inside us . . . we cannot fail to be conscious of it. Moreover, the idea of force bears the mark of its origin in an apparent way. In fact, it implies the idea of power which, in its turn, does not come without those of ascendancy, mastership and domination, and their corollaries, dependence and subordination; now the relations expressed by all these ideas are eminently social. It is society which classifies beings into superiors and inferiors, into commanding masters and obeying servants; it is society which confers upon the former the singular property which makes the command efficacious and which makes *power.* (Durkheim 1965, 408–9; emphasis original)

Power can be understood as a "function" of religious experience or preferably as the "purpose" of the sacralization process. Durkheim presupposed power, which results from a patriarchal world based on domination and subordination. From this came his idea of religious force.

Religious force is a product of domination. Durkheim found that the idea of force is religious because the force isolating the sacred from the profane lives in the minds of the believers:

> [The cult] does not have the sole object of making profane subjects communicate with sacred beings, but it also keeps these latter alive and

is perpetually remaking and regenerating them. . . . The things which the worshipper really gives his gods are not the foods which he places upon the altars, nor the blood he lets flow from his veins: *it is his thought.* (Durkheim 1965, 388; emphasis added)

The very idea of sacred force is necessary to maintain the separation between the spheres and the superiority of the sacred sphere. Religious force (the force of collective opinion) creates a collective force (from a membership that upholds the sacred by means of violence) used to legitimate domination, and it establishes gendered power and gendered social life. Without this concept of sacralizing force, Durkheim would have no theory of social life.

Religious force gives us power to control social activity and responses through abstract thought. As Durkheim has shown, this new power increases "potency." The added potency develops as material forces are increasingly disengaged from material conditions and become idealized as spiritual forces that explain and maintain social realities. This powerful religious force is seen as giving birth to a new reality that is valued because it is not of a material world: it belongs to an ideal world.

Durkheim's observations appear to have been biased by his acceptance of the universality of a particular way of thinking that belongs to a masculine worldview created and sustained by the exclusion of women and the communities they shelter. On his own terms, then, religion cannot be a universal social fact. There is still something to which religion can be reduced. Durkheim reduced religion to collective life; yet behind religion lies the will to exclude the profane, the feminine. Religion is further reducible to exclusive groups that dominate the excluded. Religion is the mechanism through which this exclusion is ensured. Religion is what makes "man."

The Souls of Men

Puberty Rites and Menstruation

In *The Elementary Forms*, religion is the primary supporter of gender and gendered power created in the collective conscience of men. Durkheim found that gendered life, once differentiated, becomes an ongoing reality. Men accomplish this process through religious rites that resemble the reproductive life of the profane, animal world, from which they have just recently come (and which they have been required to reject), and thereby co-opt the meaning of that reproductive function.

During the initiation, the adults open their veins and sprinkle the novice with their blood; and this blood is so sacred a thing that women may not be present while it is flowing; the sight of it is forbidden them. . . . Hair has similar properties. The natives wear belts made of human hair . . . as soon as a man is dead, they cut off his hair and put it away in some distant place, for neither women nor the non-initiated have the right of seeing it: it is here, far from profane eyes, that the belts are made. (Durkheim 1965, 160–61).

The noninitiated lose their profane status in the initiation rite when they are taught how to be a member of sacred society and then designated as a member. Initiation also requires a rite Durkheim translates as "to fecundate" or "to put into good condition" (1965, 367). Young men cross the boundary into sacred existence when they see and learn how the sacred is reproduced by the rites of the clan members. This is a fertility rite assuring the reproduction of the sacred. In this way, the boy learns that the existence of the sacred depends on the faithful performance of rituals by men. Although men depend upon the sacred, the sacred also depends upon the men. The mystery of this relationship produces fear and awe. Members fear that each man must do his part or the sacred will die and disappear. The boy learns that this is an awesome responsibility. In the initiation rite, boys acquire an ability to reproduce their sacred selves. Physical reproduction is still the requirement of the profane world from which boys come. The boys learn how to fecundate not only the totemic species but themselves as well (Durkheim 1965, 371). This process of "putting into good condition" requires a symbolic ripening of the womb as seen in the theatrical performance of menstruation. Flowing blood is used in initiation ceremonies to reanimate the young and "to assure the regular production of the totemic species" (Durkheim 1965, 371).

Then, in the initiation process, the initiate dies and is reborn (Durkheim 1965, 54); he is himself no longer. The death associated with initiation, like the death associated with menstruation and funeral rites, requires the shedding of blood. It seems to me that what must die in the initiation process is the young boys' communal identity and attachment to the profane, animal world of the mother, a world represented by menstrual blood. In this genderization and differentiation process, the boy becomes a man when he is admitted into sacred society. Once a man, he leaves the communal life of the mother for what Durkheim has called "the collective" comprised of sacred men. The initiation rite ensures that the genderization process is completed.

Memory Records Sacred Force and Violence

Gendered and individualized, the young man is given a soul that is distinct from his animal body. He is given a spirit that partakes in the sacred, in the totem. He is now a member of the totem, a spiritual brother to all other men. From being a member in the feminine community of his mother's house, he becomes a religious brother in a society of men. He has his god to thank for this new life: a god that requires in return control and sacrifice and gives him power to impose his will over—to exclude by violence—the nonsacred, the profane, in the name of the sacred, as a means of protecting the sacred from the profane.

The mock-menstrual and birth rites serve to give the young boy the religion he will need to keep this process going. This "religion," wrote Durkheim, is a product of "delirious imagination" (Durkheim 1965, 107). However imaginary, the product is given objective value. Durkheim found that objective value is enshrined in exclusive rites that firmly anchor belief in the origin of the entire sacrificial system and that facilitate the creation of an artificial kinship.

Without the young man's sacrifice of the original bond with the mother, that is, without leaving the profane world for the sacred world, social life would be impossible. Religion, then, creates social life, a social life that is built on and requires separation from and exclusion of women. This exclusion requires a divinely ordained force that commands the young man to do violence to his natural inclination to stay with the mother and her house, to stay in community. Mothers and their children belong to the natural world; men belong to society. Upon initiation, a man becomes a different person, who can no longer think or act in his previous profane way but must now follow new rules and regulations upon which his new life depends. His new life no longer depends on the community from which he came but upon a force outside himself, a force that created the men's society to which he now belongs.

He is himself no longer. He is a being transcended, a being redesigned in order that he might dominate two worlds: the ideal, moral world and the ordinary, everyday, animal world. The sacralization process that divides the believer into many parts facilitates the domination of the ideal and natural worlds. Although Durkheim has not explicitly described the parts and the forces that keep the parts separated, one might use his existing model to interpret this process as filling the adherent with an atomizing tension that breaks the bonds between himself and the maternal community from which he comes, and allows him to do violence to his natural inclinations and to the profane world. This soul-bearing man is not only a fractured being; he also belongs to a sacred order that can be "subdivided," while "each of its parts remains equal to the thing itself" (Durkheim 1965, 261). The sacred order reinforces the mental and physical realities of atomization; the smallest division is considered sacred. "This conception of the religious, finally, allows us to explain an important principle found at the bottom of a multitude of myths and rites, and which may be stated thus: when a sacred thing is subdivided, each of its parts remains equal to the thing itself . . . each of these partial souls is worth a whole soul" (Durkheim 1965, 261). Social life, it seems, would not be possible without this monumental symbolism of the great sacred power that shelters, even celebrates, fractured lives. Yet there is "a memory of a time when the part did not equal the whole"; the history of origins is stored in the "memory" (Durkheim 1965, 116).

Even though the initiation process appears so powerfully complete, Durkheim repeatedly stressed its ambiguous nature (1965, 455). I believe that this ambiguity, which showed Durkheim that beliefs can be changed or forgotten, is rooted in a memory of prior experience that includes union with feminine sexuality. The imitation of the rite itself ensures such a memory. The flowing of blood in initiation rites parallels the death that occurs at each menstruation, and finally the celebration of fecundity and the joy of birth complete the cycle. Durkheim also found that ambiguity surfaces in death and funeral rites. In these practices, the sacred and the profane become two poles of religious life (Durkheim 1965, 460). Morris (1987) protests Durkheim's "rigid" distinction between the sacred and the profane. But, we must ask: Are they not rigidly separated in society? The masculine and the feminine are so rigidly separated in society that often on the first day of school kindergartners are lined up in sex-segregated lines. So, as we are taught from the very beginning of our social life, although there exists ambiguity about the sacredness of the order, we are sure that the profane world is not to be confused with the sacred.

If the worlds do come into contact, the profane contaminates the sacred. Durkheim elaborately analyzed the encounter. The profane, when contaminating the sacred by its actions, becomes the focus of sacred anger and violence. The contaminated sacred object cannot become sacred again until processed through expiatory rites. "Offended and irritated by the profanation implied in this abusive and unnatural extension, it [the collective sacred sentiment] becomes aggressive and inclined to violences: it tends to avenge itself for the offense suffered. . . . But if the anger thus aroused is satisfied by an expiatory rite, it subsides" (Durkheim 1965, 460). The profane person's act of touching the sacred angers the whole collective sacred society. The profane becomes the target of collective anger and violence, whether or not the action directly affects the collective sentiment or only the sacred individual. Further, the sacred fills the profane with anger and harmfulness. The sacred can be purified only through rites of expiation. Purification and violence are often found together. The penalty paid, expiation reestablishes a boundary between the sacred and the profane.

Violence is seen as a natural or inevitable outcome and precondition of any contact between the sacred and the profane. Since religion creates social life and its institutions, and social life creates religion, the potential for violent contact exists everywhere. Takla and Pope's (1985) search for the role of force in Durkheim's sociology stopped short of making the connection between gender, force, and violence. However, as we have seen, the differences between masculinity and femininity are maintained by those social forces that promote and sustain acts of violence. These forces create social identity through sacralization processes. This act of naming requires no less bravery than living every day.

According to Durkheim (1951, 385), the woman, unlike the man, is less a social being and more a product of nature. This inability to fit into men's society is related to the sexual division of labor, a division supported by religion. As we shall see, between the forces of religion and the realities of the division of labor, women are rendered neither sacred nor social, an identity ensured by a threat of violence. The theory of power funded by violence found in Durkheim's work equates power with domination. But we must challenge this notion of domination as power, claiming that domination is simply violence (Hartsock 1983).

The inevitability of domination is held in tension with its somewhat voluntary nature. Durkheim found that on some level of consciousness there is in man a voluntary and coexistent understanding that he is both man and animal; on some level all men agree that the totemic identity is their identity (Durkheim 1965, 157, 409). Men—and it is important to establish which ones—wish to produce and reproduce an ideal world that can exist only if they segregate themselves from the natural, profane world and marshal that world into meeting their needs by using a part of it to symbolize collective power and collective force. Not explicitly recognized by Durkheim, this segregation maintained by force and violence destroys the wholeness of sexuality, creating two sexes in tension with each other.

One would anticipate that this elemental tension informs the whole of Durkheimian sociology. Indeed, there are consequences of the sacred/ profane dichotomy in Durkheim's theory and in social practice.

3

THEORETICAL

AND PRACTICAL

CONSEQUENCES

I can hear the sizzle of newborn stars and know anything of meaning,
of the fierce magic emerging here. I am witness to flexible eternity, the
evolving past, and I know we will live forever, as dust or breath in the
face of stars, in the shifting patterns of the winds.
— Joy Harjo, *Secrets from the Center of the World*

Robert Bellah's opinion that Durkheim's *Division of Labor in Society* is
the "original trunk" of his subsequent work has been well accepted.
It is not until *The Elementary Forms* that Durkheim names the sacred/
profane dichotomy as elemental in the production of all social life. At
this point it is instructive to examine briefly the social realities Durkheim
had in mind as he located their origin in religion. It will be confirmed
that even a secular feminist understanding of social oppression cannot
ignore religion. The sacred/profane dichotomy determines the major
part of the social agenda important to feminist analyses of gender
inequality. In addition, it is important for theorists who agree with and
use Durkheimian concepts to be aware of his gender blindness.

Marriage

The social institution of marriage has been well studied by feminists.
We have come to understand that it is in society's best interest to control
individual sexual relationships, even to the point of denying access of

some individuals to others, as seen in our cultural homophobia. Marriage, according to Durkheim, is necessary for the moral order. Like many feminists, Durkheim wondered how something so good for society can be so bad for people. Marriage affects the sexes differently. Durkheim was disturbed that in France women attempt suicide more frequently than men, although men complete suicide more often than women (Durkheim 1951, 176–97). Given that solidarity protects against self-murder, it is obvious that anomie is greater for women. Divorce counteracts female suicidal tendencies; on the other hand, in Catholic countries with no divorce, men have a greater chance for survival. In his monumental study on suicide Durkheim was forced to conclude that an ideal situation would consist of married men and widowed or divorced women, both with children.

These data led Durkheim to ask, "What is marriage?" Marriage "regulates the life of passion," creating a "moral equilibrium from which the husband benefits" (Durkheim 1951, 270). On wives he wrote: "She thus does not require so strict a social regulation as marriage, and particularly monogamic marriage" (Durkheim 1951, 272). The threat of divorce protects her from the unreasonable behavior of a spouse who needs her. Marriage law restricts a man's passions and keeps him within the moral law of society. Single men, during "the sexual period" of ages twenty to forty-five years, exhibit a high rate of suicide, whereas women of this age do not. Women, it seems, do not mind being alone (Durkheim 1951, 274), although Durkheim found that they would probably satisfy needs for intimacy with close friendships. Moreover, Durkheim wrote, "there is no compensation or relief for the woman" (1951, 272). Marriage is a "profitless yoke for her" (Durkheim 1965, 274).

But why this dissimilar impact? Durkheim concluded that it is not because men are "evil," although the thought did cross his mind: it is because "their interests are contrary, one needs restraint and the other liberty" (Durkheim 1951, 274). In addition, liberty torments the man; marriage ends this torment. Woman did not need to "abandon" her liberty. But by "submitting" to "society's rule," for reasons Durkheim cannot name, "it is she who made a sacrifice." Conjugal anomie (Durkheim 1951, 17, 241–76) produced an "insoluble antinomy." This conclusion forces Durkheim to develop a new theory of marriage (see Durkheim 1951, 275–76).

Durkheim hesitated to protect women because the way to decrease suicide among women is to make divorce easier, which would increase the risk of suicide for men. He asked, "Must one of the sexes necessarily be sacrificed, and is the solution only to choose the lesser of the two evils?" (Durkheim 1951, 384).

Durkheim concluded that the principle of divorce is acceptable but that divorce by mutual consent is not. The unsolvable problem arises from the role of the institution of marriage, which functions to keep society regulated. The antagonism between men and women "originates in fact because the two sexes do not share equally in social life. . . . [Marriage] cannot simultaneously be agreeable to two persons, one of whom is almost entirely the product of society, while the other has remained to a far greater extent the product of nature" (Durkheim 1951, 385). A solution would require social equalization of the sexes. In his theory, as in social practice, women are the ones sacrificed; they must be prepared to become more social, more capable of living in a man's world. In his observation of marriage men take on an identity described earlier as sacred.

Given Durkheim's comprehensive descriptions of the disparity between the happiness of husbands and wives, one can see him potentially equipped to develop an explicit theory of gender. The husband's superior position in marriage, which is due to the division of labor, mirrors a superior place in Durkheim's sociology, which is not deliberately weighted toward improving the quality of men's lives, but which has that effect. One suspects that a different sociology would have emerged had Durkheim lived a few years longer and had he engaged the developing thought of women intellectuals such as Marianne Weber.

Division of Labor

As we have noted, religion generates the power to atomize the network of human relations into distinct "individuals." This process then sacralizes certain "individuals." The division of labor not only reinforces this atomization; it receives support in religious rites and rituals.

In *The Division of Labor in Society* (1984) Durkheim maintains his profound commitment to the autonomy of the individual. The autonomous individual is an important historical product: "In fact, if in the lower societies so little place is allowed for the individual personality, it is not that it has been constricted or suppressed artificially, it is quite simply because at that moment in history *it did not exist* (Durkheim 1984, 142; emphasis original). Durkheim thought it was possible to retain both the autonomy of the individual and the true social solidarity of the primitive community simultaneously (Lukes 1972; LaCapra 1985; Morris 1987). Important to community life is the division of labor.

Durkheim asked: What causes the division of labor? He concluded that it must make man happier:

> Indeed we know that the more work is divided up, the higher the production. The resources that it places at our disposal are more abundant; they are also of better quality. . . . Now, man needs all these things. Thus it seems that he must be happier the more of them that he possesses, and consequently be naturally induced to seek them. (Durkheim 1984, 179)

The sexual division of labor makes marriage happier:

> It is the sexual division of labor which is the source of conjugal solidarity, and this is why psychologists have very aptly remarked that the separation of the sexes was an event of primitive importance in the evolution of sentiments. This is because it has made possible perhaps the strongest of all disinterested tendencies. (Durkheim 1984, 18)

These "disinterested tendencies" find that women were not "weak" but became so as "morality was progressed" (Durkheim 1984, 18). This progress influenced the evolutionary, physical form of people, people who were once more alike than different:

> These anatomical similarities are concomitant with functional ones. In fact, in these same societies the female functions are not very clearly distinguished from the masculine ones. But the two sexes lead roughly the same kind of existence. Even now there is still a very large number of savage [*sic*] peoples where the woman takes part in political life. . . . Similarily we see very frequently the women going off to war with men, stimulating them to fight, and even participating very actively in fighting. . . . Among these same peoples marriage exists only in a very rudimentary state . . . it is very likely that there was an era in the history of the family when marriage did not exist. . . . The state of marriage in societies where two sexes are only slightly differentiated thus bears witness to the fact that conjugal solidarity is itself very weak. (Durkheim 1984, 19–20)

On the other hand, said Durkheim, modern life finds marriage developing into a much more regulated and nondissolvable union. As the division of labor grew, women can be seen to have "withdrawn from warfare and public affairs . . . the two great functions of psychological life had become as if dissociated from each other, one sex having taken over the affective, the other the intellectual function" (Durkheim 1984, 20). As women began again to be involved in the arts and literature, Durkheim found men leaving these disciplines for science. Woman's work and sexual role is largely related to her inferior and less developed psychological state, a state that makes marriage possible. Reducing the sexual division of labor and strengthening her psychological life would cause marriage to disappear. Durkheim further determined that this liberation would cause not only economic disadvantages, but social and moral disadvantages as well. In other words, his sociology of marriage suggests that the empowerment of women threatens the modern nation-state.

Education

To aid what he saw to be a morally disastrous situation in France, Durkheim attempted to shore up the institutions of marriage and education. Education, like marriage, required constraint of desires. Constraining desires makes for a "happier child" and for a "secured moral order." Schools, he wrote, "must be the guardians par excellence of our own national character" (1973a, 3–4) while making "original contributions" to our national life (1973a, 7). An original contribution requires discipline and constraint. Acknowledged is that constraint does "violence to the nature of things" (Durkheim 1973a, 35). Morality is a system of prohibitions that limit the range of actions considered appropriate. This limitation is necessary for the order of society.

Therefore a child must be taught to "rein in his desires, to set limits to his appetites of all kinds, to limit and, through limitation, to define the goals of his activity (Durkheim 1973a, 43). Schools, then, must first and foremost teach the child to "restrict natural inclinations." Although criticized by specialists such as Piaget who believed that he did not understand children, Durkheim maintained that children must be prepared for (often painful) social life by adults. Adult authority regulated a child's life so that moral order and collective life would become acceptable goals in the education process (Durkheim 1973a, 130). In Durkheim's sacred/profane model the existence of a superior role (adult authority) assumes violence in the relationship. He argues that in social life with no previously established limits, "whenever two populations, two groups of people having unequal cultures, come into continuous contact with one another, certainly feelings develop that prompt the more cultivated group—or that which deems itself such—to do violence to the other" (Durkheim 1973a, 192–93).

In Durkheim's ethnography children belong to the profane order, a category used to its status as recipient of violence. Beating a child is permissible in the goal of teaching moral significance (Durkheim 1973a, 201). In the case of children, Durkheim distinguished anger from passion. He warned against punishment "in anger" saying that it must be "passionate" punishment. Passionate punishment is goal oriented.

Passionate commitment to morality meant everything to Durkheim, a father who loved his children, a patriot who loved his country, and who sincerely wanted France to survive the crisis of a traditional society being reshaped by the forces of rationalism, industrialism, and individualism. As Pickering suggests, he wanted this "progress" without the negative consequences of anomie: unequal opportunity and inadequate organization. (On this point, it is interesting to note that his own "gifted" daughter was denied opportunities to pursue her own education [Pickering 1984, 19]). It is now well known that Durkheim believed the social chaos of the times to be linked to the failure of religion:

> He believed that the moral and social uncertainty of the times was in part due to the failure of traditional religion—Catholicism, Protestantism and Judaism—to offer a satisfying system of beliefs and rituals, which could even approximate to the intellectual demands of the day—demands based on reason and science. [Durkheim looked for] a religion without God, but which at the same time contained what might loosely be called a "spiritual element." (Pickering 1984, 21)

If modern society required a progress no longer grounded in religion, what would the basis for this new moral order be?

A New Moral Order

In his introduction to *On Morality and Society*, Robert Bellah calls Emile Durkheim "the philosopher of order." Durkheim's interests led him to a new basis of social order. Arguing that the exchange and contract theories are not the moral basis of this new society since they themselves need a foundation, he puts forth his theory of justice: "A stable form of organic solidarity requires an institutionalized system of enforcing good faith and the avoidance of force and fraud in contract. It requires, in a word, justice" (Durkheim 1973b, xiv). Justice is the new faith, the new common conscience. For many, Durkheim became a "prophet of some newly born new religion" that Bellah calls "civil religion." Civil religion stabilizes *organic solidarity* by requiring enforcement of its laws. Such is the requirement of a religion of individuals whose aim is keeping individuals associated, because if their atomized union disintegrates, so does society (Durkheim 1973b, 53–54).

Mechanical solidarity, on the other hand, is the solidarity of the "homogeneous masses," the "horde." Durkheim saw the masses as "devoid of definite form," "like protoplasm" (1973b, 63). Durkheim's distinction between the masses and society, between mechanical and organic solidarity, can be taxonomically presented in this way (Durkheim 1973b, 63–85):

MECHANICAL SOLIDARITY (political-familial) primitive/mass	ORGANIC SOLIDARITY (nonpolitical-familial) modern society
1. adults of both sexes have equality	1. rigid division of labor
2. no superiority of chiefs; chiefs administrate	2. hierarchy
3. kinship is not organized over generations; "common origin" is politically important to community	3. heredity causes "common origin" to disappear; heredity fixes properties
4. child is bound to the mother equally as to other members of the adult community; natality organized	4. family groups are rigid; organized around occupations; child cannot change parentage
5. unanimous adhesion to particular beliefs causing the absorbing of the individual into the group	5. "individualism had developed in absolute value by penetrating into regions which were originally closed to it" (Durkheim 1973b, 85)

It can be seen that in much the same way as women who "give up" their independent status to become wives, the horde (a community operating under mechanical solidarity) becomes a clan (a community of organic solidarity) when it gives up independent status and becomes a sectional community. Durkheim found the movement from mechanical solidarity to organic solidarity to be voluntary and motivated by religious sentiments (Durkheim 1973b, 63–69).

Durkheim continued to ask why this dual existence, which society uses to associate the mechanical world of the masses with evil and the organic world of ideas with the good, is necessary and therefore survives. He answered by pointing to the division between the sacred and the profane, which facilitates all the categories of life (Durkheim 1973b, xliii–xliv). Mechanical life is not directly and explicitly equated with the profane, but its description resembles the definition of the profane. Likewise, the organic life mirrors the sacred life.

Inasmuch as this model represents Western society, Durkheim's model rested on a highly fractured civic morality, itself incapable of producing agents. Human agency, when directed toward worldly ends only, requires knowledge, even hope, of some reconciliation or resolution of conflicts that threaten social life and are not—indeed, cannot be—allowed by Durkheim's Nietzschean understanding of the antinomy between the individual and society, the sacred and the profane, the masculine and the feminine. For Durkheim, society is built on an unresolvable conflict between the natural and the ideal. These poles represent groups of people in tension with each other. If agency requires a vision of resolution, none is possible here. Inherent in Durkheim's sociology is an unresolvable tension between men and masculine society, just as there is an unresolved tension between the masculine and the feminine, the sacred and the profane. If agency belongs to people with the ability to choose to act on what they know to be true, it is difficult to see the Durkheimian masculine actor as a fully endowed moral agent.

As we have seen, Durkheim found religion surrounded by ambiguity. Within Durkheim's own thought this ambiguity functions as a barrier between what one suspects is true and the necessary action to confirm it. Durkheim would probably agree that as long as there is ambiguity there is a suspicion that one's life is not authentic, that there could be other choices, that the sacred might not be sacred at all. In this context, agency would require people to act on a way of knowing that the future between individuals and society can be one of equality, that the split between mind and body can be healed, that desire for mutuality exists between and among "individual" members of society.

However, men in sacred society have little potential for being free. Some women have experienced that acting on a memory, on a way of knowing, on a suspicion that one's life is not authentic, is not easy. The hegemonic forces ("representations" to Durkheim) appear to have a regenerative quality. Once they exist, representations exist in themselves "if they have the power to react directly upon each other and to combine according to their own laws" (Durkheim 1953, 23).

The social facts to which these representations refer are not material; they are exterior to the individual, who sees them imposed by a higher power. There is, however, a "limited autonomy of the mind" that is for Durkheim the "positive content of our notion of *spirituality*" (Durkheim 1953, 28; emphasis original). Spirituality is the "distinctive property of the individual . . . one should say that social life is defined by its hyperspirituality" (Durkheim 1953, 34). Hyperspirituality claims the individual for society's ends. Durkheim is not interested in spirituality but in hyperspirituality.

Hyperspirituality or religion helps the believer to understand, accept, and speak the language of society. As it creates a new language, religion remakes the soul.

Contemporary Feminist Theory as Interpretive Lens

The Elementary Forms contains a rich collection of observations that implicitly document the role of religion in the processes of sexual differentiation and the social production of misogyny. The question "Why sexual differentiation?" is bound up with Durkheim's questions "Why religion? Why the sacred?" He answered that religion, particularly the concept of the sacred, mobilizes the fulfilling of society's needs, which he concluded to be universal ideals. Society meets these needs through religion. Also, society creates universal ideals by treating social ideals as sacred. To address the universal needs and ideas, Durkheim presented a universal theory of social life. In reality, liberation thought has established that universal theories support particular needs. Following is a comparison of the particular needs suggested in the Durkheimian material with the ones outlined by Chodorow and Hartsock.[1] Nancy Chodorow (1978) sees in Western society's "capitalist needs" the root of women's oppression. On the other hand, Nancy Hartsock (1983) argues that the "social need" is the oppression of women, of which capitalism is a significant by-product.

---

1. I have limited my comparison of feminist theorists largely because of space. A selection of feminist theorists who have been instrumental to my overall perspective is listed in the Bibliography.

Chodorow: A Certain Kind of Life

Durkheim's implicit gender theory is given a type of confirmation by Nancy Chodorow, who charted the psychological dynamics of early childhood. Chodorow's *The Reproduction of Mothering* (1978) is a feminist interpretation of Freudian pre-Oedipal theory. Rooted in the psychological dynamics of early childhood, the sexual division of labor produces gender differences and is in turn produced by them. The division of parental labor, the split between private and public tasks, is rooted in women's oppression. Women's oppression, resulting in their role as primary caretaker of children, produces men and women with incompatible emotional lives.

In the pre-Oedipal experience, where the mother is the primary figure, girls are encouraged to remain attached to the mother. Boys are required to separate from her, indeed, to reject her, and to develop sharper ego boundaries. This asymmetrical development produces girls prepared for a life of imminent caring, self-sacrifice, and mothering. Girls narcissistically overidentify with the mother and emotionally never detach. Boys are more differentiated, and are prepared for a detached, individuated, public life concerned with transcendence, rules, order, law, and alienating capitalist production.

In Chodorow's analysis mothers and mothering are responsible for the creation of men who know that they are distinctly different from their mothers and sisters. Boys are thus civilized and prepared for the world of men. The capitalist world continues to exist because women continuously supply it with differentiated boys. Thus women participate in their own oppression.

In this collusion women "find" themselves socially located in the family. They continue to "find" themselves there because other women, their mothers, directed this process for them.

The differentiation process described by Chodorow, which prepares girls for life in the mother's community and boys for life in men's society, parallels the function of puberty rites described by Durkheim. Durkheim's analysis of social life shows that the religious man and his somewhat voluntary division of the world into the sacred and the profane is responsible for women's oppression. Chodorow argues that capitalist, male-dominated society requires a kind of mothering that creates sex-gender systems, heterosexual asymmetries, a psychology of male dominance, and a fear of women. Her solutions rest on shared parenting roles and a radical change in the sexual division of labor. In both cases boys are seen to be dramatically and violently separated from the primary attachments to the mother.

Carol Gilligan's *In a Different Voice* (1982) takes up Chodorow's basic argument and hypothesizes that differentiated individuals must have a differentiated moral development and, therefore, a differentiated social ethic. Utilizing Lillian Rubin's *Worlds of Pain* (1976) and Janet Lever's "Sex Differences and the Games Children Play" (1976), Gilligan argues that differentiated ethics is first noticed in children's play, which demonstrates a variable sense of reality. Boys' play is "'pragmatic' . . . regarding a rule as good as long as the game repaid it. Girls are more tolerant in their attitudes towards rules . . . more easily reconciled to innovations" (Gilligan 1982, 10). Girls are more interested in sustaining the relationship among the players than the game itself. Boys play games that teach, support, and promote independence, competition, and organizational skills. Girls play games that teach, support, and reinforce intimacy, cooperation, and harmony. The ritualized preparation of children through play can be seen as preparation for the puberty rites and rituals that prepare the child for adult roles as described by Durkheim.

Chodorow and Gilligan recognize that these asymmetrical and differentiated social ethics, one masculine and transcendent, the other feminine and immanent, are social constructions sponsored by the social division of labor, which is fundamentally rooted in the oppression of women. Chodorow, Gilligan, and Durkheim are certain that a change in the sexual division of labor will change moral development and therefore social life as well. However, neither Chodorow nor Gilligan explains how women's maternal role, which "is responsible for" gendered members of society, became so obedient to the social cause of oppressing women. Durkheim argued against Marx that the source of social action rests not literally in material conditions but in thought, in religious thought that separates the sacred from the profane, men from women.

Josephine Donovan's critique of Chodorow (1985) argues that neither Freud nor Chodorow pursues the idea of the positive aspect of the strong, powerful mother-daughter bond which "they indicate . . . has been obscured or made marginal in patriarchal society" (Donovan 1985, 112). Neither of them evaluates the bond as a source of "resurrection." The mother-daughter unit allows women to be subjects to each other while the "father's drama" names them as objects. Of course, the mother-daughter bond would not be something of immediate interest to Durkheim. His focus was on the interrelationships of sacred society.

Hartsock: A Certain Kind of Death

Nancy Hartsock, in *Money, Sex, and Power* (1983), goes further in the effort to discover how the materiality of motherhood became such an effective tool in women's oppression. Although she also focuses on sexual division of labor, Hartsock is less dependent upon a psychological model. She asks how the relations of production are constructed; how they operate; and how social theory and practice justify and obscure them (Hartsock 1983, chapters 1–6).

As other feminist social theorists have done, Hartsock tests the usefulness of currently functioning economic models. She rejects exchange theories that legitimate domination; rational economic theories that ignore institutions and need "the other"; and market theories that see relations of the sexes as voluntary action for mutual gain. She settles on the Marxist theory of historical materialism because it is the most advanced power-domination theory, even though it does not address issues of sex and race.

Adopting Marx's analysis of economic oppression of the proletariat and concluding that women's oppression is also material and historical, Hartsock asks why men oppress women even within the proletariat class. The gender-blind Marxist categories are based on the masculine experience of the production of commodities, an experience taken to be general human experience. However, this one-sided view cannot explain gendered power. Hartsock argues that women's lives are defined and structured by *eros*; eros could be a universal choice for all people. The sexual division of labor, which profoundly affects their lives as well as men's lives, is founded on negative eros. She asks how eros and power are connected and how they are interconnected with negative eros and domination. "In the contemporary Western world, the gender carried by power associates masculinity with domination and by means of this connection, fuses sexuality, violence and death" (Hartsock 1983, 151).

This gendered power is considered ideologically and institutionally to be "normal" heterosexuality. Utilizing Freudian theory, Hartsock further claims that eros has three aspects. First, it has the aim of "making one out of many" (Hartsock 1983, 166), and the repression of genital eros "is required for the development of civilization" (Hartsock 1983, 167). Second, eros is concerned with social life. However, public life has found little place for it. Third, eros is the "creativity and generation of children through social relations"; civilized life seeks to control reproduction through prescribed social relationships (Hartsock 1983, 197).

In principle, Hartsock's work agrees with Durkheim: civilization depends upon the suppression of that part of social life which has been relegated to women and that which is called "feminine."

Hartsock traces the transition from tribal community to class-divided community through fifth-century Homeric literature and evaluates the changing understanding of politics and power: "Most fundamentally, the establishment of the *polis* takes place through a process of domesticating and subordinating the dangerous and threatening female forces that surrounded what is to become the political community" (Hartsock 1983, 190). Like Karl Marx, Hartsock returns to the Homeric narratives in order to capture early historical value conflicts. Hartsock found that the complex social changes involved "domesticating the female forces of disorder—forces whose symbolic sources are the earth and the night, forces seen as deeply connected with fertility, sexuality and reproduction" (Hartsock 1983, 192).

In these narratives the males are threatened by: (1) the female representation of an older, clan-based order; (2) the disruption woman causes when in her mismatch with the new law and jury system she operates outside of the proper (masculine) system; and, (3) her sexuality, which is not controllable (Hartsock 1983, 192).

The female represents the old (pre-totemic) religion, the primitive, lawless, earth and nature forces that the male is leading into the new future, to the world of reason, law, and order. "Failing domestication, they [the men] feared, the male community would not survive" (Hartsock 1983, 192). Faced with the fact that these unruly females were needed for the continuation of the polis, "a safe and separate place" was made for the masculine political community (Hartsock 1983, 193).

Like Durkheim, Hartsock argues that it is not a coincidence that the polis is also founded on opposition to nature. "The warrior-hero lived on the boundary and confronted nature as a hostile force" (Hartsock 1983, 193). The fear for physical well-being necessitated a separate, safe physical space as well.

Unlike Durkheim, Hartsock is aware that the masculine experience is only half the story. In perhaps a too-generalizing manner, she claims that when one listens to male sexual language and looks at how sexual excitement happens and is characterized, one finds that the community of men is based on negative eros, rape, sexual murder, and pornography. On the other hand, women's sexual language depicts a community based on positive eros: energy, capacity, and potential.

Hartsock reviews women's notions of power and finds power to be: (1) the glue that holds community together; (2) the means by which community is constituted; and (3) the means by which immortality is obtained and death overcome (1983, 218). In contrast to Durkheim's theory of power funded by violence, Hartsock holds that, for women, power is not the ability to command and dominate but the property of a group. Women's power is found in the group. The group determines who and what shall be surrendered for the good of all. It also understands that (1) violence can destroy power; (2) violence and power are opposites; and (3) violence and power are not commonly found together. *Therefore, not only do women argue against power as domination, women know that domination is not power, it is simply violence.* Violence-domination and power are ancient enemies.

One could push Hartsock to say that power is itself eros. Violence is the negation of eros. As Audre Lorde writes: "When I speak of the erotic, then I speak of it as an assertion of the life force of women" (as quoted by Hartsock 1983, 225). The negation of eros—that is, the negation of power by violence—is the negation of the life force of women. Hartsock asks why this life force is feared; why and how men, as men, come to want and expect the right to dominance and will defend this right by violence.

Hartsock disagrees with Hannah Arendt's claim that men are searching for immortality and seeks instead to locate the tension in reproduction. Reproduction is clearly linked with death (Hartsock 1983, 244). "Reproduction implies the existence of *'discontinuous'* beings," she writes, quoting Bataille. "In reproduction sperm and ovum unite to form a new entity, but they do so from the death and disappearance of two separate beings" (Hartsock 1983, 244). "But what kind of vision can take reproduction, the creation of new life, and the force of life in sexuality, and turn it into death, not just in theory but in practice of rape and sexual murder? [And] give pride to the place of killing?" (Hartsock 1983, 245). Recognized here is an "inverted order," a refusal to see the reality of life activities that need both production of goods and the reproduction of human beings. In her model, men feel that they do not have the capacity for creating life. Their warrior role, whether chosen or mandated, reinforces death. "The search for life, then, represents the deeper reality that lies beneath the glorification of death and destruction" (Hartsock 1983, 245).

Perhaps Hartsock is too generous in placing the burden of misogyny on men's relationship to reproduction instead of on men themselves. Controlling reproduction is a significant factor in men's dominance over women. Durkheim suggested that the "life" men are searching for and wish to reproduce is a life set apart from the ordinary, set apart from the production of goods and the reproduction of human life. He found that man understands himself as both man and animal (Durkheim 1965, 157). However, the nonanimal part of his nature is sacred. Animals only know the world, men know the ideal (Durkheim 1965, 469). The ideal is not interested in the animal act of reproducing life. It does not wish to take over the function of childbirth or attempt primary conurturing.

Men do not necessarily agree with feminists such as Eisenstein, who wrote: "Differentiation is not distinction and separateness, but a particular way of being connected to others" (1987, 13). In fact, the "new men's studies" research takes men's motives for coparenting to be less pure than do feminists such as Chodorow and Hartsock. Brod argues that it is not clear if men's attempts to share women's experience are

> supportive or subversive of women's reproductive powers. From a comparative anthropological perspective, much of the "new fathers" childbirth involvement, usually accepted as a benefit to women, appears suspiciously like a couvade ritual [of pre-state societies] down to the laborious panting and counterfactual "we're pregnant" announcement. It remains unclear how much of the "new fathering" ethos is an attempt to surrender or re-establish male power in the face of feminist gains for women. (Brod 1987, 16)

Although one is tempted to ask if these rituals could be interpreted as men's empathy with women's experience or men's desire to claim the child as being as much his as hers, Brod's work cautions against too quick an assumption of goodwill.

According to Durkheim, for reasons of power-dominance men (and it is important to establish which ones) wish to produce and reproduce an ideal world that can exist only if it marshals the natural, animal world into meeting its needs.

Durkheim explained that men wish to create the ideal world because their desires are "normal, natural." However, his archaeological digging has produced evidence that seems to suggest that the reasons are related to a desire to establish a collectivity that materially enriches its members and makes them powerful. Hartsock, on the other hand, suggests that misogyny prompts men to leave community for men's society. What both of these views recognize is that violence and a search for power are necessary for maintaining the separation of human community into gender-specific persons with gender-specific functions. This forceful manipulation, unrecognized by Durkheim, destroys the wholeness of sexuality.

This violence receives sacred support in a religion created by men for the purpose of suppressing the feminine—suppressing all those people, male and female, who are not necessary to sacred masculine life. By disregarding immortality, Hartsock leaves religion unexplored and therefore misses the seat of socially gendered power. Durkheim found that gendered life, once differentiated, becomes an ongoing reality. Men accomplish this process through religious rites that resemble the reproductive cycle of the profane, animal world from which they have just recently come (and have had to reject) and, in so doing, co-opt the meaning of that reproductive function. Here, Brod's warning is helpful. The goals of rituals that take the reproductive experience of women and assign it to men instead of using men's reproductive experience might not be favorable to women.

Although in real life Durkheim wanted the best possible existence for French women, he could not see these issues because his search for origins produced a universal solution. The "why" question finds its answer in the inevitable social distinction between the sacred and the profane. For Durkheim this distinction was inevitable because of the universal human need that pushes toward idealization. Durkheim's answer can legitimately claim to have addressed Hartsock's issues of reproduction and shared parenting. Women's experiences are rendered transparent, nondiscursive, not a part of the system of idealizations.

Chodorow, too, provides a universalized psychoanalytic answer for her "why" question. It is similar to Hartsock's: shared parenting and a nongendered division of labor. For both Chodorow and Hartsock the center stage shifts from women as victims to their complicity in the victimization to the expanded role of men in nurturing functions. Once established as authoritative, the centralized and universal role of reproduction in Hartsock's and Chodorow's theories renders religion (and other factors) transparent. There are compelling reasons to insist that both reproduction and religion be retained as primary stars in the many-starred constellation of patriarchy; Hartsock and Chodorow do not pay attention to the latter, nor Durkheim to the former. But the brightness of these stars is partly a reflection of other stars. There will always be, in a world of great particularity, a why behind the why.

History suggests that long after sacred religion has ceased to be a dominant actor on the social scene, the reason the sacred survives in a secularized form (e.g., Bellah's "civil religion") is that people have found a new use for an old tool: to retain domination in the hands of oppressing powers. So too, experience suggests to us that when issues of reproduction and coparenting are solved, sexism will reappear and require new solutions. Experience, including religious experience, is not necessarily (and most likely not) continuous.

Even the experience of oppression is not continuous. As the Durkheimian postmodern school suggests, universal theories will not work to explain oppression. Oppression must be proved on its own terms at each moment in history. Hartsock's, Chodorow's, and Durkheim's work neatly fits together because they share a common worldview that is not intimately focused on or empirically established from within the concerns of all oppressed persons. Hartsock acknowledges that she left out the impact of her theory on lesbian life, and Durkheim states that he will not explore magic-mass because his interest is in the future of civilization. Their worldviews allow for a blindness that makes the reality unseen invisible, not important to the "major" subject under research. Hartsock, like most white feminists, would like to believe that women make decisions based on a shared notion of eros. As feminists have learned, we must ward against falsely universalizing "women." We do not have to look far back into our history to discover that white women regularly ignored slave women's desires. White feminists might want to count the number of "women of color" who have affected their lives; the number of non-Anglo-Saxon women who participate in professional conferences; or the number of nonwhite women they claim to have collegial relationships with. This is an issue that feminists cannot push off on classism or patriarchy. The current reasons for white women's exclusion of black and other racial and ethnic women are not the same as those at the turn of the century. These reasons must be continually reinterpreted. Hartsock and Durkheim are right. The answer is not class. But neither is it sexism.

The deeper disorder is found in the lives of all of those who create, dominate, and oppress people.

The Soul of a Dead Man Is a Sacred Thing

The purpose of religion is to remake the people's soul. The remade souls of believers become sacred, whereas the souls of the profane are denied. The notions of society, the sacred, and the soul are continuous in Durkheim's documentary sociology, in which dead men have souls and living women do not. Resistance to the demands of the sacred men and their society is absent from particular men, men who are called to be, who wish to be, and are thereby becoming sacred members of a sacred society. At times Durkheim seems to suggest that participation in sacred society is voluntary; at other times he finds that young men are "compelled" to join, or, as he has also noted, that "all young men wish to join." If nothing else is clear in *The Elementary Forms*, we know that Durkheim found that religion is also the product of men who at some point had to, and still choose to, act in particular ways to retain the privileges of sacred society.

As my pro-feminist (male) students and colleagues begin to document the sacralization process in their own lives, I hear Durkheim's observations validated. My community organizer's ear listens for points of intervention where pro/feminists might offer those men who are not convinced of their sacredness a way out, a way to say "No", a way to accept shelter from the threats of violence aimed at compelling them to join the sacred society of sacred men. I have learned from people like John Stoltenberg that men teach each other the advantages of misogyny. Some gay men who are otherwise not inclined to anti-woman behavior, learn that they can fend off violence aimed at them if they act out misogynistically.

Viewed through a feminist lens, Durkheim's analysis of religion reveals religion's sacralization process as a tool used by particular men to create and sustain society from which women, and the rest of the profane collectivity, are excluded. In his model, men come together and, in the excitement caused by the closeness of these individuals, choose to leave women and the feminine and to be associated together in men's sacred society. Once formed in a separate time-space, the meaning system is divided into the sacred and the profane, into religion and magic. Magic become "dangerous"; its threat of contamination helps to keep the groups in tension.

The profane can be, and often are, temporarily sacralized to provide services required of the sacred and to perform certain roles in sacred rituals. Their profane status remains, however, and the threat of de-sacralization is always present should the profane, uninvited, come into contact with the sacred.

The masculine and the feminine are kept apart by the tension created by the religion/magic, sacred/profane dualism that is itself created when the separation of men from a more encompassing community takes place. The separation created "masculine" and "feminine" persons, who, though different, "tend to confuse themselves with one another" (Durkheim 1965, 360). The sexual division between masculinity and femininity is ambiguous but reinforced by powerful social forces. Women and those called feminine are relegated to the nonsacred world of magic, which is dark and fearful. Of this world Durkheim writes little.

In many ways Durkheim was a modern man par excellence. Like Max Weber, also one of the last great voices of modernity, he believed that rules should govern desires, especially sexual desires. When choosing a model for the reconstruction of French society, Durkheim selected the rationality of religious thought over the profane, magical, erotic worldview. To salvage French society, Durkheim guided the forces of religion and science to the altar of public life where, for his love of the French people, he sacrificed much of himself as well. Most commentaries agree that the First World War energized him into an increased dedication to national life. But it also consumed him. The reality of the human need for religion stormed through his life when his son became a wartime casualty.

> At such a time of misery and desolation, Durkheim yearned, it is said, for the consolation of religion. He had written objectively about the functions of religion and the help that it gave at such occasions as he was experiencing. Now he only encountered utter misery in the form of a personal vacuum. . . . It is remarkable that having rejected the truth value of all religions he should come to them in seeking consolation at the hour of crisis. . . . Clearly the edifice of the cult of man in which he had consciously based his beliefs had crumbled. The brittle foundations had given way in the face of the holocaust of the war. . . . Society, which he seemed to worship as a quasi-deity, offered no comfort but betrayal. (Pickering 1984, 28–29)

We are told that after the death of his son his "stern exterior" showed an "almost feminine sensibility" (Durkheim 1973b, liv). "When

Durkheim died in 1917, the medical diagnosis of his death was a stroke, but it was commonly said that he died of a broken heart" (Pickering 1984, 27–28). Durkheim's personal story reminds us that there is something about death, and therefore religious thought, that feminists cannot ignore. The feminine, however much a manipulated and forced product of religion's sacralization processes, appears to be that social space where death resides and is comforted in its darkness.

Durkheim's model understands the feminine as the quality of existence remaining after the men have fled a common life (community or the feminine collectivity). Women and men are gendered at that point in time when the sacred and profane world come into being. The feminine does not constitute the "original community." What the feminine possesses is a memory of it, that, in its authenticity, empowers it to resist and to seek wholeness. However, instead of "wholeness" Durkheim saw "confusion" of the sacred and the profane, of the masculine and the feminine. Instead of wholeness Durkheim saw "magic." He did not recognize that behind "magic" is also the belief systems of oppressed persons, a type of "folk religio-experience of the masses." Folk experience does not call itself "magic"; it is given this name by "the sacred."

Folk experience is considered profane from the standpoint of orthodoxy, and it is not the same experience we have thus far called "religion." If we can see that "religion involves the making of lasting commitments between a number of ultimate loyalties in a way that affects all that we do" (Brown 1987, 5), we can see that the ultimate loyalty to which Durkheim's sacred is committed is masculine life. Religion is the way in which masculine identity is sacralized.

Masculine life differs from feminine life. According to Mol (1976), who accepts the Durkheimian paradigm, religion stabilizes difference. "Religion restores wholeness to lives fractured by change" (Mol 1976, 95). One could argue that the boy-become-man who was torn from his home and his mother's community suffered an act of violence that is addressed in religion's sacralization process, a process that stabilizes the initiated. However, Mol does not see that one man's wholeness is one woman's death. Valuing science and difference, Mol defends religion's "objectification" against its alienating aspects (1976, 11 and chapter 14). Objectification allows mundane life to be made orderly and to seem timeless. Religion's sacralization process "may actually contribute to the incapacity of society to reinforce norms and values or to provide a stable system of meaning" (Mol 1976, 35). Within itself religion is viable only when it "both initiates sacralization and defends stable patterns" (Mol 1976, 37). Religion assists the individual in finding a "stable niche . . . in a potentially chaotic environment" (Mol 1976, 65). It depends for this stabilization upon sacralized identity (Mol 1976, 92).

To promote stability, religion takes over legitimation of identity created by clan and family. "[C]onversion, charisma and the rites of birth, initiation, marriage and death are all essentially mechanisms for incorporating, rather than annihilating change. All of them desacralize (or emotionally strip) a previous identity, and sacralize (emotionally weld) a new one" (Mol 1976, 263). Religion, it seems, does what it must do for the sake of survival.

It takes acts of violence to create and sustain the sacred and the profane—to create and sustain the gendered world. This violence receives "divine support" in religion created by men for the purpose of suppressing the feminine—that is, all people, male and female, not necessary to sacred, masculine life. According to Durkheim, religion has a tremendous need to repress and suppress, or to make unconscious, its link to the patriarchal order, to domination and violence. Through sacralization of violence the lives and voices of the profane are made invisible and inaudible.

In an effort to create and sustain the violent, dominating force of men's society, religion remade the soul. The soul is no longer connected to the community of natal origin, and it is given to believe what Nietzsche called the great lie: that the separation between the masses and the elite, the dominated and the dominators, never occurred. In fact, the profane world is now understood to be soulless. Soulless people are expendable people. Durkheim did not offer a theory of religion that names tools of expendability: sexism, racism, classism, and homophobia. Perhaps his ability quickly to dismiss race and sex patterns as "biological and not social" accounts for this lack. The modern soulless profane world contains not only women, but also cultural, sexual, racial, and ethnic minorities, slaves, children, and the aged. In fact, the modern collection of invisible persons mirrors Durkheim's ethnological outline of the primitive profane.

At the very least, a feminist sociology and theory of Western rationalized religion would do well to view religion as that space in social life where gender is created. In addition, the standpoint of a liberating praxis may not be women and women's lives, as current feminist thought would suggest, but rather the whole profane community. Not separated into fractured existences, the profane collectivity, which can be at times a community, has the greatest potential for remembering the cause of their exclusion. The "profane" are not hard to find. They are sheltered in women's houses, slave quarters, and all of those places where women and men of the "profane" world gather together. Because Durkheim did not give these people and these worlds voice does not mean that they were voiceless. As Part Three will show, the political act of filtering these voices out of the story and reclassifying them as a separate voiceless group serves as a kind of anesthetic against the effects of violence done to others and therefore to one's own body. Some of the excluded voices live this story and, "finding" themselves selfless, voiceless, soulless, seek to establish themselves as individuals with voices and souls. One example is "white women" whose racial or ethnic identity has been replaced by middle-class suburban life. But here I am more interested in those who found some way to keep their own story from being subsumed into the marginalized identity they were offered. I am interested in those who kept speaking in the dark— in those who have no need "to move from the margin to the center."

4

THE SACRED

AND

THE PROFANE

"If a woman," a Kurnai headman said to Hewitt, "were to see these things, or hear what we tell the boys, I would kill her."
—Mircea Eliade quoting A. W. Hewitt in *Birth and Rebirth*

In order to underscore the sociological observations of Durkheim and Weber and to emphasize the interdisciplinary nature of their interpretations of religious forms, let us briefly explore selected works of an Austrian medical doctor, Sigmund Freud; a German historian of religion, Rudolf Otto; and a French historian of religion, Mircea Eliade. All of these major thinkers, writing after Durkheim and Weber and sharing a very "Durkheimian" twentieth-century paradigm of religion, can be said to have founded a discipline or significantly shaped one. I will focus most closely on Freud, whose ability to produce a social philosophy from the point of view of the Germanic-Westernized psyche builds an interesting (although historically backward) bridge to Weber's sociology of religion and his construction of a modern warrior spirituality.

Between Love and Civilization: Sigmund Freud

Emile Durkheim's sociological approach to totemism has now become as classic as Freud's personal, psychological approach. Most explicitly in *Totem and Taboo: Some Points of Agreement between the Mental Lives of*

Savages and Neurotics (1950), Freud compared totemism with psychological illness, beginning by looking at incest. He stressed that he was not confusing the mental lives of "savages and of neurotics," which are not quite identical even though their need to control incest is quite similar (1950, 31). The "horror of incest" is a natural link between "savages and neurotics."

Freud agreed with J. G. Frazer's types of totems and was particularly interested in totemic incest taboos. Because incest is frequently permitted between fathers and daughters (if the daughter's totem comes from the mother) and not then permitted between the mother and the son, Freud argued that the female descent line is the oldest form of inheritance. What interested Freud is that the whole clan is restricted and not just the family. The family, in fact, does not exist: the clan is the family. Kinship language indicates that the relationship runs between the individual and the group, not between individuals. This clan group marriage is held together by men's ownership rights over women. Society's way of forcing the emotional separation between men and women is found in the incest taboo (Freud 1950, 17). In general, the taboo's obsessional prohibitions are basic to its laws; for example, its laws against killing the totemic animal or sleeping with its women are radically enforced. So basic are these particular laws that Freud claimed them to be "the two oldest and most powerful human desires" (Freud 1950, 32). Taboo and desire are connected: "one would not need to be restrained from doing something one does not wish to do."

Although Freud acknowledged that he could not prove it, he believed that taboos are imposed by external authority, whereas neurosis has internal prohibitions. He discovered that taboo restrictions included food and women.

In all cases, contact with the sacred can be deadly, as Freud found in ethnographic studies:

> A Maori woman having eaten of some fruit, and being afterwards told that the fruit had been taken from a taboo place, exclaimed that the spirit of the chief, whose sanctity had been thus profaned, would kill her. This was in the afternoon, and the next day by twelve o'clock, she was dead. A Maori chief's tinder-box was once the means of killing several persons; for, having been lost by him, and found by some men who used it to light their pipes, they died of fright on learning to whom it had belonged. (Freud 1950, 43)

Yet people are not totally taken in by these beliefs. They understand that taboos act like a language that shields and changes reality so that "interlopers" are forced to stay on the margins. Freud claimed that taboos, like neurotic symptoms, have a dual nature; they restrict, protect, betray, and conceal action.

In general taboos (1) project unconscious hostility (evil impulses) onto demons. The projection deals with emotional conflict and, in defense of the persons, leads to neurosis; (2) "build up the external world" and in a nondefensive way detach "survivors' memories and hopes from the dead" (Freud 1950, 65); (3) remain an ambivalent word (Freud 1950, 67); (4) are the conscience itself and are related to what is conscious (Freud 1950, 67); (5) are related to something forbidden but whose desire is located in the unconscious.

The difference between taboo and neurosis is that in fearing generalized contamination, culturally constructed taboos punish the self, whereas neurosis fears sexual "touching" and punishes others. Social instincts that create taboos combine egoistic and erotic elements into "wholes of a special kind" (Freud 1950, 73). Examining them both, Freud quipped: "In this, psycho-analysis is no more than confirming the habitual pronouncement of the pious: we are all miserable sinners" (Freud 1950, 72).

If this is true, then collective sin must have a collective, social consequence:

> The neuroses exhibit on the one hand striking and far-reaching points of agreement with those great social institutions, art, religion and philosophy. . . . The divergence resolves itself ultimately into the fact that *the neuroses are social structures; they endeavor to achieve by private means what is effected in society by collective effort.* If we analyze the instincts at work in the neuroses, we find that the determining influence in them is exercised by instinctual forces of sexual origin; the corresponding cultural formations, on the other hand, are based upon social instincts, originating from the combination of egoistic and erotic elements. Sexual needs are not capable of uniting men in the same way as are the demands of self-preservation. (Freud 1950; emphasis added)

Like Durkheim Freud found that the reason behind taboo and cultural religious institutions is that it "makes man feel good. . . . The real world . . . is avoided. . . . To turn away from reality is at the same time to withdraw from the community of man" (Freud 1950, 74). But the memory holds all that is repressed.

Freud believed that as men found themselves spending more time directing civilization, largely because women were considered incapable, they instinctively sublimated sexual desire. "In the course of development the relation of love to civilization loses its unambiguity. On the one hand love comes in opposition to the interests of civilization; on the other, civilization threatens love with substantial restrictions" (Freud 1961, 50). Between love and civilization lives an "irremediable antagonism." There is an "inverse relation holding between civilization and the free development of sexuality" (Freud 1961, 6).

Not only is civilization shaped by its repression of love and sexuality, but it also endeavors to oppress familial life even further by requiring the family to hand over the individual; but "the family will not give the individual up" (Freud 1961, 50).

> Detaching himself from his family becomes a task that faces every young person, and society helps him in the solution of it by means of puberty and initiation rites. We get the impression that these are difficulties which are inherent in all psychical—and, indeed, at bottom, in all organic—development. (Freud 1961, 50)

Because women claimed their children, they produced an unintentional, exclusive family unit that after much labor and love is now threatened by civilization:

> Furthermore, women soon come to opposition to civilization and display their retarding and restraining influence—those very women, who, in the beginning, laid the foundations of civilization by the claims of their love. Women represent the interests of the family and sexual life. (Freud 1961, 50)

In order to maintain civilization, the man "withdraws from women and sexual life . . . and [finds himself] estrange[d] from his duties as husband and father" (Freud 1961, 51). Civilization does not steal energy from sexuality unnoticed:

> Present-day civilization makes it plain that it will only permit sexual relationships on the basis of a solitary, indissoluble bond between one man and one woman, and that it does not like sexuality as a source of pleasure in its own right and is only prepared to tolerate it because there is so far no substitute for it as a means of propagation of the human race. (Freud 1961, 52–53)

Like Max Weber, Sigmund Freud thought that "primitive man was better off in knowing no restrictions of instinct" (Freud 1961, 62). Freud realized that only ruling men were the "happy" primitives: "We must not forget, however, that in the primal family only the head of it enjoyed this instinctual freedom; the rest lived in slavish suppression" (Freud 1961, 62).

A major element in the ability to enslave is the effective taboo regarding virginity and its ability to shape memory. "The demand that the girl shall bring with her into marriage with one man *no memory* of sexual relations with another is after all nothing but a logical consequence of the exclusive right of possession over a woman which is the essence of monopoly on the past" (Freud 1958, 187; emphasis added). A taboo means danger; "it can not be disputed that the general principle underlying all the regulations and avoidances is a dread of woman" (Freud 1958, 194).

> Perhaps this fear is founded on the difference of woman from man, on her eternally inexplicable, mysterious and strange nature, which thus seems hostile. Man fears that his strength will be taken away from him by woman, dreads becoming infected with her femininity and then proving himself a weakling . . . but in any event taboos described are evidence of the existence of a force which, by rejecting woman as strange and hostile, sets itself against love. (Freud 1958, 194)

Despite noting the anguish caused by it, Freud did not want to appear to be an enemy of civilization. Rather, he desired to fix it up, acknowledging that it can never be suppression-repression free and that some parts of it will resist all reform (Freud 1961, 62). All civilizations exist between two instinctual poles; one represents life (eros) and the other represents destruction (death). Out of the struggle between eros and death, civilization is formed.

The One-sided God: Rudolf Otto

Rudolf Otto's *The Idea of the Holy* (1923) asked the question: What do religious people have in common? Otto discovered that people operated with rational and irrational experiences (beliefs and feelings, respectively), both of which are necessary components of religion. In Christianity he saw a gradual yet definite recognition of the rational as superior to the irrational—a movement of logic that created a "one-sided god" (Otto 1952, 4).

What makes religion a separate category of experience is its "peculiar category of interpretation and valuation" called "Holiness—the Holy" (Otto 1952, 5). As in Durkheim, the Holy, the sacred, the numinous state of mind is sui generis, irreducible. Otto's ethnographic observations, like Durkheim's, found the sacred an entity "set apart" from everyday life:

> The *mysterium tremendum* of deepest worship is "thrillingly vibrant and resonant, until at last it dies away and the soul resumes its "profane," non-religious mood of everyday life." (Otto 1952, 12)

Not only is the sacred "religious" and the profane "non-religious," the sacred *is* identity. In addition to *tremendum* (awfulness, terror) and *majestas* (majesty), there exists in the holy a third element, which Otto called "urgency" or "energy." One sees it in " 'wrath,' and it everywhere clothes itself in symbolic expressions—vitality, passion, emotional temper, will, force, movement, loss of my own identity, excitement, activity and impetus" (Otto 1952, 23).

Thought is rationalized expression originating in the nonrational, feeling consciousness. Otto found that when rationality and irrationality are kept together as a unit, their resulting combined energy further unites with majesty, providing Martin Luther's profoundly explosive experience of the *omnipotentia Dei*, which became an active, compelling, alive force. This force appears in mysticism of love as the "forcibility" seen in that "consuming fire of love whose burning strength the mystic can hardly bear, but begs that the heat that has scorched him may be mitigated, lest he be himself destroyed by it. . . . 'Love,' says one of the mystics, 'is nothing else than quenched wrath'" (Otto 1952, 23).

Otto wrote that magic is surpassed by the numinous, the sacred. (That is, it is a mystery how the holy Other became the wholly Other.) This transcendent life moves on, carrying with it a red thread inherited from magic. Through Kantian introspection and critical reason Otto discovers that as "different as these [religious phenomena] are, they are all haunted by a common—and that a numinous—element" (Otto 1952, 117). Included in this common thread between the magic and the sacred are residual elements of:

Pre-Religion
  1. the magic of pre-religion, the very primitive experience of un-reflective, nontheoretical behavior;
  2. the worship of the dead;
  3. ideas of souls and spirits;
  4. idea of *mana*, power;
  5. feeling animate or alive (i.e., the primitive awareness of his or her "alive" status);

6. fairy stories, fanciful, wonderful, miracle, miraculous;
7. rise of the "daemon"; "divine" beings; separated life begins and inaugurates religious feeling;
8. notions of clean, unclean, pure, and impure develop; numinous feelings of impurity bring "natural" emotions of disgust and thus "social teachings of loathing" (Otto 1952, 123–24).

Religion
9. emergence of sense perception (feeling) and cognitive awareness of the numinous;
10. numinous awe, facilitating an awareness of "places set apart" (Otto 1952, 127); this awareness and its psychological "self-attestation" (130) are connected to historical traditions and a dim memory of "primeval revelation" (131).

Seeing magic as a place of terror, Otto was surprised that beings, "born originally of horror and terror, become *gods*—beings to whom men pray, to whom they confide their sorrow and happiness, in whom they behold the origin and the sanction of morality, law and the whole canon of justice" (Otto 1952, 136–37; emphasis original).

How does this happen? It happens "through innate ideas of 'numina.' " There is something in human experience that naturally perceives the sacred. As long as these numinous ideas live, religion is prevented from total rationalization. These experiences of the sacred are not derived from history (Otto 1952, 136–42). The sacred preexists. Here Otto's work reflects a faith perspective lacking in Durkheim, who found the sacred a natural historical production of the collective experience.

The Profane Lifts Up the Everyday: Mircea Eliade

Eliade utilized Otto's insights in a ground-breaking work titled *The Sacred and The Profane: The Nature of Religion* (1959b). Noting Otto's definition of God as "a terrible power experienced as wrath" and the numen as "wholly Other," Eliade analyzed this sacred reality that is power itself. In order to understand the modern Western Weltanschauung, which is Christian, he paid close attention to Christian notions of the sacred and the profane, which are for all religions two modes of being. But like Durkheim he first had to understand primitive, elemental experiences; and in close affinity with Weber he found material conditions (economy, culture, social organization) to be explanatory factors in the "Mother Earth" concept developed by agricultural peoples and in the absence of "Mother Earth" among hunting peoples. His work may be graphically presented in this way:

SPACE AND TIME: TWO EXISTENTIAL MODES OF BEING

SPACE

Sacred	Profane
real	nothingness (unreal) (94)
being	chaos (absolute nonbeing) (64)
power	empty dissolution (nonpower) (64)
idea	nature (64)

Nonhomogeneity of space, a break in existence-experience	Neutral homogeneity of mass, of mass experience, no differentiation of space (22)
Creates the world to be lived in (23) which is threatened by disorder, darkness, chaos (49); this world is created as a matter of choice (51)	No true orientation, no world, just fragments of the universe
Values holy hierophanies interruption of the sacred resulting in detaching the territory from surroundings making it qualitatively different; "sacred space" is consecrated space, "centers the world" (42)	Values places such as birthplace, first lovemaking site, first youthful journey to a particular place; these are not "everyday experiences" (24–26)

TIME

Sacred	Profane
Myth	History
Sacred time is reversible, "it is a primordial mythic time made present"—reactualized "in the beginning" (68–69)	Historical present, feels temporal rhythms of music, being in love, and waiting for a sweetheart
Not temporal, is recoverable, repeatable; it is possible to participate in the original sacred moment (69)	

Attitude "suffices to distinguish religious from non-religious man" (70)

Sacred time is indestructible time, strong time (81); regenerates, fecundates a sterile womb, heals, allows one to prepare for war, is poetic inspiration (86)

Its eternal presence makes possible and explains the existence of profane duration of historical events; e.g., the divine hierogamy makes human sexual union possible (89)

Is anxious before the danger of the new, refuses to accept responsibility for historical existence; rather, it accepts immense responsibility on the cosmic plane (93)

Primordial memory preserves .... Historical, personal memory
true history; does not involve
personal memory (61)

Cyclic time of the profane is .... Cyclic time is time itself
terrifying to the sacred because
it is desacralized time

Life repeats itself .... Life leads to death

| |————————————————————————| |
| | | |

Mixing the two modes

Judaic-Christian Time (Eliade 1959b, 110–12), via God (YHWH) is not cosmic, but exists in nonreversible historic time. Christ is incarnated, a historically conditioned human existence—not reversible or repeatable. History becomes a theophany.

SEXUALITY

Sacred	Profane

Sexuality is distinguished in .... Sexuality is apparently not a
Eliade's observations as dis-   distinct category
tinctive activity

Because cosmos is proof of
sanctity, it becomes a paradigmatic image

Marriage is valorized as a hierogamy of heaven and earth
(165); so, woman is assimilated into the soil, seed to the se-
men, virile and agricultural
work to conjugal union

These experiences are not just
ideas. "The Hindu who, em-
bracing his wife, declares that
she is Earth and he Heaven"
experiences the relationship

Eliade noted that both men's and women's societies are religious
(1959b, 193), even though there are two kinds of sacredness (1987,
127). There are differences between the gendered expressions of social
life. The sacred superheroic world of the supreme being "All Father"
is "unknown to women" (Eliade 1973, 7). A man enters the men's
society as a matter of "choice; not all those who have undergone the
puberty initiation will enter the secret society, though they may all
wish to" (Eliade 1959a, 192). Like Durkheim, Eliade found that initiation separates the child "from the profane world of childhood, where
he was under the care and guidance of his mother . . . there will be
disclosed a sacred history which eventually will bring about the understanding of his own spiritual identity" (Eliade 1973, 85).

The mother does not sit by without protesting against the process
that tears her child from her. In some ceremonies the protest is so strong
that mothers bring spears to threaten "the men who are approaching
to take the young boys away" (Eliade 1973, 87). As the boy is led
away he is taught that he must die to the profane world. "The mothers
and the womenfolk, as well as the initiates, understand this ritual death
literally. The mothers are convinced that [never again will the boys]
be their children" (Eliade 1973, 88–89). Eliade documented the rituals
in which the young man physically abuses and threatens to kill his
mother in an effort to show that he is now separate from her and no
longer cares for her (1958, 7, 11, 27). These messages of death are
meant for the mother as well as for the son. Initiation rites establish a
belief that once women terrorized men, now it is men's turn to terrorize
women. What cannot be reconciled here is the differing purposes of
women's rituals. Whereas men's rituals seek to place men at the center
of the world, granting them sacred space and deepest meaning, women's
rituals continually fall apart and remain simple actions profoundly
connected to "nature."

In examining women's initiation ceremonies, Eliade found that the young girl at first menstruation is separated from the community in a dark hut. She is separated as an individual; the young boys are separated as a group. In their initiation, all of the girls, unlike the boys, are brought into the collectivity of women. All of the boys will not join the collectivity of men. Women's collectivities form their own "mystery associations," which took a long time to disappear; for example, they reside in the witch covens in the Middle Ages (Eliade 1959b, 195). However, they are very fragile and did eventually disappear (see also 1987, 112–16). The men's associations, unlike the women's, did not disappear.

Eliade confirmed that the religious life "always entails death to the profane condition, followed by a new birth" (Eliade 1958, 201). He recognized that women are excluded from the religious. Eliade understood the profane by comparing it to the sacred; the profane is what the sacred is not.

Summary

Freud, Otto, and Eliade showed that the sacred has particular social realities attached to it. In agreement with Durkheim, they found the sacred and sacred people to be separated from the profane and profane people. Eliade and Freud show more closely than Otto that the sacred in social life describes masculine identity.

As with Durkheim's observation that the sacred and the profane inhabit different space-time frames, so in Eliade we find that they are separated in social life into different "modes of being." Eliade described the sacred as offering to the adherent what is "real" and what is "powerful." The sacred offers itself over and against the profane, which is chaotic nothingness and powerlessness. The sacred enjoys differentiation of space, the profane does not. The sacred chooses to create an orderly world; the profane is just as happy without a world—it exists in "fragments of the universe." The sacred centers the world it created and keeps it spinning in a newly established space that brings with it reversible time. Whereas the profane lives in the present, the sacred is able to go back to the beginning of time. Whereas the profane moves from heartbeat to heartbeat, the sacred is able to repeat and recover experience. Sacred time is strong like a warrior and eternal. It allows the gods and humans to become one. Sacred time captures "true" memory over and against the profane, which only has a "personal" memory. For the sacred, time is linear and can repeat itself. But the cycles of the profane lead to death.

An all-powerful and renewable space-time frame facilitates the concept of sexuality as a distinct activity of life. It struggles against the profane, which does not experience sexuality as an isolatable experience. Here Freud has claimed that knowledge of sexuality is repressed in order for the sacred, civilization, to go on its merry way. Based on Freud, one might say that the sacred must not remember that it created this concept and then repressed it. The act of not remembering takes its toll on physical and psychical life. Freud connects the sacred with psychological illness. The sacred and its taboos control the memory, which, in turn, threatens civilization. When women remember that their bondage results not from a decision to love patriarchy but from a desire to protect their children, they become increasingly inaccessible to the sacred order. Whereas the sacred order requires the death of their memory, the repressed, suppressed, oppressed Other fans the flames of memory by choosing love over civilization.

Feminist Notes

Judith Van Herik's *Freud on Femininity and Faith* (1982) uncovers the theory of gender buried in Freud's theory of religion. Both theories are rooted in his oedipal theory of development wherein (1) masculinity is a general human norm; (2) the general human subject is masculine; and (3) this subject is of greater value (31). Freud linked masculinity with the intellect, which develops from its ability to renounce; further, he connected these to Judaism (to his father's Hasidic milieu). Freud related the notion of sacredness or holiness "to the will of the father . . . it demanded painful instinctual renunciation" (Van Herik 1982, 182). Femininity is linked to wish fulfillment, emotionalism, and Christianity, especially Catholic folk piety (like that of his nanny).

Estelle Roith, in *The Riddle of Freud: Jewish Influences on His Theory of Female Sexuality* (1987), claims that the main source of Freud's sexual ethic is traditional Judaism, which sees women as inferior, enemies of civilization, and sexually deficient—that is, wishing for love. Freud and the Jewish traditionalists saw Christian "bourgeois romantic love" as "bizarre, hypocritical and unhealthy" (Roith 1987, 126). "Freudian sexual doctrine had its origins in the encounter between two cultures that differed radically in their sexual ideologies" (Roith 1987, 127).

Freud wrote that "the ascetic current in Christianity created psychical values for love which pagan antiquity was never able to confer on it" . . . and while this statement might seem to us to strike a faint personal note of envy, the phenomena of romance, courtship, and indeed, fore-pleasure depend, as Cuddihy persuasively argues, on the principle of delayed consummation which, in both Freudian and the Jewish doctrines, is constantly deplored. (Roith 1987, 127)

Even though in *Civilization and Its Discontents* Freud had great difficulty finding a psychological meaning for "maleness" and "femaleness" (1961, 54), he continued to operate with a psychological value system favoring masculinity. For some researchers there seems to be little doubt that Freud's understanding of holiness, as it related to people, originated in his Jewish cultural identity (the Hebrew word for holy, is *kadosh*, meaning "apart"; a *goy kadosh* is a *people apart*, that is, a "holy people" [Cuddihy 1987, xi]), which attached masculinity to the sacred and set it apart. This set-apart condition is necessary for men whose goal it is to create and maintain culture and civilization.

In *Totem and Taboo* Freud found that the longing for the father gives rise to religion, and religion gives rise to and depends upon culture. In *Future of an Illusion* Freud decided that it is not just the father but "human weakness and helplessness and need for protection" that is the "chief part" in the formation of religion (Freud 1929, 41). Religion, which fulfills the wish for protection, is therefore an illusion. Illusions are not errors, but rather they disregard their relation to reality (Freud 1929, 55). Some people are more prone to acting on "illusions" than others; these people can be dangerous.

Educated "brain workers" are not to be feared; but there is a danger that

the masses of the uneducated and suppressed, who have every reason to be enemies of culture . . . will attack the weak point which they discover in their task masters . . . so follows the necessity for either the most rigorous suppression of these dangerous masses in the most careful exclusion of all opportunities for mental awakening, or a fundamental revision of the relation between culture and religion." (Freud 1929, 68–69)

Not only women but the oppressed in general oppose culture. Science can balance this threat. As Weber will confirm, it is science's capacity to stamp out wishing and magic—that is, to stamp out the lifeblood of the masses—that proves science to be an effective tool for political leadership. For Freud belief in science is not an illusion. What science cannot give to humankind cannot be obtained anywhere (Freud 1929, 98). Science presents culture with a kind of freedom. Scharfenberg (1988) finds Freud caught between wanting, through psychoanalysis, freedom from the law: wanting a spiritual freedom. Yet Freud feared that dispensation from guilt would threaten religious and moral value systems and therefore the future.

Examining Freud's interest in art, Scharfenberg finds him clearly understanding that civilization requires restrained imagination and spiritual asceticism. Freud saw a need in civilization for a Moses who overcame his passions and subdued his rage. "Overcoming one's own passions in favor of and in fulfillment of a destiny to which one has committed one's self" is the "highest possible achievement" of people (Scharfenberg 1988, 46). Achievement requires repression. Scharfenberg argues that from Wilhelm Fliess Freud picked up the idea that what is "repressed is the nature of the opposite sex which is present in every person" (1988, 57). Fliess based his idea on mathematical and biological theories, concluding that humans were bisexual. Freud, unable to work with these models, chose to stay with the language of the "soul" and the "dark unconscious" (Scharfenberg 1988, 58).

Discovering that the "world formula" is reduced to the "struggle between destruction and love" (Scharfenberg 1988, 61), Freud wanted to heal society through language and therapy (76). As Weber wanted to know why people obey, Freud wanted to liberate people from the compulsion to repeat. Scharfenberg sees in Freud the Weberian prophet who instinctively links the revolutionary with the traditional (121). Also, like Weber Freud was interested in the obedience taboo as an especially German political problem. Both men wanted German men to rise up and become strong leaders, realize the fate of the times, and renounce that which distracted one from the goal.

Yet Freud found problems with his rational foundation because "no one has the authority to force therapy on the masses" (Scharfenberg, 1988, 131). Freud knew that people had to be freed from taboos and given means to develop "traffic codes" for personal interaction (Scharfenberg 1988, 132). Also necessary to the future was a sublimation of aggressive instincts, which were to be replaced with "social ones," that is, with "eros" (1988, 132). In the end Scharfenberg finds Freud searching for "a technology of life based on the happiness value of love" (1988, 133). This technology had to be based on reality.

The problem with religion was that it was filled with delusion that signaled not "an illness of the psyche" but rather its attempt to heal itself. This healing could not happen because, as in neurosis, only the currency of neurosis (or religion) has value. The delusion is created linguistically from a specialized language system.

Freud's most critical evaluation of religion proclaimed that religion had lost touch with reality. "To the extent that it is distorted, one may term it *delusion*; to the extent that it brings a return of the past, one must call it *truth* (Scharfenberg 1988, 140; emphasis original). In Scharfenberg, Van Herik, Cuddihy, and Roith, Freud's "return to the past" means "strengthening masculine identity." The sacred past does not contain feminine or profane identity.

Largely because the feminine is linked to wishful thinking, which often turns into "the pleasure principle," Freud was skeptical of religion; it sought "the very fulfillment of the oldest, strongest, most urgent wishes of humanity" (Scharfenberg 1988, 144). Needing to affirm reality radically, he had to free himself from wishful thinking. Scharfenberg suggests that Freud sought, in place of wishful thinking, a kind of faith that was free from dogma, a faith constantly ready "repeatedly to plow up the vineyard" (1988, 145). This ability to respond to historical existence was not wishful thinking but suffering; "as long as a person suffers, he can still accomplish something" (1988, 145).

In agreement with Freud, a kind of wish fulfillment is at the heart of magic, at the heart of the spirituality of the oppressed, for whom not suffering but struggle and surrender are required. What is truly "spiritual" in profane life is the struggle for life, and in this struggle the oppressed suffer. About Freud, Van Herik concludes:

> The next reason to encounter Freud may be to consider carefully the challenge of his claims that culture is renunciatory and that in renunciatory culture femininity represents fulfillment. . . . [This] dilemma might be a useful basis for asking further questions, within the context of feminist social theory, about how gender works in our moral economy and about how gender and uses of God are thereby intertwined. (Van Herik 1982, 200)

From Freud it can be concluded that the sacred exists apart from the everyday; the social and psychological sickness created in this separation is responsible not only for the continuing genderization of social life but also for the abuse of people called women and feminine. The everyday and that which is created by separating itself from it maintain distinct authority systems. We will now turn to Max Weber, who studied one of these authority systems very well.

Part Two

MEN, BEASTS, CATTLE, AND SEEDS
Max Weber

5

RELIGION

AND

MAGIC

The realm of values is dominated by insolvable conflict, hence by the necessity for continuous compromises. Nobody can definitely decide how the compromises should be made, unless it be a revealed religion.
Max Weber, letter to Wilbrant as cited by Wolfgang Schluchter

Women are encouraged to know her will, to believe that her will is valid, and to believe that her will can be achieved in this world.
Carol Christ, *Laughter of Aphrodite*

Max Weber on Rationality

Max Weber's lifelong project (1864–1920) was to "locate meaning and progress in the absence of meaning" (Freund 1968, 20). Weber considered his time to be confronted with two choices: (1) to go back to the old churches and therefore to abandon the intellect; or (2) to face the future with courage, meeting the fate of the times. Meaning and whatever happiness one can find are located in one's own greatness. Utilizing ascetic Christianity's path to greatness, Weber suggested a path to national greatness.

Max Weber's interest in the developmental history of the West created a powerful analysis of bureaucratization and rationalization. He found the world divided into several "value spheres," all related to and affected by each other, yet each operating within its own value system. Hence it is possible for these value spheres to form "constellations" that give rise to particular social phenomena shaped by a particular ethic. For example, in his well-known *Protestant Ethic and the Spirit of Capitalism* (1958) Weber finds that Protestantism, or religious rationalization, and urban autonomy are necessary preconditions for capitalist formation. These are factors in a constellation of factors that brought about the great transformation of thought toward "world mastery and world domination." Although this particular reality of modern rational capitalism cannot be denied, other realities could have been equally possible had the constellations appeared in another configuration.

Weber wanted to know why people engage in "practical rational conduct of a certain kind, a lifestyle of inner worldly asceticism that combines active self control with world mastery" (Schluchter 1981, 143). In other words, how is it that people are able to squeeze the magic out of their lives? He found a possible answer in ascetic Protestantism's reinforcement of a particular relationship between economic and moral action that created the possibility for capitalist accumulation—one necessary precondition for our modern Western economy. Weber concluded that other "constellations" of factors contributed to modern capitalist culture as well, such as (1) the history of ascetic Protestantism; (2) the history of humanist rationalism; (3) the history of modern science and technology; (4) the ascetic impact on non-economic spheres; and (5) the impact of economic and cultural conditions on Protestant asceticism (Schluchter 1981, 147). The question is whether there is an overlooked but fundamental conflict, or constellation of conflicts, involved in religious rationalization, in demagicalization, in the Protestant rejection of the world. Required in asceticism and religious rationalization are the repression and suppression of nature and all that is feminine. In his historical survey of religions, Weber recognized that in the process of replacing magical motivation with an abstract, universalistic ethic, it was necessary to develop an antipathy toward sexuality. By implication, this means toward women and the feminine. Implicit in Weber's sociology of religion is a theory of gender inequality.

It is important to remember that Weber was a supporter of the feminist movement in Germany. His wife Marianne played an important role in developing German feminism. Max Weber provided legal defense for women with compelling causes who were unable to pay legal fees, and in general he sought to include women's concerns in his justice-making activities. He gathered a following of women who would sit in on his lectures. Thus it is even more painful to realize that the foundation of his thought thoroughly excludes the feminine—an exclusion that ultimately works against a liberating social program for women.

Weber's *Sociology of Religion* (1963) moves from a review of religion in general to a specific analysis of ascetic Protestantism. (For an extended discussion, see R. Stephen Warner 1970.) This direction is shaped by the questions he asked in service to his interests in modern vocational culture and political economy. Weber sought to perfect rational ascetic religious practice in order to create a strong German nation. (Roslyn Wallach Bologh's *Love or Greatness: Max Weber and Masculine Thinking—A Feminist Inquiry* [1990] fully evaluates his quest for greatness.)

Historical Development of Rationalized Religion

Weber found that the model for ascetic Protestantism, Roman religion,[1] was adverse to orgiastic or mystery religions. In it magical activity was confined to personified gods, and everyday religious behavior was organized around sacred law (Weber 1963, 11). New experiences pushed Roman religion into developing a pantheon of gods.

Gods of the Heaven and Gods of the Earth

In general Weber found that the gods quickly become hierarchically ranked. Gods of the earth, like the deities that controlled the harvest, have "customarily borne a more local and popular character than the other gods" (Weber 1963, 13). The inferior earth gods, who controlled wealth through the harvest and served the dead, were no match for the celestial gods, who resided in the mountains and clouds and presided over fixed laws. The development of ancestral gods maintained patriarchal economy as the domestic community bond grew. As life became more settled and localized, the primary "classical bearer of the important phenomenon of a political local god was of course the polis" (Weber 1963, 17). As political activity and the polis grew, the stronger the god of conquest needed to be. Weber cites as an example the establishment of Israel and its election by Yahweh. This Israelite polis,

---

1. Weber's profound interest in Greek and Roman religion parallels that of Nietzsche; see Robert Eden's *Political Leadership and Nihilism,* University Presses of Florida, 1983.

like others, was a political association headed by a civic god. Weber points out that the polis was not only politically and externally but also internally exclusive. Anyone not belonging to the "society of patres" could not hold office or establish legitimacy. The society of patres determined societal and household norms.

Clear to Weber is that "purely economic considerations do not uniquely determine the form of primitive appropriation and division of labor, but military, religious and magical motives enter" (*General Economic History* 1984, 26). The universal god of the polis was slow to lose its magical qualities. Rational thought had to reach a certain "critical mass" in order to challenge magic's powers significantly. The power of the god as a personal overlord grows as the "rational striving for order on the part of secular individuals grows" historically (Weber 1963, 22–27). As new religions develop and are supported by secular or religious powers that suppress competing cults in favor of the new, the need for differentiation between the polis-cult-religion and kin-sorcery-magic grows. The priesthood grows with this differentiation and serves to maintain it. Here Weber found the origins of the sociological phenomenon of the "organized and permanent enterprise concerned with influencing the gods, in contrast with the individual and occasional efforts of magicians" (Weber 1984, 28). As the division between the polis and kin organizations is intensified, so is the division between religion and magic. As religion grows away from magic it has to develop its own ethical framework, built on a new authority that no longer appeals to the kin-magic experiential continuum.

God and Ethics

Men, said Weber, placed increased ethical demands on the gods as:

1. the quality of power increased as orderly legislation effectively controlled large pacified groups;

2. the rational comprehension of an eternal and enduring cosmos increased;

3. the increasing regulation over new types of human relationships brought rules for interaction; and,

4. the reliable necessity of "one's word" in relations and transactions became vital (Weber 1963, 35–36).

Weber distinguished between this rational ethical behavior and the religious behavior of the nonprivileged classes. The degree of magical activity depended upon the congregation (Weber 1978, 447) and its economic status. The peasantry remained more magically inclined.

In comparing religion and classes, Weber found a greater diversity of religious expression among the nonprivileged and less intellectual groups. He also noted that women found the greatest equality in deprived class religion. In any class the exclusion of women in cults is also related to the degree of pacification or militarization within the culture (Weber 1963, 104). Increases in militarization decreased the chance of women's participation. Weber pointed out that access to participation does not mean that women have access to privilege. Privilege in Judaism, Christianity, Islam, and official Buddhism belonged to men. He concluded that salvation religion tended to glorify nonmilitary virtues and thus attracted and included deprived groups, especially women, as followers. As religion rationalized (in Christianity, as early as Paul) and left behind those deprived of status, it required a new ethic rooted in an intellectual framework compatible with demands of rationalized culture.

God and The Intellectuals

When salvation religion takes hold among groups of high social privilege, it is characterized by (1) an intellectual qualification for salvation; (2) mysticism; (3) "a strong devaluation of the natural, sensual, and physical"; and (4) "the exaggeration and impressive refinement of sexuality . . . the suppression of normal sexuality" (Weber 1963, 123–24). As intellectualized religion suppresses magic, there arises "a growing demand that the world and the total pattern of life be subject to an order that is significant and meaningful" (Weber 1963, 125). Even so, wrote Weber, one of the long-lasting tenets of and struggles within Christianity is its anti-intellectualism. The religiosity of the less intellectual and lower classes is more likely to be characterized by magic, pacifism, and feminine participation.

Asceticism, Mysticism, and Salvation Religion

The destiny of religions was influenced by intellectualism, the priesthood, and political authorities when the ruling, noble, and middle classes lost their political power to the bureaucratic, militaristic state.

The rationalist, intellectual bureaucrats sought contemplation as they sought political and economic goals, by "avoid[ing] interruptions caused by nature and the social milieu" (Weber 1963, 170). Weber saw that the salvation sought by intellectuals was based on an "inner need" that was filled for them by asceticism and mysticism.

The ascetics were of two kinds: the world-rejecting ascetic who withdraws from the world, and the inner-world ascetic who participates responsibly in the world but is not of it. When enjoyment of the world was forbidden, work became the focus (Weber 1963, 166). Ascetics and mystics reject the world's empirical order of "creatureliness" and ethical temptations of sensuality, reliance on natural joys and gifts (Weber 1963, 175). Both affirm individual, rational activity within an institutional framework and resign themselves to the order of the world. For example, legal marriage was seen as not an erotic but an economic arrangement and "subsequently as a carrier of the cult of the dead" (Weber 1963, 241).

The ascetic finds salvation in rational action, in an ethic of vocation. Work was elevated from a contemptible activity of slaves, women, children, and other despised groups to the valorized, sacralized activity of "men." In this way the work ethic could compete with or replace the warrior ethic as a source of masculine identity. For Weber this is the unique contribution of ascetic Protestantism (Weber 1963, 182).

Religion, Politics, Sexuality, and Art

Once religions acquire status equal to that of political associations, tension appears between the two spheres of religious and political life (Weber 1963, 223). The god of war, who is also god of the fathers (for example, the Christian God), reminded Weber how intimately interdependent politics and religion are. The "magical religions," he remarked, "had no conception of religious wars" (1963, 224). "But for magical religion, and even for the ancient religion of Yahweh, political victory, and especially vengeance against the enemy, constituted the real reward granted by God. The more the priesthood attempted to organize itself as a power independent of the political authorities, and the more rationalized its ethic became, the more this position shifted" (Weber 1963, 224). Priests now introduced and legitimated the "religious war."

The growing contradiction between "brotherly love" and an "ethic of war against the outside" surprisingly did not turn in on itself, but facilitated a notion of just and unjust wars (Weber 1963, 224). In service to the politically powerful, the priests needed to maintain a congregation of demilitarized peoples and hence preached an ethic of pacification and resignation to the great powers as desirable to God (Weber 1963, 225). As Weber, through Troeltsch, recognized, the religion that becomes privileged among political powers is one in which grace and hence salvation are controlled institutionally (Weber 1963, 232). Weber found this action important for maintaining the power of the priest as opposed to that of the prophet or magician.

This institutionalizing action-organization of the church power structure brought with it a need to control the world and all irrationality. Irrationality threatened the church's power and godliness; it did not function with or serve ethical, rationalized religion. For Weber the most irrational power sphere was that of eroticism, which served nothing but amoral pleasure (Weber 1963, 236). The long and intimate relationship between religion and sexuality moved Weber to search through it for traits with "sociological relevance." He decided that necessary for his understanding of the effect of ascetic Protestantism on social behavior was "leaving out of account as being rather unimportant for our purposes the innumerable relationships of sexuality to magical notions, animistic notions and symbols" (Weber 1963, 236).

He decided that not important to his study are

> the communal religious behavior of the laity at a primitive level . . . cults and rites of the various functional gods who control reproduction, whether of man, beast, cattle, or grains of seeds. [From erotic experiences and] from other magical practices the notion that sexual surrender has a religious meritoriousness . . . need not concern us here. . . . On the other hand, the permanent abstinence of charismatic asceticism and the chastity of priests and religious virtuosi . . . is a symptom of charismatic qualities and a source of valuable ecstatic abilities . . . for the magical control of God. [Mysticism and asceticism] have frequently operated together to produce hostility toward sexuality. (Weber 1963, 236, 237)

For the mystics sexuality blinded one to the goal; for the ascetics sexuality destroyed the ability to plan and control life. As between religion and sexuality, so does a basic affinity exist between religion and art that is destroyed when art "creates values of its own . . . usurping the prerogative of religion" (Freund 1968, 152–3). Weber wrote that "ethical religion enter[s] into a strong polarity with the sphere of art. . . . Religion has facilitated art by magicians and sacred bards . . . as well as the artistic creation of temples and churches," which he called "the greatest of artistic production" (Weber 1963, 242).

But, he adds,

> the more art becomes an autonomous sphere, which happens as a result of lay education, the more art tends to acquire its own set of constitutive values, which are quite different from those obtained in the religious and ethical domain. Every uninhibited, receptive attitude toward art springs from the significance of the content, which may lead to the formation of a community. But the conscious discovery of uniquely esthetic values is reserved for an intellectualist civilization. (Weber 1963, 243)

As with sexuality, religion's violent rejection of art is done in the name of fighting sin. Sin is an alien concept in magic. As rationalized religion increases, emphasis on ethical actions, on sin, increases as well (Weber 1963, 266).

The ultimate conflict is seen in the reaction of asceticism to art; art is required to surrender to esthetic values. Weber recognized that the religious devaluation of art is attended by "a devaluation of magical, spiritual, orgiastic, ecstatic, and ritualistic elements. . . . The more the god proclaimed by the prophets was conceived as transcendental and sacred, the more insoluble and irreconcilable became this opposition between religion and art" (Weber 1963, 244). Weber's discussion of art included music, particularly singing, pictorial arts, dance, and poetry. Freund sees "profound affinity" between magic, sexuality, art, and the erotic. All of these come under attack in societies that negate the position of women (1968, 184).

Rationalized Religious Asceticism

In Weberian sociology rationalized religion is demagicalized religion. Religion, having developed from magic, carries suppressed appreciation for magical elements. The highest form of rationalized religion is the ascetic Protestantism of social and religious elites. Because of its goal orientation (the vocational "calling" as a task), it hostilely suppressed all competing knowledge of or ways to God. It is hostile to magic, sexuality, and art, to the masses (and to what feminists call the sociable body), and to all that is opposed to the society-polis.[2]

---

2. In my framework community represents the sociable lives of people who live together and work toward the group's well-being. The society-polis represents a group whose control over others rewards certain people at the expense of the dominated. The society or polis tends to be male-dominated; community has traditionally been the sphere of women. Community does not place the same value on rationality as does the society-polis.

Ascetic Protestantism supports a rational world order in that it seeks to work out salvation in this life through an individual's vocational calling. Mitzman concludes that Weber (along with Marx and Nietzsche) saw that aristocratic religion, which focused on one's own vocational calling, leads to a rationalism that reifies institutions and values and leads to a "destruction of essential aspects of human personality: grace, dignity, personality, ultimate meaningfulness" (Mitzman 1969, 187). However, Weber was deeply divided between the value of Protestant ethics, which were critical to the accomplishment of modern life, and the more personally fulfilling erotic, magical life. Mitzman attributes this division to a conflict between the young, puritan Weber and the mature nonpuritan Weber.

Weber may have accomplished this thoughtful movement toward eros by the time of his death, but to what extent it is still difficult to say. In a move not conditioned by eros, personal and national greatness became a new meaning system for Weber. This new meaning system, ascetic modernity, is never divorced from Weber's overall desire to strengthen his ego (Mitzman 1969) and to facilitate the achievement of greatness (Bologh 1991). It is these desires that formed the base of what Troeltsch called "neuropathological asceticism."

Even though Weber acknowledged that magic still survives, his developmental scheme placed it at the historical beginning of religious expression. However, the increasing purpose of religion is to rid itself of magic and

> from purely magical efforts at controlling the supernatural to increasingly rational attempts to comprehend the relationship of the gods to the order of nature. Weber's juxtaposition of "religion" against "sorcery," "gods" against "demons," "priests" against "magicians," and "religious ethics" against "taboo" all reflect his effort to view religious development in terms of the progress of Reason. (Mitzman 1969, 201)

This progressive, rational behavior is religiously motivated by a transcendental God who makes ethical demands on "his" followers, and economically and politically motivated by a social elite that needs a passive mass lacking in competing sources of power and knowledge, which it can then direct. However, magic does not disappear as religious expression develops; it continues to reside in the religion of the masses.

As Durkheim distinguished between mechanical and organic solidarity, Weber distinguished between the magical religion of the masses and bureaucratic religion. The inherent tension between the two is summarized as follows:

MAGICAL RELIGION OF THE MASSES	BUREAUCRATIC RELIGION OF THE ELITES
– close to spirits and magic	– tolerates mass magic if it fits into its religious agenda
– as social class decreases, salvation and magical religion increase	– as social class increases, interest in prophets and "other world" decreases
– role of women is varied and more equal	– women's role is suppressed
– attracts women	– less attractive to women
– serves community	– serves society-polis
– seeks union with the holy	– seeks to be a tool of the holy
– values the natural, sensual, and physical, including ecstasy	– devalues the natural, sensual, and physical
– wants to control reproduction of men, beasts, cattle, and seeds through community control and requests for surrender	– resists outside control of reproduction, controls via individual action, resists surrender to community
– is experience-oriented	– is intellectually-oriented
– is the preference of demilitarized, pacified people	– is the expression of militarized people

Weber sought to alleviate the tension by providing the masses with a rationale for supporting bureaucratic life. He argued that the values of the leadership of this sphere, by being best suited to create a great nation, would be most capable of protecting the masses.

In "Science as a Vocation" (Gerth and Mills 1946) Weber continued his interest in virtuoso elites who direct the development of modern vocational culture. The tension between the elites and the masses is responsible for the process of creation and destruction of values that establishes our material existence. The fate of science is that it must live knowing that this building-up and tearing-down process means that its works will be continually outdated. This realization led Weber to inquire into the value of science: "Why does one engage in doing something that in reality never comes, and never can come, to an end?"

(Gerth and Mills 1946, 140). Even science itself cannot provide meaning for the demagicalized, calculating, and technological society it helps to create. For Weber science does not answer Tolstoy's question: "What shall we do and how shall we live?" (Gerth and Mills 1946, 143). Therefore scientists must be value free since science cannot answer questions of value. Science, then, rejects the "religious bond, [and] does not know of the 'miracle' and the 'revelation'" (Gerth and Mills 1946, 147). Yet not science but "fate" (the fact of modernization) is responsible for the preempting of the gods, demons, and magic.

The problem with meaning is this irreconcilable tension between the meaninglessness of the modern world and the need for meaning. The problem is resolved for Weber by choosing "science as a vocation" rather than a return to religious experience, as the German youth of his day were seeking to do. The youth wanted the transformation of science and scholarship into instruments of relevance and personal meaning. Weber denied this possibility and argued that the task was to face "the fate of the times like a man" (Gerth and Mills 1946, 156; see also Alexander 1987, 185). It is precisely because Weber understands their despair, which he experienced in a total nervous breakdown, that he committed himself to answering their dilemma. The answer was rationalism: "Rationalization is at once enervating disenchantment and enlightening empowerment. It had led to increased freedom and at the same time facilitated internal and external domination on an unprecedented scale. This ambiguity is intended. Rationalization is at once a terrible condition, the worst evil, and the only path for human liberation" (Alexander 1987, 187).

There is great similarity between Weber's question, "How have we come to a condition of 'icy darkness,' which threatens to extinguish life and is at the same time a condition in which human freedom is possible?" (Alexander 1987, 187) and Durkheim's questioning of the consequences of the division of labor on social solidarity: "How could autonomy of the individual . . . be reconciled with the necessary regulation and discipline that was required to maintain social order in modern differentiated types of societies? How, in other words, could social bonds be maintained without submitting individuals to the distasteful guidance of tutelary institutions that would repress human autonomy and individuality?" (Coser's introduction to Durkheim 1984, xiii).

Their answers for meeting the demands of the day are similar: science and rationalization. At the same time, Weber decried the rationalization of the world and the parceling out of the spirit. He wanted leaders, heroes, to reinspire life with their charismatic authority. Yet the great losses of World War I forced him to conclude that people could only bear the fate of the times—there was to be no charismatic escape. The other option that kept pulling at him was the world of erotic and magical living. However, he could not understand how its values could stand up against the machinery of the modern age. In addition to being populated by the socially weak, the magical world's "weak" character did not appeal to Weber. His description of magical "religion" and its community, which includes the actual participation of women and all oppressed members in society—the aged, children, and demasculinized men—includes a description of practical action based on valued experience descriptive of the feminine life. Weber's study demonstrates that rationalized, bureaucratic, ascetic religion and masculine experience mutually create and constitute each other.

In Weber's sociology the tension between the community and the society-polis, between magic and religion, expresses a fundamental tension between feminine and masculine experience. In his adequate causal analysis, ascetic Protestantism (or masculine experience) gives rise to modern vocational, bureaucratic, capitalist culture. In order to do so, it must suppress magical community and that which gives it power: for example, sexuality and art; it must suppress the feminine. There are several layers of conflict that are implicitly and explicitly found in Weber's work:

religion vs. magic
masculine vs. feminine
society vs. community
elites vs. masses

Weber suggested that these conflicts can be overcome by choosing either (1) to subject radically and absolutely the natural world to the demand of religion, thereby intensifying the conflict; or (2) to relativize the conflict so that coexistence is organically possible (Schluchter 1987, 113f). As Schluchter points out, Weber's preference for relativizing the conflict (creating separate spheres) is based on the retention of virtuosi and mass groups that remain on different levels. As in Luther's doctrine of the two kingdoms, the masses are expected to submit to virtuoso leadership. The weak feminine is subject to the strong masculine, the community to society, the masses to the elite.

The Challenge of Troeltsch

In many ways Weber's sociology was shaped by Ernst Troeltsch, with whom he shared a house and who often was the only one who could humor him on his darkest days (Marianne Weber 1975). The collegial debate between these two ascetic personalities rested squarely on whether one could find ultimate meaning in Christianity. For Troeltsch, an heir of Hegel and a student of Marx, ideals are found only through historical investigation and are never realized until the end of history. Weber found that ideals are directly available: history is not necessary for understanding them—one may obtain them firsthand. For Troeltsch meaning primarily comes from history. Weber's "value-free" method prevented him from agreeing with Troeltsch, who found no "charismatic persons" from whom to get firsthand information; instead he found only charismatic essences (Morgan and Pye 1977). Troeltsch maintained that because meaning is linked to particular historical expressions and experiences, it is not value free.

In this regard Troeltsch insisted (see *The Social Teaching of the Christian Churches*, vols. 1 and 2, 1960) that the "essence of Christianity" leads one to pacifism. As we know from Marianne Weber and Mitzman, Troeltsch moved out of the Weber home over an argument relating to Weber's war-related activities. Troeltsch maintained that the "essence of Christianity" led to a particular, "ideal type" behavior; other behaviors are related to one's social position. Weber apparently argued against Troeltsch's desire to examine the leadership potential of types other than the virtuoso elites.

Weber's sociology of religion does not deal with the "essence of Christianity" as a matter of personal conviction, as does the work of his friend. Rather, as a sociologist with a political strategy, he studied and adopted one type of behavior, the partial viewpoint of rational asceticism, itself related to one social position, that of virtuoso elites. It is this view that Weber found responsible for modern rational capitalism and to which he turns for resources to face "the fate of the times." It is this ascetic worldview that Troeltsch found least valuable for the times.

Troeltsch did not deny Weber's findings that asceticism was a strong force in early Christianity, nor did he deny that asceticism is closely connected to the contrast between the world and the church. But he carefully called "erroneous" any claim that asceticism rose from this contrast. Troeltsch acknowledged in the introduction to his *Social Teaching* that he developed his argument in dialogue with Weber, Simmel, and Rickert. Troeltsch, as church historian, theologian, and philosopher, painstakingly prepared a broad picture of Christianity and insisted that Weber take his research seriously. However impressed, Weber left the works to footnotes. This polite if active dismissal of Troeltsch assumes significance when we understand that Troeltsch claimed a broader and more varied asceticism than the one that denied the world and hence found itself in Weber's sociology. Weber's sociology is shaped by his focus on the cause of world mastery and on the solutions to problems of modern states and leaders. He omitted from his work those religious forms most critical to the ethical formation of the mass experience.

Most important here is Troeltsch's evaluation that asceticism was not an inevitable outcome of Christianity: "He [Jesus] glorif[ied] poverty for its own sake. But he teaches quite plainly that food and work are only of value in so far as they are necessary for life; otherwise they have no value. . . . The ethic of Jesus is heroic rather than ascetic" (Troeltsch 1960, 59). "He unquestionably accepted the world and its simple and innocent joys . . . full of hope that the ideal would very soon be realized" (1960, 102). This ideal was a life undifferentiated from the world by "language, locality and customs" focusing on the "lot which falls to the individual," not on the idea of "calling" (Troeltsch 1960, 124). Christianity's goal, typically Eastern, was a "humanity which renounces all self-will, opens the heart to the inflow of sacramental grace" (Troeltsch 1960, 108). Jesus "did not encourage asceticism but an indifference towards the natural conditions of existence," an indifference that required a life-style of simplicity and intimacy. These acts of simple and intimate living in the face of the world required a heroic personality (Troeltsch 1960, 107). The difference between asceticism and indifference is that the former implies resistance and repression, domination and control; the latter does not. One problem for Weber apparently was that the Jesus worldview was not successful. One can see why asceticism in Weber's scheme is heroic (gendered masculine). But why, in Troeltsch's (historically unsuccessful) scheme, are indifference, intimacy, and simplicity, which usually characterize the feminine, heroic? Because to live indifferently is to live on the fringe of society, to expose oneself to the wrath of the socially powerful, who feel threatened by intimacy. Indifference enables one to resist the temptation of "status," the temptation to be regarded by others as different and better based on social distance and power. Living against repression and domination is the more difficult task. It is this resistant posture that Troeltsch recommended for the times.

In Troeltsch's framework force and domination lose effectiveness, although persecution may actually increase if those controlled simply love the dominator and go about life as if this oppressor did not exist.[3] However, as Troeltsch reminds us, within the Christian framework this indifference is intended as a life-style not only for the subjugated, as Weber and Nietzsche argued, but for all persons.

Asceticism did not rise out of the central religious aim of Christianity but out of a particular ethical rigorism that was a response to "larger and more complicated social conditions" (Troeltsch 1960, 103). The evangelistic ethic of Jesus required ascetic self-denial. But this self-denial was seen as a positive action of love of God and of humanity. It was most adequately expressed as a "non-attachment, a freeing of self" from material goods. In this context salvation of self is found in a loss of self that is the prompting act precipitating the salvation of the world. Genuine asceticism, then, is practiced by a group that keeps itself from slipping into the dangerous world of materialism, egoism, and self-will. (Examples of contemporary, "genuine" ascetics might be the Mennonites, the Amish, the Moravians, the Brethren, and the Hutterites.) In the spirit of Troeltsch, W. H. C. Frend, in *The Rise of Christianity* (1984), describes genuine asceticism as having a social motive that asks: "Why do the rich grind the faces of the poor?" (1984, 423).

Troeltsch found the self-denying, world-rejecting asceticism experienced and documented by Weber to be an early historical and practical "mistake" that shaped "the whole concept of asceticism" (Troeltsch 1960, 103). This mistaken formulation took the original and genuine message and created a self-denial that was severe and contrary to nature: a denial that included everything and was seen as required by God. Troeltsch called this "overstrained piety" founded on the preservation of its own moral system, which became an end in itself (Troeltsch 1960, 103).

Troeltsch believed this "self-denial-become-good-work" asceticism to be "most peculiar" and "permanently nourished in the increasing

3. This heroic person is not gendered for Jesus, who knew "no Jew nor Greek, slave nor free, male nor female." The Jesus movement (surrounding him and up to about 45 A.D.) was predominately made up of men rejected by the dominant culture and of women. Jesus was not a "warrior," and the movement sought reconciliation, not revenge. The apostles quickly moved to make his a universal ethic and as they rose to power moved to suppress the Jesus movement, which remained an underground tradition as the apostolic tradition became authoritative. With the apostles, the suppression of the feminine became official. See Fiorenza (1983) and Theissen (1978).

emphasis on Original Sin and on virginity" (Troeltsch 1960, 103). This peculiar structure needed "extraordinary effort of will and enthusiasm" to maintain itself, and it became capable of the "wildest eccentricities" (Troeltsch 1960, 104). Nongenuine forms facilitated a "particularly strange" rise in a belief in the existence and presence of demons (which Troeltsch acknowledged is partly due to the decline of faith in old religions). These new spirits were no longer "morally indifferent"; they became dangerous and wicked. The methods developed to repel these demons "robbed life of all spontaneity . . . thus detachment from the sense life leads to an asceticism, which, however, is not really based on a metaphysical dualism of spirit and matter" but on a practical dualism of Satan and God. It could also result from the "neuropathic weakening of vitality, due to a certain weariness and slackness of the sex instinct, caused by ignorance of the laws of sex" (Troeltsch 1960, 107). Troeltsch showed how the mind/body dualism penetrated Christianity and recognized that something is terribly wrong when the body (matter) is considered sick and the dualism is not thus seen to be entirely destructive.

Troeltsch found this "ideal of chastity" difficult to explain but ultimately caused by a civilized world suffering from a "nervous disease" that sought "purification and support in religious ideas." In any case the stress laid on the "purity" of the "virgin" state opened the door to stillborn asceticism. When the ideal of celibacy began to "appeal to the healthy and the strong, it produced a system of physical self-torture whose one aim was the repression of the sex instinct. This, of course, became combined with all the abnormalities of the perverted sex instinct" (Troeltsch 1960, 107).

According to Weber (1963) the church needed celibacy to be a prevention against clergy offspring inheriting church wealth (238), while inner-worldly asceticism did not need celibacy or poverty but the "avoidance of all erotic pleasure," and the "elimination of all idle and exploitive enjoyment of unearned wealth"—the avoidance of "surrender to the beauty of the world" (183). For Troeltsch genuine asceticism's notion of purity was founded on a humble openness to grace. This peculiar form was founded on "a higher degree of perfection, in which complete asceticism, poverty and celibacy can be particularly or wholly obtained . . . a special *Charisma* [most important for clergy]" (Troeltsch 1960, 109; emphasis original). Genuine celibacy and genuine asceticism have their place in history when they work to provide positive freedom to achieve goals. However, asceticism was not originally a Christian concept; Weber himself mentioned the asceticism of the Romans and its influence on Christianity. Troeltsch also argued that it was taken up as believers met the surrounding culture on its own terms. Once adopted, the whole ethic of the church changed; it lost its original security and confused worship with ethical behavior. Troeltsch maintained that alongside of

> Christian thought upon the idea of the Family there were, however, quite different voiced ideas of Christian asceticism in the ideal of celibacy . . . the influence of asceticism . . . led to a grotesque exaltation of sexual restraint, which again led to the well-known ideas about the danger inherent in the female sex and to a low estimate of women—these ideas certainly arose . . . not out of the thought of Christianity. (Troeltsch 1960, 131)

On the other side of this grotesque "non-Christian" development were found convents for women that facilitated what Troeltsch considered "advantageous" increases in scope and influence for women in religious life. Among the "genuine" forms he listed gnostic groups whose techniques included frenzied and ecstatic movements (Troeltsch 1960, 105).

Weber documented the life issues of women more clearly in his political and economic sociology than in his sociology of religion. His lesser ability to see women's issues in religion facilitated his interest in learning how frenzy and ecstatic forms are rejected because ecstasy facilitates a withdrawal from nationality and rational organization by providing a more immediate source of meaningful and expressive behavior than do nationalism or rational organization.

In light of his friendship with Troeltsch and Troeltsch's scholarship, it occurs to us to ask why Weber was so interested in how society goes about denying the feminine, the expressive, the irrational, the spirit. Could it be that the puzzle Weber (and Weberian actions in society) caused for Troeltsch was caused by something in addition to a "nervous disease"? Could it be that, given Freud's understanding of the incest taboo and Weber's attraction to his female cousins, Weber's own needs for sexual intimacy could not be satisfied by women? Did Weber's attraction to his "unavailable" cousins prevent a personal recognition that his desire rested elsewhere?

Weber on Primitive Social Organization

Weber's study of primitive life documented the long history of tension between women and women's spirituality and the needs of men's society. He outlined two different bases for appropriation of land and goods in primitive life: (1) the physical means of laboring with the soil are implements belonging to the kindred of women (Weber 1984, 26); (2) the land is treated as territory that has been conquered and is protected by the man: an agnatic man or some masculine group (Weber 1984, 26).

The man owns land by right of conquest; the woman owns her tools, which she uses to work the land. Divided along gender lines, individuals belong to a multiplicity of groups that further define appropriation (Weber 1984, 26).

Weber described the then-current theory outlining transition from "group marriage" to a theoretical *mother right* (*Mutterrecht*) as a commonsense one. However, the subsequent transition to *father right* (*Vaterrecht*) took place through the institution of marriage by capture. Common sense is replaced by violence. In addition, he found mother right occurring only occasionally, and not at all in general. Patriarchal law of social groups established legitimate marriage, which gave legal standing to children of a certain wife of a man. Weber listed these social groups as the household community, where only children of a certain marriage could inherit; the clan, where only legitimate children could share in blood vengeance and inheritance; the military group, where only children by marriage had the right to bear arms; the class group, of which only these children were full members; a religious group, where only legitimate children's sacrifices were acceptable to the god and only they could perform ancestor rites (Weber 1984, 36–37).

Weber contrasted the "house communities" with the hunting and fishing house societies, which, he maintained, were led by "charismatic leaders based not on kinship but on war-like qualities" (Weber 1984, 39). His observations might be presented in the following way:

HOUSE COMMUNITY	MEN'S HOUSES
Housework/Fieldwork	Hunting/Fishing
Women	Men
1. Magic kinship	1. Practiced totemic religion, magic*
2. Family lived in the house; young, old, all women	2. Only men of age could be active
3. Women's world	3. Women kept out by fear and threats

4. Leader was of ranking kin	4. Charismatic leader
5. Subject to exposition (held accountable)	5. No demand for accounting
6. Usually elderly	6. Young, strong male
7. Communal consumption and centralized work	7. Exclusive, valuing individual consumption
	8. Warrior group may or may not be the same as men's society
	9. Owns land by virtue of warrior role
	10. Therefore has citizenship

*Weber's work lists different stages and varying degrees of magical influence, from the most influence found in group control of copulation magic, as in fertility rites, to totemic religion and clan taboos of men's societies with decreasing use for magical elements, to rationalized religion, which is demagicalized.

Membership in the men's societies lasted twenty-five to thirty years and frequently included polyandrous marriage by capture. Like Durkheim, Weber found women excluded from these societies. "Women are forbidden to enter the men's house, in order to guard its character of secrecy. It is kept sacred by fear-inspiring surroundings" (Weber 1984, 40). Women raise young boys until novitiate age when they "are taken out of the families . . . receive the consecration of young manhood, and take up their life in the men's house" (Weber 1984, 40).

Any man who fails the test of strength, or cannot "submit" to the practices of the men's society, or "is not received into the cult," is thereafter a "woman" and not given "men's privileges" (Weber 1984, 43). When too old to serve the men's society or military institution, the men go back to live with their wives (Weber 1984, 40).

The men's house creates not only totemism but also the matriarchate, in which children are alienated from the father. Where totemism does not exist, Weber found the patriarchate (Weber 1984, 41). The "growing tendency towards the patriarchate" (away from any association of maternal succession) was "decided according to established land tenure" (Weber 1984, 41). In both the matriarchate and the patriarchate "the woman always remains under the authority of a man" (Weber 1984, 42).

Under patriarchal authority a woman was little more than a "field slave"; alongside of the woman were her children, slaves, and demasculinized men. Men are ritualistically separated from women and rejected men (Weber 1984, 116). Men and women were even separated economically within the clan by sex-differentiated money (Weber 1984, 238).

In Weber's evaluation the growing religious claim (the strengthening of the warrior class and totemic gods?) and the increasing bureaucratic administration of the men's societies facilitated the demise of the clan (Weber 1984, 46). Urban life required activities that cut across and broke down clan taboos. Likewise, urban life promoted congregational religion, which cut across clan lines. Religious force brought by prophecy encouraged the individual to build up the church membership over and against clan membership. Religious groups competed with clans for inheritances. The second force, political bureaucracy, also moved against the clan. With uneven success, states come to disallow clan authority. Western religion facilitated the dissolution of the clan into the polis and into the state. Judaism assisted this dissolution by discrediting fertility magic and "stigmatizing it with a character of decadence and godlessness" (Weber 1984, 361). Judaism gives to Christianity a "magic free platform" and thus contributed an "important service from the viewpoint of economic history" (Weber 1984, 361).[4]

We can see that the suppression of magic became crucial for the elevation of a Protestant religious order that relied on the police power of the state to protect its growing material interests and its "capitalist" ownership of salvation. The suppression of magic attempted to deny the masses access to an alternative knowledge of, understanding of, and way to God. The breakdown of magic was defended and maintained by political and institutional violence. Warrior religion had to fight a community power of shared action to prevent a radically different community vision facilitated by sexuality and art. So too did the new warrior religion of ascetic modern rationalism find itself called on to suppress, repress, and control the irrationality of the mass, of a worldview described by Weber in feminine terms. Weber's theory of social domination, describing types of social action, authority, and domination, shows how he thinks social control is possible.

---

4. Rational capital is facilitated by rational religion which rises above the community (Nietzsche's "herd") and in its will to dominate convinces the rational actor that he or she has a right to be independent of community. Rational religion tries to camouflage its actions by claiming that it is really responding to an older, more sacred order than the community. Perhaps Nietzsche, Weber's silent mentor, says it most succinctly: "The herd instinct is inherited best, and at the expense of the art of commanding. If we imagine this instinct progressing for once to its ultimate excesses, then those who command and are independent would eventually be lacking altogether; or they would secretly suffer from a bad conscience and would find it necessary to deceive themselves before they could command—as if they, too, merely obeyed. This state is actually encountered in Europe today: I call it the moral hypocrisy of those commanding. They know no other way to protect themselves against their bad conscience than to pose as the executors of more ancient or higher commands" (quoted by Eden 1983, 174).

6

AUTHORITY,
POWER,
AND DOMINANCE

The people's voice is God's voice.
—Max Weber,
Economy and Society

The question of dominance quickly becomes for Weber a question of what makes Western rationalism unique. Weber's "sociology of domination" forms a macrosociology on an idealist, Nietzschean base; all reality is founded on individual action. To explore his power-domination model one must begin with a general examination of its conceptual foundation, Weber's effort to distinguish three overlapping dimensions of social life: authority, material interests, and value orientation (Bendix 1977, 286). The distinction between power and domination will be made, supported by an understanding of the legitimization of domination in its traditional, rational, and charismatic types. Given Weber's individualist base, has the power-domination model adequately addressed collective power and collective domination?

The Sociology of Domination

Weber's examination of power and domination is based on a definition of sociology that concerns itself with "the interpretive understanding of social action and thereby with a causal explanation of its course and consequences. . . . Action is 'social' insofar as its subjective meaning takes account of the behavior of others and is thereby oriented in its course" (Weber 1978, 4). Weber's methodological foundation for this individualist approach softened when he had to distinguish between "types of meaning." He expanded the meaning of an action, which is the meaning that a particular actor personally gives to it, to include reference to a general meaning that a group of actors may give to it (Weber 1978, 4). A second type of meaning was developed as a theoretical tool to aid in abstract analysis of "pure" meaning attributable to hypothetical actor(s).

Here Weber developed two useful ideas. First, he was able to separate the importance of "recapturing an experience" from the interpretation of that experience. When the recapturing is impossible, the social scientist strives for clarity of observation and accuracy of comprehension that can be rational, emotional, or artistic (Weber 1978, 5). Second, his ideal model of "hypothetical actor(s)" operating with "pure meaning" appears to serve the purpose, similar to that of Marx's concept of "proletarian false consciousness," of facilitating a way of understanding values and human action orientations different from one's own values and orientations. The "ideal type" removes ambiguity and highlights action deriving from "irrational factors." Weber warned of the danger of "pure types," clearly intended as a methodological tool, creating rational action where none exits (Weber 1978, 6).

Weber further distinguished meaning from understanding. Understanding has two forms: observational understanding of subjective meaning and explanatory understanding of motive (Weber 1978, 8). Rational observational understanding of actions (what you see is what it is) has a commonsense quality about it. What Weber did not clearly articulate is that this understanding is based on particular familiarity with a particular culture. "Irrational" action rationally observed "out of context" may not be "irrational" in its culturally specific context. This blind spot allowed him to concede that cephalic index and skin color might be shown to correlate with the degree of certain kinds of rationality (Weber 1978, 8), although he was always reminded that his desire for "statistically conclusive proof" would crumble before the possibility of subjective determinations of irrationality. Likewise, intended or motivational meaning must be qualified and understood within the complexity of meaning.

Buried in Weber's discussion of meaning is a self-correcting possibility that could counter the nonvalid claims of biological determinists or superiority theorists wishing to use his model: that is, his notion of the "interpretive grasp" that must acknowledge that it rests on the borderline of meaning (Weber 1978, 9). Meaning cannot be stated as fact. Weber saw that we grasp meaning in three ways: (1) historically (we discover the intended meaning); (2) sociologically (we can produce an average or approximation of intended meaning); or (3) scientifically (we can formulate a pure [ideal] type). Each of these interpretations seeks clarity, but none "claim[s] to be causally valid interpretation" (Weber 1978, 9).

To overcome the borderline handicap, one must utilize comparative interpretative methods (Weber 1978, 10). When this is not possible, the "imaginary experiment" using ideal types is employed with the reservations already mentioned. How, then, does one determine "correct" or "typical" behavior? Weber suggested that we must form verifiable generalizations from our experiences and calculate the probability of the action's occurrence.

Causal interpretation might be "correct" when action and motives have been correctly apprehended and their relationship is meaningful. If the relationship is not meaningful, the attached statistics are not sociologically meaningful. Nonmeaningful actions become conditions, stimuli, or hindrances of action. All action is the behavior of one or more human individuals. Of action we can only know the function; the phenomenon itself escapes us.

Once actions have been generalized, it is possible to designate "laws" (Weber 1978, 11). Laws, like "correct behavior," are observable probabilities holding typical motives and typical intentions. In the case of laws based on experience, the relationship between the means and the ends is clear, especially when the means are observed to be "inevitable" (Weber 1978, 18). It is through the creation of laws that sociology formulates the uniformities of the empirical observation (Weber 1978, 19).

Types of Social Action

Weber defines social action to be only that which is not related to inanimate objects and which is oriented to the behavior of others. For example, religious behavior is not social if it is contemplation or solitary prayer (Weber 1978, 22). It is here, at the beginning of *Economy and Society*, that one might question his definition of social action. Weber has not made a clear or definite enough correlation between individual action (for example, contemplation or solitary prayer) and the social motivation of individual action.[1] In all major religions one prays because someone else is praying or has prayed. Types of prayer are constructed in communities, and individual prayer is prayed in communities. The most chilling examples of the social significance of individual prayer are found in the Asian and Latin American people's movements, in which individual resistance fighters kneel and pray to a deity for assistance as they prepare in their poverty to face armed militia, while they themselves are unarmed.

This is social action; action supported by the power that individuals gather over time to face sure death; powerful social action based on an authority unknown to Weber. A challenge to understand this authority might lead one beyond Weber to hypothesize that all action, as all thought, is social and originates in an authority base unique to it. Weber's problem is humorously solved, however. Like Marx's self-acknowledged cover to Engels—whenever I get in trouble, I call it a dialectic—Weber helps himself out of this trouble by saying that the borderlines (this time between the individual and the social) are indefinite (Weber 1978, 24).

Weber distinguished between four types of social action:

1. *instrumentally rational* action determined by expectations of behavior used as conditions or means for rationally chosen behavior;

2. *value-rational* action determined by a conscious belief for its own sake, independent of the outcome;

3. *affectual orientation* determined by feelings; an uncontrolled reaction to stimuli, producing irrational or meaningless behavior;

4. *traditional orientation* determined by habituation, and bordering on meaningfulness.

A social relationship, then, is that behavior between actors that constitutes other-oriented action described above. A social relationship exists where there is a probability of meaningful social action. This

---

1. Bendix disagrees (287), saying that Weber's position in *The Theory of Social and Economic Organization* (New York: Oxford University Press, 1947) extends social orientation even to activity when individuals are alone, as long as they take into account the actions of others, including probable actions; however, this is not the explicit statement of *Economy and Society*, and indeed Weber's *Sociology of Religion* is ambiguous on this point.

social action is oriented toward usage, custom, and self-interest. The probability of a social action is guided by the actor's sense of a legitimate order as context. In the case of laws the relationship is stated as clear. Legitimate order is constituted by convention as well as by law; belief in the validity of the order also constitutes a valid order.

The bases of legitimacy are tradition, faith, subscription to values, and enactment. But Weber does not elaborate upon this belief system. The question of who must believe in order to create legitimacy is not clear. Must the staff believe? the ruler? the society? combinations of them? none of them? Does the struggle begin when the staff does not believe? How is it that men control women and those deemed feminine who have ceased to, or never did, believe men's actions were legitimate? In the very tension of the belief-disbelief continuum, social relationships are maintained.

Legitimation and Social Action

The social legitimation of action was of personal and professional concern to Weber. Still more intriguing for him was the fact that people create or help to maintain power structures, some of which dominate them (see Mitzman's *The Iron Cage*, 1969). Although he never fully discovered *why* they do this, he accumulated a massive and compelling description of *how* they do it. Notable here is the contrast between Weber's search for reasons for obedience and Marx's search for reasons for revolt. Both men question these actions in their personal and professional lives. The question constellations of "Why do I?" and "Why do *we*?" seemingly appear to sponsor powerful social theory.

How people act "in society [is] with and against each other on the basis of their material and ideal interests and . . . in a relation of authority and obedience on the basis of shared understandings" (Bendix 1977, 286). People are oriented toward each other and toward norms.

Within social relationships, whether or not they are conflictual, competitive, selective, open or closed, traditional or enacted, there exists an expectation of mutual responsibility and response. The form of responsibility and response changes with the organization of the group. Regardless of group formation, for Weber *power* remains the probability that an actor's will can be imposed in the face of resistance by others. *Domination* is the probability that the actor's command will be obeyed by the group in either a political or a hierarchical setting.

The Phenomenon of Power

Weber divided power relations into three categories: (1) he outlined power based on constellations of interest (market or status groups); (2) power holds a base in established authority (legal, traditional, and charismatic power); (3) power is held on the basis of leadership. The first two categories will be discussed later in their relation to dominance. The third requires brief mention here.

Weber's supposed "great man theory of history" really results from an underdeveloped idea that suggests that "history alternates between the charisma of the great men and the routinization of bureaucracy" (Bendix 1977, 326). The rise and fall of charisma is related to the relative importance of individual action. The decline of charisma must be taken case by case and its cause located in the communities to which it is appropriate. When society decides not to deal with a charismatic leader, "heresy" charges are established. Collins quite insightfully claims that these charges are more than intellectual, they are symbols for organizational power and politics. The symbolized heresy is an attempt to prevent the shattering of social solidarity (Collins 1986, 213). In other words, charismatic leadership itself draws attention to deviations and risks of deviations damaging to the dominant power structures. At certain times communities or states are more or less willing to suffer the consequences of following the charismatic leader.

Domination and Legitimacy

The probability of the imposition of will in the face of resistance of others was not as interesting to Weber as the source of the ability of the powerful to dominate. Weber's search for an answer to the question of obedience led to his articulation of three types of dominance, each maintaining their own forms of legitimate authority: traditional, legal-rational, and charismatic dominance. Dominance is not simply "having power or influence over others." Each type of dominance implies some level of compliance based on an interest in obedience (Weber 1978, 212). Weber saw compliance as voluntary action "based on ulterior motives or genuine acceptance."

Dominance, then, is a reciprocal relationship between the ruled and the rulers. The most important aspects of this relationship are (1) the power to command; and (2) the meaning each attaches to the authority relationship (Bendix 1977, 292). Here one waits for Weber to explore the second aspect of the relationship with the same depth as the first.

By abandoning the topic Weber implicitly concedes primacy to the dominance of rulers. For the ruled it is crucial to challenge the notion of complicity and to discover the meaning they attach to the authority relationship. It is necessary to go beyond Weber's notions of tradition, rational legality, and charisma. A Weberian analysis can be used to support theories that the poor comply in the acceptance of their relegated poverty. The meaning of obedience for ethnic and racial minorities, women, the poor, and the ruled, is regularly attached to life-and-death decisions (that is, nonobedience entails risking one's life), whereas the ruler frequently chooses the action as a possibility for personal gain.

Regardless of the motivations of the ruler, the maintaining of dominant authority frequently requires a loyal staff bound to obedience by custom, effective ties, or personal self-interest. But these reasons for obedience are not in themselves totally reliable. In addition, domination of the staff is necessary and is maintained through the staff's "belief" in "legitimacy." Each form of domination nurtures its own belief and establishes a trained staff to protect it (Weber 1978, 213). Once a staff is in place, the relationship between the leader and the followers is mediated by the power of the staff to impose through force the leader's will on the "followers," who now become subjects or masses. The creation of the leader-staff-mass relation moves patriarchy, with its degree of mutuality, to a patrimonial situation with no mutuality.

Types of Dominance by Authority

Weber established the existence of three types of authority that claim validity based on legal-rational, traditional, or charismatic legitimacy. Legal-rational authority receives obedience due to the legally established order. Authority is held in the "office," whereas authority in traditional dominance is held by a "person occupying a sanctioned role." The obedient person complies out of loyalty to the custom. Charismatic authority is gathered by an individual leader who is trusted for his or her unique qualities engendering personal belief.

Weber's study found historical epochs to be characterized by types of dominant authority, as follows.

Legal-Rational Authority

The modern administrative epoch is dominated by legal authority. The legal-rational system has separated office from home and "ownership of the means of production" from individual ownership by the official. Social action is governed by a system of rules and laws applied to everyone as valid members of the group. If this is the case, then we have a highly useful concept to employ on behalf of the oppressed: we can expect to find those not considered "valid members of the group" dominated by a system of rules or laws that do not apply to them. For example, it becomes clear that when suffrage is systematically denied any particular group, those people are not valid members of the state and they retain no real legal recourse within the state. Membership in the state, community, organization, and so forth, requires conformity and the possibility of conformity. Within the organization a hierarchical system of obedience is established in which the highest level determines "correct" behavior for valid and nonvalid members. The validity of membership itself is determined by dominant authority.

Organizational entities, whether the state, the church, or economic enterprises, have all adopted modern forms of bureaucratization. Whether socialist or capitalist, superiority within the bureaucracies depends on their ability to assimilate technology. The ultimate question is, of course, Who controls this massive machine? Technical specialists are the power brokers in bureaucracies. Their role increases in capitalist systems that require the modern bureaucracy to plan, control, and calculate.

Socialist systems would require a similar dependency in order to carry out their programs; in fact, Weber argued, they would need a higher degree of formal bureaucracy. In centrally planned bureaucracies, the risk would be "dictatorship of the bureaucrats rather than dictatorship of the proletariat" (Bendix 1977, 459). For Weber bureaucratic administration was simply domination through knowledge. Technical knowledge and experience facilitate the striving for power. However, the flip side of bureaucratic social action is the leveling of status, which replaces the status holder who is dependent on privileges and appropriations.

Further, bureaucratization foreshadows mass democracy (Weber 1978, 226). For Weber democracy meant choosing a ruler through the dictate of parties organized as machines. Weber's highly cynical analysis of what democracy is or could be in the modern world is perhaps healthy. When one looks at the highly bureaucratic societies of the United States and the former Soviet Union, one immediately becomes skeptical of correlating bureaucratization and mass democracy.

Traditional Authority

Whereas the legal-rational system claims authority for itself, the traditional authority has legitimacy claimed for it through personal commitment to age-old rules, values, and powers. The person in authority is a "master," and is legitimized through traditions that construct the content of the command as well as its limits. The obedient are also obligated and choose to obey the master in the unlimited areas in which tradition claims no rules but general authority; even so, resistance to authority is against the master and staff, not the traditions (Weber 1978, 227).

It is important to distinguish between Weber's idea of "individual freedom of choice" in conformity with custom (Bendix 1977, 295) and the inability to choose freely due to conditioning. For example, blacks born into slavery may believe that they are inferior because the dominant authority has conditioned them to believe it. Even after a successful challenge to dominant belief, prior conditioning that did not allow them to experience success can foreshadow the oppressed's ability to believe in their capabilities, eventual success, and equality. However, they are not free to choose status inferiority until they are indeed equal.

Traditional authority is given; we are born into it (Bendix 1977, 287).[2] When we challenge it, as Weber did symbolically in the challenge to his father, we must pay the price: we must start over and create or accept an alternative authority. To do this without a notion of what lies ahead can be revolutionizing and devastating, as it was for Weber, as demonstrated in Mitzman's *Iron Cage*.

Acceptable or not, traditional authority can be maintained with or without a staff. A staff is collected by patrimonial recruitment of kinsmen, slaves, ministeriales, clients, coloni, or freedmen; it is also possible to have extrapatrimonial recruitment of favorite persons exhibiting personal loyalty, vassals, or volunteers. When a staff does not exist, we have the oldest forms of *gerontocracy*, rule by elders in a noneconomic or nonkinship system, or *primary patriarchalism*, rule by inheritance in an economic and kinship system. In both cases a type of checks and balances exists. The master does not assume personal control but is given control by the willingness of persons to submit for their own benefit; therefore, the master has no staff and must rely on the goodwill of the members.

---

2. Traditional authority is *present;* charismatic authority *erupts;* and legal authority *develops* (Bendix 1977, 287).

Patrimonialism and extreme sultanism often arise when traditional authority develops a staff of administrators or militia that are not selected by tradition and given authority by the membership, but are personal controlees of the master. The members of the group then take on "subject" status.

Another form of patrimonial authority is *estate-type domination*, in which the staff appropriate power and economic assets. Complete appropriation finds government divided between the ruler and the staff, who control through personal right. In contrast, a gerontocracy or elementary patriarchal system is administrated by the group on behalf of the group. Appropriation by the master distinguishes patrimonialism from patriarchalism. It is obvious, then, that patrimonial systems require more maintenance and a strict concern with safeguarding their legitimacy.

Charismatic Authority

Weber realized that it was impossible to establish the origins of charismatic authority; somewhat before traditional authority because examples of charismatic leadership and communities appear throughout time. He came to see, as Gerth and Mills (1986, 245) write, that charismatic authority is a permanent type, appearing as response to psychic, physical, economic, ethical, religious, and political distress. Charismatic authority is concretized through a community belief in observed supernatural, superhuman, or exceptional abilities. Often the leader claims divine origin or appointment, or magical or prophetic abilities (Weber 1978, 241). Charismatic authority derives from "proving his powers in practice" (Weber 1978, 1114). Being so able to affect the everyday world, (he) fulfills (his) "responsibility to the ruled," proving "that he is indeed the master willed by God" (Weber 1978, 1114). However, "the people's voice is God's voice," and his authority quickly disappears when the people disagree (Weber 1978, 1115).

The followers or disciples freely subject themselves to charismatic authority, locating proof of its legitimacy in an event—a miracle, for example—as guarantee for meaningful devotion. The subject is obliged to recognize the authority and to organize appropriate behavior.

Appropriate behavior often requires the creation of charismatic communities staffed by persons chosen for their charismatic qualities. As these communities are frequently communalistic, administration is lacking in any organized form. The goal of the community is to create new obligations or rules that are always in contest with other charismatic communities.

Charismatic authority is antithetical to rational, bureaucratic, or traditional authority. A revolutionary force, charismatic authority is irrational, said Weber, in its repudiation of rules and of the past. As long as personal charisma is proved, the authority is retained and it does not need to appropriate power. Economic considerations do not exist, as people follow a call, a mission, or a spiritual duty.

During traditionalist eras charismatic force is the primary revolutionary force (Weber 1978, 244). The revolutionary force of reason works externally, affecting life situations; the force of charisma affects the subjective, internal life that seeks reordering to address unhappiness, suffering. When successful, charismatic readjustment to the problems of the world requires a new look at all attitudes. The degree of revolutionary action depends upon the degree of *metanoia* (Weber 1978, 1117). Powerful revolutionary force "overturns notions of sanctity," abandoning the sacred for the inner knowledge of the Divine.

However, charismatic authority is not stable authority. Succession becomes a major problem, and eventually charismatic authority takes on traditional or rational characteristics. As the ideal and material interests of the community must be maintained, leadership authority is transferred to a new leader, who is revealed or designated by the previous leader, or granted to an "office." This routinization of charisma allows followers to appropriate powers and economic advantages in addition to participating in the charismatic community. Once routinized, charismatic authority does not seek revolutionary change. A charismatic staff becomes a necessity, and its antieconomic beliefs are altered toward *prebendalism.*

Feudalism and Prebendalism

Weber discusses the prebendal structure of feudalism because out of it often develops a structure different from charismatic or patrimonial authority. This structure has two types, one based on fiefs (*Lehensfeudalismus*) and the other on benefices (prebendal feudalism); all other forms have a patrimonial character (Weber 1978, 255).

A fief includes the appropriation of powers and rights in exchange for services within the master's household. However, vassals are not always controllable. They often lose political struggles if the master develops a local administrative staff. This staff is patrimonial, extra-patrimonial, or a group of trained specialists organized around fiscal issues, not the fief. Once developed, the administrative staff also presents the feudal chief with a struggle for administrative power.

Benefices and prebendal feudalism have a fiscal basis; individuals are awarded appropriate benefices according to income and service. Rather "sultanistic," prebendal feudalism does not involve "free" contractual relationships of "personal loyalty" (Weber 1978, 260). Rather, the financing is of a type aimed at stabilizing income—often of a civil administration or a royal treasury. Frequently, benefices include military groups of dependent knights (e.g., the Samurai), which significantly makes them different from fiefs (Weber 1978, 262).

The Complexity and Constellations of Dominance

Weber's analysis of domination extended to the constellation of interests in which types of domination merge to form a greater controlling force. These mergers are endless in possibility. The most significant constellation Weber used in his analysis of capitalism was domination by economic power and authority.

Domination by Economic Power and Authority

Domination is pervasive in all social action. From language to sexuality to economics, rational association is a result of the exercise of domination. "Domination constitutes a special case of power . . . economic power is a frequent . . . consequence of domination as well as one of its most important instruments" (Weber 1978, 942). Domination, then, has another possible type in addition to domination by virtue of authority: domination by a constellation of interests (Weber 1978, 943), the purest form of which is monopolistic domination in the market. This domination is supported by individual pursuit of self-interest. Although Weber does not refer back to it, it is important to remember that his *The Protestant Ethic and the Spirit of Capitalism* shows the social preparation necessary for individuals to choose this constellation.

For Weber the borderline between economic and authoritarian domination is a fluid one. However, economic domination is easily converted into domination by authority; this domination is "identical to the authoritarian power to command" (Weber 1978, 946). As in all domination, the rulers must command the ruled so that they obey, believing that they, the ruled, created the content of the command. It is not difficult to extend Weber's monopolistic domination, the possession of goods or marketable skills, to the monopolistic possession of ideas. Again, economic power is derived from ideas or norms that subjugate the ruled. Further, the subjugation is maintained through the dominant ideas of inferiority.

In summary, administrative staffing is vital for all forms of authority beyond that of traditional authority, if it desires to continue functioning. *History is the expression of the struggle between chiefs and their staffs for appropriation and expropriation of the means of administration.* Weber found that our historic journey is toward increasing the ability of the rulers to dominate with less struggle.

Culture has developed around the solutions to this struggle and is marked by the constellation of officials who need the chief and aid him in the struggle against the feudal classes and others desiring power (contrast Marx's class struggle). From this conflict resolution have arisen major cultural forms, including, most significantly, kinds of education and status groups.

Despite the permanency of bureaucratic and patriarchal structures, this rationalizing process is not static. "In this respect, they are both institutions of daily routine. Patriarchal power especially is rooted in the provisioning of recurrent and normal needs of everyday life. Patriarchal authority thus has its original locus in the economy. . . . The patriarch is the 'natural leader' of daily routine" (Gerth and Mills 1946, 245). Given this, the bureaucratic structure is the "counter-image of patriarchalism transposed into rationality" (Gerth and Mills 1946, 245). Bureaucracy is created to meet calculable needs. It is created to be what magic is not.

The noncalculable needs find their provision in charisma. Change in the bureaucratic provisions is still possible through charismatic leaders who again take up the internal challenging of values in pursuit of genuine revolutionary change.

In a real way Weber maintained Hegel's notion that history ends in the present, not in the future (Bendix 1977, 388). His notion that the paradise of premodern organic life, with its absence of technological, capitalistic, bureaucratic machinery, had been lost apparently created a personal state of *disenchantment-demagicalization*. It is probably more correct to say that Weber, in true conformity with his Calvinist upbringing, extended general spiritual disenchantment to the material life! It is here that Calvinism deviates from other forms of Protestantism, and other forms of Christianity, for that matter.

Liberalism and Disenchantment-Demagicalization

Gerth and Mills find that Weber's "disenchantment"[3] thesis embodies a liberalism and an enlightenment philosophy that found "history as a unilinear progress towards moral perfection . . . or, towards cumulative technical rationalization" (Gerth and Mills 1946, 51–53). Bologh confirms her analysis that it is neither "liberal nor illiberal" values "but manliness that accounts for Weber's politics" (Bologh 1990, chapter 2). Where others see liberalism in "individualism, independence, power and greatness," Bologh sees an idealized conception of manliness. However, she finds that "Weber's realism or rationality often coincides with liberal political positions and values" (Bologh 1990, chapter 2). Bologh explains these apparently contradictory evaluations as "two sides of Weber" that "can be integrated into or subsumed by a single overriding value and fear: the value of manly independence and the fear of servile dependency" (Bologh 1990, chapter 2). Because bureaucracy threatens manliness, it was important to Weber that throughout the rationalization process the charismatic individual is enabled to interrupt the bureaucratic trend in order to become the "sovereign of history," the heroic man (Gerth and Mills 1946, 53).

But is this the case? In order to be the sovereign of history, one must rise above society. To maintain, develop, or control social life, predictability is necessary: "Predictability is the skilled accomplishment of lay actors—not a phenomenon governed by mechanical forces. . . . The 'accomplished' character of the social world always involves 'effort' on the part of the actors, but is at the same time 'effortlessly' a part of routine, taken-for-granted nature of everyday life" (Giddens 1983, 64). Whether it is planned or not, an individual becomes a charismatic leader only when recognized by others. Individuals cannot stand apart from the corporate accomplishment of everyday life.

---

3. Talcott Parsons's translation of *Entzauberung* in *Sociology of Religion* as in Gerth and Mills's *From Max Weber* (see *Gesammelte Aufsätze zur Wissenschaftslehre*, Tübingen: Mohr, 1922: 536, 554), uses "disenchantment" rather than Schluchter's choice of "demagicalization," thereby preventing a more powerful impact of Weber's startling insights into the nature of this conflict.

It is dangerous to reduce the notion of charisma to a relationship between individuals and society. The charismatic leader or authority must be distinct enough to be set apart from society, yet a charismatic community is needed to give substance to the leader. Often the leader becomes one and the same with the community.

Let us turn more directly to Guenther Roth's discussion of charismatic communities. Today the most common of charismatic communities is the ideological one. *Ethical* (applying political, transcendent standards to the powers that be) and *exemplary* (providing exemplary conduct) forms see the world as a meaningful totality requiring "an extraordinary correspondence between belief and action" (Roth and Schluchter 1979, 131).

Roth extends Weber's religious virtuoso concept to include ideological virtuosi, true believers, people of virtue. Ideological virtuosi "are, so to speak, highly accomplished technicians in matters moral . . . whose spiritual needs cannot be satisfied by piecemeal social amelioration or political compromise, in contrast to the majority who accept routines and rules of politics" (Roth and Schluchter 1979, 131).

The virtuoso task is to discover how to motivate the majority and how to survive during politically stable periods that render them isolated. Weber's interdisciplinarity becomes instrumental in the analysis of the partial worldviews involved in social maintenance. In Weber's "structural-functionalist" system it is "only through institutionalization that material and spiritual wants receive a socially relevant solution" (Schluchter 1981, 270). Weber's method allows one to examine the "power distribution among partial orders (the natural, economic, religious and political) [which] results from their position within the control hierarchy of society. The power distribution within partial orders results from the position of an actor vis-à-vis the means of production of material and spiritual goods" (Schluchter 1981, 35).

In addition, there is another type of authority that characterizes a masculine individualism, plays by the rules and follows the leader, and, if all else fails, threatens some act of violence to ensure obedience. Weber's model is a Western patriarchal model that does not understand or even see the feminine model(s) of authority held by the oppressed, which are rooted in eros-sociability.

Domination can be seen as sheer enforcement of particular will instead of as a "contractual and reciprocal relationship." Traditional authority is not given but taken; it is required from the dominated for daily living. The development of legal authority is not as natural as

Weber understood it. It is based upon the exclusion of voices unnecessary to the political life of the virtuoso elite. On the other hand, charismatic authority can be seen to belong to the world of oppressed persons as well. It is the only type of authority in Weber's framework that is potentially controlled by mass response. However, as Weber described it, this charisma is dependent upon individual charismatics: charismatic authority disappears with the demise of the charismatic individual. But there is another kind of charisma. The charisma of community, of sociability, depends upon the charismatic potential of the group that does not follow a leader, even though charismatic qualities of individuals are necessary to the community, but that plots its own course through negotiated wills. Meaning in this system is indeed, as Weber suggested, attached to an authority relationship. However, in contrast to Weber's notion, this relationship is not between a leader and the masses but among the members of a community. It is the glue of charismatic community. It needs no staff to protect it; protecting communal authority is the ongoing accomplishment of the community itself.

7

EROTIC

SOCIABILITY

AND BEYOND

The need for deep sharing is a human need.
—Audre Lorde

Mitzman finds Weber's attempt later in life to reconsider mysticism or cosmic love to be a way of creating an "alternative to the dry hyper-rationality that resulted from an ethic of worldly asceticism" (1969, 198). Weber's consideration of cosmic love ended in a rejection of its requirement to become "a part of the cosmic All." Accepting cosmic love held grave consequences: it would be tantamount to suicide (Mitzman 1969, 198). Weber's perceived loss of individuality, consciousness, and responsibility is, in a Chodorow-Gilligan sense, the anticipated loss of masculine identity that Weber attempted to "ennoble," not "dissolve" (Mitzman 1969, 198).

Weber's choice was consistent with his desire for a strong German nation over against a weak, "old womanish" one. Just as the nation is substituted for the tribal family, the community of warriors is substituted for the "brotherhood of love." Disharmony is chosen over a bond uniting economics, politics, aesthetics, and the erotic (Mitzman 1969, 209). Ultimate meaning is transferred to the function of war, which transcends family ties (Mitzman 1969, 212). Through death the warrior discovers meaning in the life that leads to it (Mitzman 1969, 213). Accepting worldly violence, the ascetic must reject pacifism.

In order to accept violence as legitimate, Weber drew a parallel between asceticism, which found a unique way to remain "possessed by God," and a national value of service, both of which acted to solidify power. He inadvertently recognized, in the creation of men's warrior societies, a usurpation and redefinition of feminine roles and experience. Weber's affiliation with warrior asceticism substantiates Mitzman's argument that Weber was in direct contest with his mother for his soul (Mitzman 1969, 225). Benjamin's analysis (and indirectly Douglas's observation) that society expects the son to overcome the mother and be separated from her, by violence done to himself, is an underlying analytical tension recognized by Mitzman. The boy becomes a warrior and a member of men's society by doing further violence to himself at the request of the leaders; at the same time he recognizes the incompetency of the community of men (Mitzman 1969, 225). The only choice in this unhappy situation is to obey the fate of the times, that is, to obey the society of men.

Weber, like Troeltsch, found that obeying men requires obeying one's demon. An ancient legend shows that obedience requires sacrificing one's wife (Mitzman 1969, 273). By obeying the demon, the husband acknowledges that he lacks the "grace to save her." Marianne Weber was no stranger to this analysis and in her virginal marriage quietly complained of Max's repression but also recognized that fighting it was a losing battle—a war waged against the ethic of sexual unhappiness (Mitzman 1969, 279; Weber 1975).

To surrender to one's sexual self was to surrender to nature and thus to prove one's own "animality." To be an animal was to surrender to humanity.

Yet when Weber needed a break from these tensions, he prescribed eroticism: "Love is the respite. Precisely because it is irrational, it provides the personal element that the modern individual needs, to give some meaning to a world of conflicting institutions that have become too rational" (Collins 1986, 79). The shift from meaning found in vocation to meaning found in eroticism is profound. However, erotic love between individuals is a subcategory of love found within the community, for which sexual love is but one aspect of love. Indirectly, Weber found that it was impossible to love individuals with erotic equality while maintaining a political commitment to suppressing the requirements of communal love (for the story of Weber's encounters with the erotic see Green 1974).

A Helpful Asymmetry
in Weber's Thought

Bologh (1990) demonstrates that Weber's one-sided, conflict-oriented perspective is biased toward and descriptive of masculine experience. Her understanding of Weber's concern for manliness and nationalism centers on his elevated values of individuality and independence. Weber's concern with manly greatness, strength, arms, power, and action stands opposed to the feminine life of intimacy, weakness, powerlessness, and dependency. This opposition marks his "struggle over the dilemma of manliness, the conflict between modern manliness which is a product of the modern rationalization of the world and the threat to that manliness by the continued rationalization of the world" (Bologh 1989, 27).

This dilemma is played out in his sociology of religion. Bologh recognizes in Weber's work a pattern that associates warrior ethics with masculinity and ethics of the subjugated with femininity. She concludes that the tension in his work is that between a religious (absolute) ethic of brotherly love and worldly, political activities.

However, in addition to a tension between masculinity and femininity, there is also in Weber a tension between an elitist masculinity and other masculinities. Weber often collapses the Christian faith story into the story of the masculine, ascetic, intellectual elite's story—precisely the intended hegemonic goal of the elite—and therefore only recognizes the less-than-one-sided experience of some Christian men, those men who were able to ally themselves with the forces producing modern rational capitalism. Troeltsch claimed that the essence of Christianity led to a particular ethical standpoint that was continually compromised by the social position of individuals in society.

Troeltsch maintained that the core Christian message, far from generating powerlessness and passivity, centers on noncomplicity in the worldly goals that deny individual worth and universal equality. The subjugated risk their lives by simply choosing to live toward equality instead of complying. Contrary to Weber, this alternative religious form, which understands the feminine, ethically renounces domination, not power; violence, not force; imposition of will, not negotiation of wills. In a feminist sense, Christianity shaped and experienced by women and the oppressed can be seen as a radical critique of social political order; it cannot easily be characterized as "traditionally feminine and submissive." The apparent submissiveness can be seen as a surrender to liberationist values that do not serve a heroic masculine order based on domination, violence, and imposition but serve to protect the souls of people who exist on the margins of social life.

The Revolt of the Widows

A widow in early Hebrew through early Christian societies shared more than a little in common with contemporary widows. The Hebrew word for "widow" (*almanah*) has as its root the word *alem*, "unable to speak." (It is related to an Aramaic word meaning to be in pain.) Thus the widow was the "silent one" (Thurston 1989, 9). Having lost her husband and his status, a widow was without political and economic status. To be a widow was to live a precarious existence, to live as if dead to society. But she is not really dead. She may be considered "marginal" by the "central" dominating forces in society, but she is not "marginal" to herself or her community.

Stevan L. Davies in *The Revolt of the Widows* describes first- and second-century communities of women who were voluntarily celibate, "widows" to society. Their celibacy predates the church's requirement of clerical celibacy. Living in a time that took magical authority for granted (Davies 1980, 28), they are the praying, teaching, organizing backbone of first- and second-century Christianity. The writings these communities left behind (or stories written about these communities) instruct newly converted women in how to deal with the practical problems of divorcing a spouse in light of civil society and its police force; of choosing celibacy while yet a virgin; or refusing remarriage if widowed. The writings instruct the women on how to deal with church authorities, men who frequently abandoned them in struggles with the husbands, fathers, or menkindred who wished to retain control over the independent female who had freely chosen celibacy and now sought refuge in women's communities. These refugees found diversity not only desirable, but necessary (Davies 1980, 12).

The writings indicate that women were not interested in the "structure, rules, governing laws" of the church, and were indeed prevented from those functional areas. Instead they concerned themselves with the needs of the whole Christian community, such as teaching the religious and social ways of living in community, magical healing, and raising the dead. While the apostles were concerned with "heroic virtues" (Davies 1980, 32), women and the communities that supported them concerned themselves with opposing moral order (Davies 1980, 34).

Risking execution, and often executed, women and their support communities chose to "*end family life in the sense of an end to reproduction*" (Davies 1980, 34; emphasis added). Wives were considered property, and often returned to husbands by the police, who frequently were called in by angry husbands who blamed the "sorcerer" apostle on "bewitching" wives. Oftentimes, Davies writes, the accusation of witchcraft coexists with the emergence of new values and norms that conflict with indigenous values (Davies 1980, 40). The community of "widows" chose to live outside the normal structure of their society. In some instances wealthy converts endowed the communities; but more frequently poor Christian "churches" supplied much of the widows' sustenance.

At the time of the "widows" the monastic communities that Weber discussed had not yet come into existence. Weber had no knowledge of these communities. This unusual community of women suffered persecution, torture, shame, humiliation, continual attacks by police, civil authorities, and menfolk. Yet they found comfort in the apostles who would uphold their choice: "I know that you are more powerful than those that seem to overpower you, more glorious than those who are leading you away to imprisonment . . . you understand all these things yourself, namely that . . . you are superior" (Davies 1980, 53). Whole unto themselves, the widows were encouraged to remain steadfast.

The widows described celibacy as a "treasure." "Who finding a treasure did not make use of it?" (Davies 1980, 55). Through choosing not to reproduce or to facilitate the polis-family system, women used the only resource they had to challenge the social structure.[1] In cooperation they founded community.

In support of each other they gathered to pray, to dance, and to sing. When things went wrong, it is not the apostle or Jesus—that is, no earthly male—who intervened, but God. The identity of women was no longer founded on sexuality alone. Their identity was shaped and protected in a community that threatened masculine society. Community was formed by saying "no" to patriarchy.

---

1. For an extended discussion of celibacy see Ruether 1984.

The widows' stories tell how easy it was for women to leave their husbands, while men had great difficulty leaving their wives. The mothers, wives, virgins, and widows had little problem with piety, but the men were always on a lower spiritual level. These women considered their spiritual lives to be qualitatively better than men's (Davies 1980, 63). Even when men refused to baptize them, they knew their worth and baptized each other and even baptized themselves.

Although the Christian message was one of equality, social practice left much to be desired. Christianity was "portrayed as a faith which elevates women and brings them maturity and strength" (Davies 1980, 68), while Christian men were not sustained in times of need or crisis. Women knew that they had to be better than men and formed a group "with a collective identity, the 'virgins of Christ who serve him'" (Davies 1980, 74). Davies argues that this collective identity facilitated a community of persons (made up of the widows and their supporters) who were not interested in "the problems of legitimacy and the virtues of the church officials" (1980, 79). This sentiment sat in tension with the reality that a stable church was the source of income for the widows. Even so, the resistant community was little concerned with the authority that derived from legitimacy of the office.

Many women found this semiclerical status of widows in community "attractive." When describing this life the widows often used the analogy of "marriage." Yoked in marriage to God, they committed themselves to a "true man" in an "incorruptible marriage" (Davies 1980, 84). Because of the increasing independence of these women and their growing challenge to male leadership, which was persecuted by the secular political powers because of its inability to "control the women," by the middle of the second century women are considered a threat to men's salvation, a danger to their souls.

The female-directed communities with their collective identity and support by autonomous persons became too powerful a reality and too powerful a symbol of what was ideally Christian as opposed to what was morally wrong with society. Together, women and God resisted the authority of men.

This independent vocational status directly opposed civil authority and laws that supported a man's right to maximum reproduction. As women rebelled from their marriages, they did it alone (Davies 1980, 111). The apostles provided the original message but no material support.

Seeking to retain control of the developing church hierarchy and to retain the respect of the surrounding community of men, church leaders moved to suppress the roles and functions of women in the church. By the middle of the third century female imagery for God had disappeared from orthodox Christian tradition and women were denied preaching, teaching, and healing functions. The church fathers imposed "male only" restrictions on church leadership and books written by women, and branded them heretical (Davies 1980, 128; also see Elaine Pagels's *The Gnostic Gospels,* 1981). But women survived. Their power was greater than a "power within," greater than eros. It included God.

Asian Women and Christianity

Eighteen centuries later, Korean women heard the Christian message of freedom and responded as their first- and second-century sisters did. Mattie Wilcox Noble, in *Victorious Lives of Early Christians in Korea* (1927), provides autobiographical sketches of Koreans during the time of their conversion in the early 1900s. Noble found that Korean women were attracted to the message of equality; the practice of equal education for Christian men and women; the message of freedom; the practice of watching missionary women give instructions to men; the message of salvation; and the practice of treating women as bearers of their own soul. Wrote one convert: "I also rejoiced that freedom had come to me—a woman. The day that Jesus Christ was preached in Korea, began the emancipation of women from the bondage of thousands of years" (Noble 1927, 105).

These stories tell of how Korean women found strength to resist husbands who beat them because of their church attendance. Tired of beating them, husbands sometimes gave in and let their wives attend. The women prayed for the conversion of their husbands, who they knew would stop beating them if their hearts could be truly converted. In the meantime they rejoiced in their own freedoms. They were free to leave their husbands to proclaim the gospel; free to be themselves. Contrary to traditional culture, they were now free to have their own names. At baptism they required a name. Wrote one woman: "I never had a name. Think of it, for nearly fifty years without a name. On my baptismal day I received a name, all my own—'Dorcas.' Yes, it was the happiest day of my life" (Noble 1927, 105).

Ascetic Women's Experience

Unlike Weber's understanding of Christianity as weak, the Christianity experienced by the widows and Asian women risked life, encouraged and supported life, and understood that the story of Jesus of Nazareth was about the giving of life for the good of all. In another context it is this universalized stage that Carol Gilligan calls the "highest" stage in women's moral development.[2]

It was the honor of moral integrity that Jesus, the women of the first century, and Asian women of the twentieth century sought when they risked offending the sociopolitical order. (People such as Bishop Desmond Tutu of South Africa and many South Africans share their spirit.) It is perhaps because Troeltsch recognized that the masses see the "essence of Christianity" as a movement toward liberation that Weber chose not to discuss it. He chose instead to talk about the social behavior produced by a particular faction, an intellectual elitist party, whose struggles had a message for a Germany desperately trying to save itself and its civilization.

As Bologh suggests, Weber advocated the creation of "alternative *spiritual* values that are of this world." They include self-discipline, self-control, and willingness to employ violence to achieve power. As seen in the lives of the oppressed Asian women, the widows, and the poor, Weber's values were not the spiritual values of the subjugated; the latter do not benefit from this world's riches and from this world's prescribed access to fulfillment. To achieve their goal, these women have had to create a value-authority system unknown to Weber.

Like Weber, the community of widows and the Asian women sought redemption and dignity. However, they discovered that the desire to escape natural existence is neither necessary nor desirable. The only way to live a truly human life is to live it cooperatively in communities that surrender individual achievement and salvation to the universal good. These (Christian) women's stories demonstrate that surrender happens to be a particular problem for those in hierarchical authority and for (Christian) men who understand individual fulfillment as individual gain. The feared impact of early Christianity's collective representation in the powerful renunciation of oppressive social order necessitated its active, violent suppression.

---

2. It is ironic that the cold that Weber caught, which ultimately led to his death by pneumonia, was caught on Easter Sunday, the day on which Christians celebrate the resurrection and liberation from the dead, from all those things that keep the believer from choosing universal equality and righteousness.

But its suppression was largely a measure of its success. Weber wished to suppress this power in favor of forms of political domination that facilitated an individual's rise to leadership. The "mass" was a dangerous threat to his goals: "The use of term 'mass' itself limits the conception of the people's role in politics to that of objects; it prevents them ever being seen as the potential subjects of political action except in a dangerous capacity" (Bologh 1989, 17). To Weber democracy was not created by "street politics" or by "the mass (which) is always subject to emotional and irrational influences," but through "responsible and realistic politics . . . made by a few cool and clear heads" (Bologh 1989, 17).

Whether or not we conclude that Weber's model of political democracy was restrictive, the fact remains that the idea of control by a few "realistic" persons who valued ascetic Protestantism rose to unimaginable heights of privilege within the Western sociopolitical order that disregarded Christianity's "essence." For many people this model was liberative. Christian asceticism's ideal "possessionless" existence has always been rejuvenated from below. However, once it existed as an economic model of exploitation, it ceased to be a spiritually valid option for those Christians who were themselves oppressed and were trying to preserve the teachings of Jesus. The religion that satisfies an economic calling is what Weber calls an unbrotherly religion that makes a vocation out of worldly activity (Collins 1986, 78). At the close of his life Weber found that the only relief from this historically endless set of tensions is love or escape into the arms of the old churches. What Weber really means by love is "eroticism, or erotic love." Perhaps the primary enduring theme from first- to twenty-first-century feminism is that "erotic love as relief" is not the same thing as erotic sociability.

Weber and the Feminist Notion of Eros

Bologh analyzes Weber's work as a "struggle over the dilemma of manliness"; yet it could also be said to be a "struggle over identity." In this light Karl Jaspers wrote: "We no longer have a great human being who could reaffirm our identity. Weber was the last one" (quoted by Roth and Schluchter 1979, 13). Bologh shows that masculine identity produced a particular way of knowing and acting in the world founded, according to Weber, on "warrior ethics." Feminists have spent a great deal of time explicating the different ways men and women know and act. The question always returns to: Why? Why is differentiation based on sex? This question set off a flurry of research on the "origins of misogyny."

Nancy Hartsock uses Homeric literature to assist in the search for origins. Like Weber she locates the origin of women's oppression in the development of the warrior class, which, as a part of men's society, utilized violence and domination to threaten and control women and their houses. Hartsock sees this oppression as a "division of labor" problem based on a threat to violence. Like Chodorow, she recommends coparenting as well as full inclusion of women and men in political economy.

Full inclusion is not a goal of rational capital or of rational religion.

> The first conflict is religion versus the family. . . . Weber was to emphasize that this breaking away from the family-based society was to have major consequences for social transformation; it created new forms of organization and new levels of motivation that could eventually overturn the traditional society circumscribed by kinship. But initially this took the form of a conflict. Leaving one's parents, and even one's wife and children, as the world religions encouraged individuals to do, was obviously an act of disloyalty to the family. It was proclaimed in the name of a higher ethical system, but nevertheless it was a blow to the ethical demands of the family group. (Collins 1986, 72)

Weber found that religion's attack on the family permanently transformed it. Religion's control of the family leads to transformation of society. Whereas Hartsock focuses on physical oppression via reproduction and the family, Weber can be said to focus on the spiritual production and reproduction of meaning. Weber pursued how meaning is reproduced through religion's relationship to social and economic realities such as the family. It is "meaning" that Weber could be said to find existing in the physical relationship. This system of meaning could be seen to become the cause of, reason for, or tool of women's oppression. Here Weber and Durkheim find common ground. For both there exists something above or beyond the material life that is responsible for social relations. Durkheim found that men created the ideal totemic world that excluded women.

Even so, it is clearly noted in both Hartsock's and Weber's studies of primitive life that symbol and materiality are fused: the female-feminine is a symbol of power—power of life, the power of fertility. Lost to human community is male-masculine support and appreciation for the female-feminine existence. Men perceive the continuous work of women to be of value and yet lacking in their own lives. There is no way for them to include these activities in their bureaucratic (and warrior) lives. Their reaction frequently is misogynistic.

But there is hope. The former masculine identity with its particular way of knowing and acting, of which Jaspers found Weber to be a symbol par excellence, is dissolving. In a sense, both ancient masculinity and femininity are gone. However, just as ancient men constructed men's exclusive societies, so as a matter of survival have women, excluded men, slaves, and "racial minorities" of this century consciously constructed their own communities. Although separated by intent and by the centuries, both group-forming actions are meant to protect something vital, something without which life is not possible.

This "something" is rooted in the future of identity. The future of identity for the oppressed and the excluded is partially held in the hands of the dominating elite—hands whose fingers form the constellation of religious, political, social, economic, natural, psychological, and physical oppression. The rest of the future lives in the dark unknown, to which varying constellations of people bring different lights.

Political Power and the Erotic Light

Collins finds that Weber's overall political theory understands politics as a struggle for legitimacy. Weber evaluated this struggle to be a personal one. However, since his theory of authority and power is rooted in an understanding of domination, one might say that Weber's overall theory assumes that politics separated from the community will is a struggle for establishing the legitimacy of domination. Jessica Benjamin (1987) maintains that the issues of separation from recognition by the mother in early childhood development reappear in erotic domination and affect the relations of the sexes in particular ways, as seen in a form of rationality held by men, called "rational violence" (Benjamin 1987, 42). Autonomy is achieved by dominating the other. Domination creates the threat or the possibility of violence against the other. Just as the initial break from continuity is an act of violence (see Douglas 1984 and Girard 1986), the break from masculine discontinuity into continuity requires violence as well. "In this way violence and reason become necessary parts of an act of mastery over death" (Benjamin 1987, 50).

Weber expressed mastery as "instrumental rationality" or, because it forms the base of our culture, "instrumental culture" (Benjamin 1987, 63). In this culture the world becomes disenchanted. Echoing the work of Bologh, Gilligan, and Hartsock, Benjamin associates Weber's understanding of disenchantment with masculine rationality, whose foundation is rational violence. All four feminist theorists contain themes of individuation and domination as characteristic of masculine experience.

Although Benjamin perhaps overidentifies "rationality" with "masculinity," she correctly connects the disenchantment-demagicalization process and masculine rational violence with masculine hegemony. If, as Hartsock believes, power and therefore community are based upon the feminine principle of eros, then violence and domination—the opposites of power—are also enemies of eros. One quickly feels what Weber meant by the irreconcilable tensions that Bologh has shown to be a tension between the masculine and the feminine.

Some feminist theorists recognize in most cultures a "memory" of a time when all was well between the sexes. The best-known memory of this type in Western culture is the Hebrew myth of the Garden of Eden. This memory reminds us that relations between sexes are created and not fixed. Therefore they can be re-created.

Re-creating the relations depends upon how the issues of dominance and submission are addressed. These issues can be understood as rooted in a fundamental relationship between eros and rational violence. Because Weber profoundly understood modern rationalism and clearly articulated one of its constellation's most significant aspects—ascetic vocationalism and its hostility to art and sexuality—we should expect him to have a keen insight into eros and erotic love relations. Bologh discusses this in "Max Weber on Erotic Love" (1987b). Her work may suggest that Benjamin's notion of "rational violence" is akin to Weber's notion of the conflictual, brutal nature of erotic relations. Examining Weber's *Intermediate Reflections* (Gerth and Mills 1946, 323–59), she states that Weber "describes erotic love in terms of a conflict model of interactions" (Bologh 1987b, 242). Weber considered salvation religion to be in tension with erotic love. This tension results from erotic love's brutal and coercive nature.

At this point, two of Bologh's Weberian themes—(1) the crisis in masculine identity and (2) the association of femininity with the ethic of brotherly love—can be used to show that Weber's discussion of "the erotic," in the context of its tension with the ethic of brotherly love, does not only reflect the masculine bias, understanding, and experience of eros, but it also reflects a particular masculine bias that has as its aim the perpetuation of patriarchy in its capitalist and religious forms. First, Bologh explicates Weber's notion of erotic love, which is founded on the inherent coercion and brutalization of the less brutal partner, whom Bologh identifies as the woman. For Weber, and from the point of view of the modern masculine self, erotic love is opposed to submission, affirms individuality, presupposes differences, glorifies animality, is exclusive, is an alternative way to God (salvation), is related to conflict, represents a will to possess, and involves spiritual violence (Bologh 1987b, 245–47). Previously it was seen that the development of masculine identity is based on individuation, difference, and opposition to submission anchored in a grounded notion of violence as a consequence both of genderization and of continued life with other men. Weber described erotic love in masculine terms, based on a privileged identity of what it means to be a powerful man.

Bologh questions whether this notion of erotic love must necessarily be "conflictual" and proposes "sociability" as an alternative basis for relationship. Sociability requires a pleasurable relationship of desire. "In this respect sociable relationships are identical with erotic relationships. In the latter, the desire for the other includes sexual desire" (Bologh 1987b, 257).

Describing social relationships that require "desire, action, pleasing and caring," Bologh describes feminine social experience that "presuppose[s] trust that the other will not take advantage or hurt" (Bologh 1987b, 257). That is, it does not presuppose violence. Comparing "sociability" to Weber's "analysis of erotic love relationships, we find that sociability presupposes that the imposing of the self on an other may itself be pleasurable to the other. The expression of one's desire may please the other" (Bologh 1987b, 258). Ultimately Bologh seems to be saying that for women, or for a feminist notion of sociability, there is little distinction between eros and erotic love. Erotic love is eros extended to sexual desire. Feminist analysis of community (social) relations of "desire, action, pleasing, and caring" finds that these are also the bases of sexual relationships. Both require a notion of self-interest that is not threatened but enhanced by surrender.

Bologh observes that "religion responds by challenging the basis of erotic love in sexual desire" (1987b, 250). Herein exists a challenge of interpretation: could it be that salvation religion's challenge to erotic love is also a challenge to masculine notions of erotic love and of social relations as required by the masculine notion of conflict and opposition of will? This challenge may be the religion of "brotherliness's" support of the more brutalized partner, a partner whom the religion of "brotherly love" encourages to claim for (her)self an erotic sexual love relationship based on the sociability of eros.

Rabbi Abraham Heschel, a nonfeminist Rabbi of Rabbis, seeking to clarify (what ironically Troeltsch might call) ideal Judaism, found that sexuality and sexual relationships are important metaphors for the relationship between the Holy and the human (*The Prophets*).

Ideally, the prophets argue, the God-human relationship should be like the husband-wife relation. Through the prophet Hosea God says that what is missing in the relationship is *daath*, a Hebrew word for the awareness that comes from sexual union, that is, intimate knowledge of the other. The relationship between God and Israel is a sexual one, one of shared inner joy and suffering. In describing the troubled marriage between God and Israel, Hosea finds God mourning the loss of that inward knowing and of the original relationship. Feminist biblical scholar Phyllis Trible finds the book of Hosea speaking of Israel as a runaway wife. The prophet speaks of God as wanting to

> woo her, I will go with her into the wilderness and comfort her: I will restore her vineyards, turning the Vale of Trouble into the Gate of Hope, and there she will answer as in her youth, when she came up out of Egypt. On that day she shall call me "My Friend," and not "My Husband." (Hos. 2:14-16, NEB, as translated by Trible in a lecture at Union Theological Seminary, 1981)

The ultimate relationship is one of friendship and not of master-slave, husband-wife. This friendship contrasts with Weber's study of religion's reaction to the erotic and with the ascetic and mystical opposition to erotic love and to eros. It agrees clearly with Bologh's notion of sociability.

Weber's work on asceticism and mysticism best describes his understanding of erotic love relationships involving spiritual violence (Bologh 1987b, 247). The abstract moral principle of love is foreign to eros as sociability and to Judaic and Christian notions of *daath elohim*. Humans are not bound to God; they have a free will. It is God who woos humans, but humans are left to respond as they will. The "God who owns people" is an ascetic's god. The wild, passionate love that God has for the people of God has no cause, no known source—it is beyond law and covenant love (Hebrew *hesed*: "covenant love"

[Heschel 1962]). As Weber skillfully showed us, modern asceticism's contribution to social order was the taming of wild, passionate love.

Marianne Weber described Max on his deathbed in this way: "He became the picture of a departed knight. His face bespoke gentleness and exalted renunciation" (Weber 1975, 698). In many ways Weber's own asceticism, with its renunciation of magic and sexuality, did not allow him to understand the experience and mass affiliation with Judeo-Christian *daath*. To deny the erotic sharing of pain and joy is, in this tradition, to deny the soul of the people of God. Denying the soul is an important risk to weigh in choosing "politics as a vocation."

Weber attributes to erotic love the denial of the other as a "separate self with its own soul" (Bologh 1987b, 251). Denial of the other's soul is a fundamental act of social and religious oppression—of misogyny, heterosexism, and racism. A soulless person in American history, such as a black slave, has no right to suffrage or to salvation. To be soulless means to be outside the grace of God; it means there is no God to woo you, to claim you, to avenge you. Feminist documentation of the suppressed feminine within Judaism and Christianity (Ruether 1977; Mollencott 1983; Daly 1968) finds that the feminine possession of "soulfulness" was questioned not originally but after the first and second centuries of each tradition. It is only with regard to women that the presence of soul is questioned: that is, the soul is essential to being human, but may not be a part of women. Women or the feminine may not be fully human. This less-than-human status is most vividly extended in American history to slaves whose clergy-masters justified their enslavement by claiming they had no souls (Raboteau 1978).

Rabbi Ruth Adler (1982) liturgically uses the story of the Shekina, the female counterpart to the masculine Yahweh-God, to revive the waning female Jewish interest in Judaism. Although the Shekina literature is still sparse and today contained primarily in oral and homiletic traditions—hence even mentioning it here might be seen as problematic—some Jewish feminists seem to regard her as the "female Soul of God who could not be perfect until he could be reunited with her" (Walker 1983, 932).

The cabalistic explanation of social evil is rooted in the loss of the Shekina. The Hebrew *sh'kina* signifies a "dwelling place"; therefore God has no "home" without her (Walker 1983, 932; see Exod. 25–29, Hebrew *sakan*). Cabalists linked their notion of disharmony in the divine marriage to disharmony among men and women and "taught that it was essential to bring male and female cosmic principles together again, which might be done by sexual magic, signifying union of the sun (man) and moon (woman). This was graphically expressed by the hexagram, also known as the Star of David, a magical sexual symbol for Cabalists"(Walker 1983, 401). Without the female aspect, the Goddess, humans and God lost Truth, Wisdom, and Creativity.

"Immanent energy of all emanated things" (Gaskell 1960, 469), the Shekina is eternal Grace, Glory, Fire, and Light. "The Glory of God, tradition holds, becomes more glorious when it is deliberately divorced from the Temple" (NBD 1101). However, the Temple still stands. The masculine forces won and the Shekina may be heard weeping and wailing as she wanders through the night looking for wholeness (Adler 1982).

It could well be this notion of grace, glory, fire, and light that is enshrined in the claim of Jesus, "I am the light of the world" (John 8:12, NEB). However, patriarchal tradition makes a point of arguing against the notion that Jesus is claiming this feminine principle.

Rethinking Religion

Late in life, when Max Weber discovered his love for Elsa Jaffe and his failing love for his virgin wife Marianne, he found himself moving from a strong attachment to asceticism to an interest in mysticism and mystical love. Even this brief experience of consummated love allowed Weber to entertain the notion of grace. He found the solution to his deep struggle resting in a feminine attribute. Mitzman documents this late-life discovery as Weber's correlation of charisma with pneuma ("feminine, divine, grace, the Holy Spirit": 1969, 302). Weber found the source of this power not in the "heroic warrior" but in "the primal mother."

> For if we examine carefully the ideas Weber associates with charisma, we find a number of rather archaic feminine characteristics among them. Weber presents charisma as synonymous with *pneuma*, the "breath" of the Holy Spirit. And the common quality linking charisma and the Holy Spirit is the feminine, indeed maternal, quality of divine grace. (Mitzman 1969, 302–3)

If one understands Weber's life and work to be the painful detailing of alienated, differentiated masculine life—shaped and maintained by violence—one understands what an act of grace it was that he came to know the feminine at all, much less the magic of eros.

In both economic and spiritual capitalism magic is suppressed. A reconsideration of magic might be the remedy for a suffering and alienated will. It could serve as the basis for Bologh's sociability and for our feminist eros. Weber found women, children, the aged, demasculinized or demilitarized males, and the oppressed to be attentive to magic. A defense of magic, then, may be a defense of the oppressed.

Magic

Starhawk in *The Spiral Dance* (1979) writes about the contemporary rebirth of the ancient religion of the Great Goddess: witchcraft dating back before Judaism, Christianity, Islam, Hinduism, or Buddhism. Similar to Native American or Asiatic shamanism, it has no scriptures, sacred books, or dogma (Starhawk 1979, 2). A religion attuned to the herd, it has dualistic images of "Mother Goddess, the birthgiver, who brings into existence all life; and the Horned God, hunter and hunted, who eternally passes through the gates of death that new life may go on" (Starhawk 1979, 3).

Weber's early disinterest in surrender of "men, beasts, cattle, and seeds" becomes particularly interesting here. Starhawk sees villagization and the gathering and planting of seeds as a shift in communal and religious life:

> The Hunter became the Lord of the Grain, sacrificed when it is cut in autumn, buried in the womb of the Goddess and reborn in the spring. The Lady of the Wild Things became the Barley Mother and the cycles of the moon and sun marked the times for sowing and reaping and letting out to pasture. Villages grew into the first towns and cities. The Goddess was painted on the plastered walls of shrines, giving birth to the Divine Child—her consort, son and seed. (Starhawk 1979, 4)

Starhawk believes that the growing defense of urban boundaries and the invasion of warrior peoples with their warrior gods drove the Goddess peoples up into the mountains physically and underground politically. Witchcraft became for early ascetic Christianity a symbol of women's sexuality, primarily women's reproductive power. Witchcraft claimed the feminine as divine and therefore confronted the warrior gods with the powerful female. Witchcraft's magic was a language of poetry, not theology, a language that expressed mysteries and "the secrets that cannot be told" (Starhawk 1979, 7). The saying "Men know, women wonder" reflects the basic division between dogmatic and magical religion.

The ascetic connection of erotic sexuality with animality is not missed by Weber or by Starhawk. "She [the Goddess] contains him, as a pregnant woman contains a male child. Her own male aspect embodies both the solar light of the intellect and the wild, untamed animal energy" (Starhawk 1979, 10). Starhawk does not hesitate to equate one's self with the animal world.

Starhawk's work is similar to Louis Wirth's massive *History of Cities*, which depicts nomadic peoples becoming settled and, in the process, their previous worldview, expressed in religious terms, becoming no longer adequate. Females lose their central place and their symbolic role of fertility is challenged by the "re-creative" strength of warfare. Starhawk claims that magic facilitated small group life. "Witchcraft is not a religion of the masses—any sort" (1979, 13), but "a religion of clergy" (Starhawk 1979, 14). By excluding the masses Starhawk dates her magic to contemporary and particularly American needs for individualism and isolation. Her magic is not rooted in the ancient magic, or at least not in that ancient magic observed by Cavendish, Durkheim, Eliade, Thomas, or Weber, all of whom link the masses with magic. Her magic must be about something else, perhaps about something very modern that needs to anchor itself in history. Is it about creating an autonomous female self?

> The Mother, the turning spiral that whirls us in and out of existence, whose winking eye is the pulse of being—birth, death, rebirth—whose laughter bubbles and courses through all things and who is found only through love: love of trees, of stones, of sky and clouds; . . . through love of ourselves; life-dissolving-world-creating orgasmic love of each other . . . each of us is unique and natural as a snowflake, each of us has her own star, her Child, her lover, her beloved. (Starhawk 1979, 14–15)

Witchcraft, "the other way of knowing" (Starhawk 1979, 19), allowed one to face oneself. This particular kind of magic is a relationship among individuals, the Goddess, and a select community called the coven. It is not between women and the wider community. In this sense it directly parallels Durkheim's "sacred society of men."

There are major differences in these sacred societies, of course. The greatest power, the power of death, is symbolized in the Goddess (Starhawk 1979, 78); but the Goddess does not have this power. Because she was created by the adherent, the adherent contains this power. This fact of logic contrasts with the masculine totemic cults described by Durkheim who believe quite unconsciously, but with moments of ambiguity, that God directs power to the adherent whom "he" created. "We create her," Starhawk says (1979, 81). In Starhawk's weaving of the history of magic, there is a noticeable thread that acknowledges the human role in the creation of religion and is the holy thread itself. People regard magic as a symbol of their own power over life and death. The law of the Goddess, then, is love, "passionate sexual love, the warm affection of friends, the fierce protective love of mother for child, the deep comradeship of the coven" (Starhawk 1979, 83). The Goddess chooses life; she has the power to "restore slain warriors to life" (Starhawk 1979, 84).

Mary Douglas and Emile Durkheim suggest that this power did not withstand the test of reality—of war; and men created their own men's society with its own totemic religion. The Goddess worshipers' understanding that "sacrifice is *inherent* in life" (Starhawk 1979, 84; emphasis original) is not a motto for the men's society of warriors, who appear to sacrifice the most. The image of God in witchcraft is that of the "Dying-God . . . his death is always in service of the life force. He is untamed sexuality" (Starhawk 1979, 194). This image of the masculine in service to the feminine that is found in this type of Goddess worship is reversed as the warrior gods emerge and dominate. For Starhawk, the magical unity between eros and logos is broken as witchcraft is suppressed.

Witchcraft's power rests in "the art of changing consciousness at will" (Starhawk 1979, 109). Understandably, such a power could not be allowed to exist as the developing polis consolidated its social control mechanisms.

The Power of Magic "The primary principle of magic is connection." The energy that surges through the connections is ecstatic and is often called "love and love is magic" (Starhawk 1979, 129). Since magic recognizes natural forces of equilibrium, Starhawk regards the revival of witchcraft, of magic-love, as a reawakening of "a mode of consciousness that has been dormant for thousands of years and is now coming to the fore. . . . This dormant consciousness facilitates a personal will" that allows the adherent to make her or his own decisions and to act on them (Starhawk 1979, 186). "To will is to claim our power, our power to reclaim the future" (Starhawk 1979, 184). To will today requires new myths, new liturgies, new icons, new symbols of the

Goddess, "of legitimacy and benefices of female power" (Starhawk 1979, 188). Magic, then, establishes legitimate authority that facilitates action and decision making.

The action of decision making is crucial to moral life. Carol Gilligan (*In a Different Voice*) claims that the basis of moral development is the ability to make choices, to decide among actions and consequences. Woman's ability to make choices for herself is no small matter when her structural inability to make choices allows men to make choices for her. Traditional stereotypes of women as incapable of moral decision making are rooted in the actual absence of power to make decisions. Their moral agency is established by understanding that the female self has legitimate authority.

Birth control has been the primary choice around which women have recently asserted their will, to make decisions and to be responsible for those decisions. It is in taking responsibility for the universalized impact of the decision that women achieve maturity. This sense of "taking responsibility" is not the same as Weber's notion of masculine authority standing at the helm of a ship. Steering others in and out of storms and taking on the responsibility of their lives is not the same as Gilligan's feminist notion of responsibility, which claims agency but not power through domination to direct others. For Gilligan responsibility rests on taking stock of the consequences of each action and its effect on others. For Weber the personal and social consequences were important but not primary; for the politician they were sacrificed as part of the inevitable tragedy of life.

Magic is an ancient way of establishing that "we are the world" and the Goddess is the world; therefore we are the Goddess and she is us. Magic is a way to understand feminist moral maturity. Once accomplished, this maturity is polished by the power to direct life. It is a power "from within," not a "power over" paradigm (Starhawk 1982). This power is threatened by patriarchy, which utilizes "power over" and rationalizes violence against women as sexually inferior beings.

In contrast Starhawk's Goddess finds sexuality sacred, "affectionate, joyful, pleasurable, passionate, funny, or purely animal. . . . Sexuality is sacred because it is a sharing of energy, in passionate surrender to the power of the Goddess, immanent in our desire" (Starhawk 1979, 196). Magic can be seen as a facilitator of Bologh's sociability, which is based on pleasurable desire. This joy does not fear the dark (Starhawk 1982, 196). Magic facilitates surrender, which is crucial to communal life. If the Goddess is us and we are the world, magic surrenders to power of the self, of others, and of the world. Magic creates "the circle of interdependence of all living organisms. . . . The circle is also the circle of community" (Starhawk 1979, 196).

Starhawk finds the fundamental message of magic to be:

> You are it. You are part of the circle of the Wise. There is no mystery that has not been revealed to you. There is no power you do not already have. You share in the love that is. (Starhawk 1979, 199)

The circle is protected by the Goddess, who is the "Guardian of the Threshold." In sexual analogy, she protects the woman; in political terms, she protects the community from undesirable intruders. The Guardian of the Threshold, as healer, heals the self and the community (Starhawk 1982, 69).

Here is where problems arise with Starhawk, for whom this power and healing is for a small group, the coven. This modern magic is not "of the primitive," not of the "herd" found in Nietzsche, Douglas, or Hartsock. In her discussion on the ethics of magic (1982, 437), Starhawk's ethics are concerned with "cleaning up the beer cans on your path." Although the issues of personal integrity and immanent appreciation for the diversity of "sacred wills" does lead her to mention El Salvador, there is no real description of how her magical community acted on global issues apart from participating in demonstrations against nuclear war and for a generalized peace. Lacking is what makes ethics ethics: a notion of "what is evil." For Starhawk "Power-over, violence, coercion, domination, hurtful as they are, are not evil in the sense of being part of a force in direct opposition to good. Instead, they are mistakes, processes born of chance that spread because they serve some purpose, structures that may now have outlived their usefulness" (Starhawk 1982, 43).

Pushed to its ultimate conclusion, this ethical system has no room for misogyny. The immanent justice of magic must reflect its first principle: all things are interconnected (Starhawk 1982, 44). It is difficult for most feminists to speak of the power-over women as a mistake. Whose mistake? That of the community of women and men together? Starhawk betrays her ideal image of "no sin in magic" by pointing the finger of guilt for the domination of the erotic through alienation at seventeenth-century Puritanism and wage labor (Starhawk 1982, 137). The problem is that alienation began long before the seventeenth century. Hartsock, Sargent, and Hartman have long suggested that the domination of the erotic precedes capitalism and that Puritanism and wage labor are products of misogyny. Mary Douglas's experience in African cultures and subsequent analysis that "men have agreed" to oppress women did not show a dependence upon Puritanism or wage labor. The activities Starhawk wishes to accuse are not detached from their human proprietors, who are men. Paula Gunn Allen is clearer about this.

The Sacred Hoop

Paula Gunn Allen's *The Sacred Hoop* (1986) is an energizing, vividly delightful, and consciously explicit reconstruction and remythologizing of American Indian experience. Allen seeks to know the "truth" of American Indian existence apart from Western paradigms. The difficulty of the task appears right at the beginning when the American Indian experience has to be translated into Western (dualistic) categories in order to talk about "the sacred." She quotes Keres literature: "At the center of all is Woman, and no thing is sacred (cooked, ripe, as the Keres Indians of Laguna Pueblo say it) without her blessing, her think-ing" (Allen 1986, 13). The question is: Are the American Indian cat-egories of cooked and ripe things, blessings, creation of earth and plants equivalent to "sacredness" in Western religiosity? It is difficult to equate the Hard Beings Woman genatrix, who provides a breast for the em-powering of the world, protects all thought, breathes life into men and women alike, and is both Mother and Father, with the Western sacred, which uses violence to maintain a separation between ways of knowing and the people who know differently.

The great Woman requires peace, cooperation, and sharing. She and women scold men for getting angry, leaving community, and threat-ening to destroy it by gambling and acting irresponsibly. The great Woman does not leave the community destroyed; rather, she gives her people her very heart in order that they might rebuild community. Clearly, she is not sacred in the same sense as the Western sacred God we have been discussing.

In summary, sacredness for Allen means the ability to empower a whole people.

> According to the older texts (which are sacred, that is, empowering), Thought Woman is not a passive personage: her potentiality is dynamic and unimaginably powerful. She brought corn, agriculture, potting, weaving, social systems, religion, ceremony, ritual, building, memory,

intuition, and their expressions in language, creativity, dance, human-to-animal relations, and she gave these offerings power and authority and blessed the people with the ability to provide for themselves and their progeny. Thought Woman is not limited to a female role in the total theology of the Keres people. Since she is the supreme Spirit, she is both Mother and Father to all people and creatures. She is the only creator of thought, thought precedes creation. (1986, 15)

Allen's description of that "which is sacred, that is, empowering" shares characteristics with Durkheim's and Weber's notions of the sacred as central empowering agent. However, unlike the sacred related to warrior society, which empowers individuals to act in brotherhood in a sacred society of men who gather wealth and people unto themselves, the Thought Woman empowers communities to empower themselves. Unlike sacred religion's privileging of the sacred, the god, the totem, Thought Woman spirituality is empowering and centered around the heart of a woman. This woman's heart empowers and gives authority to all the gifts she gives to the people: corn, agriculture, potting, weaving, and the like. In American Indian mythology, at the heart of "what is sacred" and empowering is the heart of people.

Allen finds that Western and American Indian notions of sacredness differ. In the latter's mythology sacredness is intimately tied to the creation of peaceful lives.

The word *sacred*, like the words *power* and *medicine*, has a very different meaning to tribal people than to members of technological societies. It does not signify something of religious significance and therefore believed with emotional fervor—"venerable, consecrated, or sacrosanct," . . . but something filled with an intangible but very real power or force, for good or bad. (1986, 72)

Having sacredness, power, and medicine is "a way of being in the world" that each person possesses; each person has the potential for being life or death.

The Lakota's White Buffalo Woman, who brings the sacred pipe without which no magic is possible and who bids the Four Winds, carries a teaching function similar to the Keres' Thought Woman. Counseling the people to live in harmony is their primary task. These beings do get angry, however! Iyatiku, the Mother of Corn, and Thought Woman have the ability to destroy with their anger. When men gamble and are scolded by women, they get angry and retire to their "kivas," to men's space where women cannot go. Secluded, the men neglect rituals and bring drought to the people. Finally Corn Woman brings a flood on her "foolish people" and they are forced to move and rebuild their houses. Men and women are punished alike. Their village is destroyed.

However, the Corn Woman leaves them her heart. She does not destroy the people. Instead, she offers herself: "She charged them always to share the fruits of her body with one another, for they were all related, and she told them that they must remain at peace in their hearts and relationships. The rains came only to peaceful people, or so the Keres say. As a result of this belief, the Keres abhor violence or hostility" (1986, 17–18).

The task of ritual is to maintain peaceableness. Gender-specific rituals allowed men and women to dominate in their own sphere, with the other gender assisting. Gender-inclusive rituals allowed both genders to share power. This balance of gender control in ritual balanced the social life of the tribes. Yet gynofocal leadership was most common in American Indian societies. Western colonial agents often misinterpreted women's primary role in tribal government as the work of "meddling old women" (1986, 33). The defeat of American Indian nations forced Western patriarchy on tribal governments. Women became "voiceless pawns" (1986, 37). Christian missionization, which recognized that its success was related to silencing women, also adopted threatened and actual violence as a means of control. Through many forms of violence and silencing, Western colonizers (including missionaries) broke the spirit of Native peoples. The "Christian" God brought to American Indians was separate from humanity and did not need the cooperation of people; "he" was a patriarch's God. The missioners and heads of federal government understood that to change people, one changed their religion. American Indians, their souls thus re-created, struggled to survive in a hostile and foreign environment. Their fire, their spirit, was not totally snuffed out; among the dry ashes of beaten lives a rekindling began. Rekindling is heard in the voice that speaks through alienation, and through the very inability to speak it is found dancing and writing poetry. The silenced American Indian voice, fragile but not timid, is continually nourished by its very survival.

Allen continually qualifies notions of sacredness as she attunes her work to the empirical reality addressed by myths. Yet, inevitably, she is rooted in Western language and thought patterns that make it difficult not to use its most elementary conceptual categories. However, she does not accept these categories as easily as Starhawk. Nor does Luisah Teish.

Jambalaya

Luisah Teish's *Jambalaya* promotes the women's movement goals of ending racism, classism, and heterosexism. Degraded and labeled as "marks of savagery," African religion was dismissed by colonists as "superstitious." African magic must be reclaimed in the fight against racism. Teish reclaims New Orleans voodoo, an ever-evolving tradition. Voodoo "contains African ancestor reverence, Native American earth worship, and European Christian occultism" (1985, x). Voodoo developed out of material and unconscious matristic life experiences.

According to Teish, African and voodoo magic continues the seeds of power. Its rituals empower those who are willing to be transformed; without personal willingness rituals would have no power. *Jambalaya* can claim sisterhood with Starhawk's text. However, there are notable differences between them. For Teish, magic belongs to the masses, to the oppressed, and voodoo, to slaves and their children. It was their secret religion, and their way of preserving what they could of African culture. Voodoo magic is about remembering. Magic is also the way the self is understood and the family maintained. The work of magic builds communities. The altar circle is not limited; any number from three to three million people can be included in the circle of common aspirations (1985, 249). Being essentially of the same essence, magic interweaves itself with other magics, there being no apparent distinction between magic and religion.

Voodoo, which inherits a pantheon of gods and goddesses from African religions, reaches across the gender and age spectrum. Nowhere does Teish mention an occasion on which any person came to be equated with any of these gods and goddesses. Unlike Starhawk's formulation of magic, neither Allen's nor Teish's has people creating gods or goddesses. People do not become gods or stand in their place.

Both Allen and Teish recognize the role that magic and religion play in acknowledging difference and reconciling it within the person and within the community. Natural and human polarities are not meant to separate people but to mark the poles inside nature. The tension between the poles creates whole beings. However, Teish does not dwell on the fact that this tension seems rarely to produce wholeness. In Teish's retelling of ancient myths it seems as if men fear women's magic more than women do men's magic; however, both sexes are capable of destroying the other's magic.

The power of magic is everywhere, and it is intoxicating. Luisah Teish "grew up tipsy," "saturated in the liquid realities of voodoo" always flowing somewhere and filling the air with its aroma. A child whose mother was gifted in magic and a member of the Sanctified church, she could hardly escape the spirits.

Teish's worklists for women and all people seeking transformation grow out of her past experiences and the needs of contemporary people. The first thing to be accomplished in voodoo is the spiritual cleansing of one's own house. Important to this cleansing is a bed made right and the search for domestic tranquillity. Of help here is the stopping of gossip and the reading of psalms.

Second, personal power is to be achieved through the gaining of altered states of consciousness. Third, useful charms and chants should be learned for practical use in, for example, the curing of depression and the creation of self-esteem. Fourth, one needs to learn to love the earth and, fifth, to connect with one's familial and community roots. Sixth, rituals for the care of extended family must be learned. Seventh, one must learn to court the seven African powers. Eighth, one learns to "make the four corners," to communicate and gain spiritual power from the living dead.

These works are directed toward empowering oneself and one's family and community. Modernized for twenty-first-century women, *Jambalaya* hopes to make the power of magic available to women so that we might change people and things. We have power to transform ourselves and others. Important to this transformation is personal and corporate ritual that clears "sacred space," much in the manner of Afrodiasporic traditions (39) by claiming that space (through dressing it) and by evoking the presence of spirits. The ninth work is "working the rainbow"; it is the putting together of all of these works into a continuum of being that fortifies and affirms.

Like Starhawk Teish creates magical formulas and rituals for the empowering of self and community. However, Teish's emphasis on family and Afrodiasporic traditions grows out of a magical way of life anchored in living communities that have throughout history irrupted into centers of magic (in this case voodoo) before and after African slavery in the West.

In contrast to Allen, who is not able to retell the rituals and the secrets of magic and how the spirit world works, Teish and Starhawk seem to know these things quite precisely. Whereas Allen can only describe reality, Teish and Starhawk are able to create it. This is an interesting difference. Teish, more so than Starhawk, has greater personal access to ongoing magical communities; yet it is Allen and her Native American tribe(s) that appear to have remained continuously and materially connected to the spirit world. The degree to which one is authentically anchored in the material reality of the oppressed people one has chosen to research appears to be an important factor determining one's ability to go beyond description of spirits and magical secrets. The more closely one belongs to a particular community, the less able one is to tell its secrets. To tell the secret is to risk losing the power. The closer one is and one's people are to being destroyed by dominating forces, the harder it is to steer the magical spirit ship out of the stormy seas and anchor it unprotected in the harbor so that oppressive agents might get a good look at it.

The Power of Women Is Power Within

Audre Lorde writes in *Uses of the Erotic: The Erotic as Power* (1978): "As women, we have come to distrust that power which rises from our deepest and non-rational knowledge. . . . Of course, women so empowered are dangerous. So, we are taught to separate the erotic demand from most vital areas of our lives other than sex" (3). The absence of eros (Lorde's "personifying creative power and harmony") is itself asceticism. The erotic functions to maximize joy and happiness—something the ascetic cannot be bothered about. The power to experience joy is the power by which we say "yes" to ourselves. It is a shared power. It is not a religion, as European Americans are wont to claim it; it is a way of being. "That power which arises from our deepest non-rational knowledge . . . the erotic offers a well of replenishing and provocative force to the woman who does not fear its revelation" (Lorde 1979, 29).

The erotic reveals the self within: the feminine-masculine unity of self. As seen in Allen's description of Indian oppression, it is this notion of and search for undifferentiated unity that threatens hierarchical power relations. Weber must suppress the feminine for political reasons; leadership depends on carrying out one's own truth, goals, and causes, which the masses have been convinced to follow. These goals are maintained by hierarchical power structures and may require the use of force and violence.

Weber found it necessary to get rid of magic, which he found everywhere he looked: "In his quest for truth, Weber everywhere removed magic from his path" (Marianne Weber 1975, 681). Marianne Weber, reflecting on Max's "radical disenchantment," found that he compensated himself with a "new truth content" (1975, 681). She referred to "Politics as a Vocation":

> Young people felt called upon to build a new world and hoped to succeed in establishing, with pure motives, an unprecedented social order whose structure would be . . . filled with ethical and religious ideals of justice and brotherhood. . . . Weber forced his listeners, first of all, to recognize without illusions the social political process . . . [which] has been at all times based on legitimate physical violence and that politics always means the striving for a shared political power. . . . Under certain circumstances every holder of political power is forced to do harm to others for the sake of his goals. This is why he cannot be subject to any absolute ethic, and least of all to that of the gospels. . . . And, above all, no matter what goals he may serve, he must always have *faith* in them if he is to escape the curse of creatural futility. . . . A politician must be ready to lose his soul. . . . The politician is one who is soul-less; is one who cannot be "touched" by another's pain; who will not surrender to the other. (Weber 1975, 682–84)

The alternative to this conflict-ridden, brutal, political world was erotic love, itself a product of conflict and brutality. The leadership men must prepare for results in violence against the feminine—a violence that costs them their soul. The erotic love of men destroys the soul of the least brutal partner. It is no wonder that Marianne Weber remarks that the then-modern women's movement, founded on "erotic love," "benefits only men" (1975, 373).

As long as hierarchical, privileged politics and privileged sexual relations exist, there will be a tension between feminine and masculine aspects of spirituality. This tension is reflected in the relationship between "magic and religion."

The struggle between the masculine and the feminine surfaced in Durkheim and Weber as a struggle between magic and religion. Sir J. G. Frazer's *The Golden Bough* demonstrates this tension in which the priest angrily pursues the magician over "haughty self-sufficiency . . . impious and blasphemous usurpation of prerogatives. . . . [The priest's] interests as well as his feelings were often injured by a rival practitioner, who preached a surer and smoother road. . . . (Thomas, 1971, 253) The agencies of clerical repression were not in themselves strong enough to cut off popular magic from its roots" (Thomas 1971, 263). Keith Thomas maintains that the battle against magic was both religious and political. He illustrates the problem by quoting a pamphlet written in 1593 concerning the local wise woman: "She doeth more good in one year than all these scripture men will do as long as they live" (Thomas 1971, 264).

The battle against magic was a battle in "affirmation of the potentialities of human labour which was to encourage men to seek a technological solution to their problems rather than a magical one" (Thomas 1971, 278). But it is far more than religion, Weber suggested, that "duped" the masses. Thomas, a historian of religion and magic, writes an almost Weberian conclusion: "It took a combination of social and intellectual forces to destroy popular magic. In this revolution the dogmas of Protestantism played some part. But the Reformation could never have killed magic without the changes in the mental and physical environment which accompanied it" (Thomas 1971, 279). Primitive beliefs became intellectually unsatisfying (Thomas 1971, 647), but the disillusionment process is hardly a crystal-clear one. The scientific, rationalist explanation is not sufficient when one also needs to address the context of human knowledge.

Thomas finds Bronislaw Malinowski's argument unfashionably helpful. Malinowski argued that "magic is to be expected and generally to be found whenever man comes to an unbridgeable gap, a hiatus in his knowledge or in his powers of practical control, and yet has to continue in his pursuit" (quoted by Thomas, 647). For Malinowski, as for Starhawk, magic restores confidence and optimism. But Malinowski goes further than Starhawk in his observation that magic is found where a people organize themselves without a police force to protect them (Thomas 1971, 650), among the masses who by design or by circumstance find themselves defenseless.

Thomas is unconvinced by Malinowski's argument that the rise of technology is ultimately and primarily correlated to the decline of magic. He suggests that the decline of magic is accompanied by a different kind of technology, that of the "natural and social sciences" (Thomas 1971, 656). In an almost Durkheimian sense, this growth was founded on a religious understanding of order (Thomas 1971, 657). Although he recognizes the "chicken-and-the-egg" nature of the "which came first" debate between changes in beliefs and changes in the socio-economic structures, Thomas notes that stress in both areas appears around disease and infertility (e.g., fourteenth-century Lollards); epidemics, bad harvests, illnesses, fires (e.g., sixteenth-century Reformation); and inadequate medical technology (e.g., seventeenth-century witch beliefs) (Thomas 1971, 657). With Mary Douglas (1984), one can see that these areas of spiritual and material security focused on the concept of "pollution." The polluting nature of profane life was also observed by Durkheim. Totemic religion understood the sacred to be the one polluted, and the profane the polluting element.

The implicit masculine/feminine tension in Durkheim's definition of sacred and profane is echoed in Weber's distinctions between religion and nonreligion. Likewise, Douglas, Allen, Starhawk, Teish, Ruether, Christ, and Goldenberg agree that Western society tends to affirm these separations.

Weber observed that these struggles are also between the "few and the many," between social and religious elites and the masses, who are comprised of women, slaves, children, aged, and demilitarized or demasculinized men. Thomas concludes that the form of popular religion, religion with a continuous understanding of magic, has not changed much over the centuries, although the content varies. Quoting from Jacob Burckhardt, he summarizes his position: "rationalism for a few and magic for the many" (Thomas 1971, 666).

Magic for the many, like religion for the few, also was concerned about controlling contagion. The issues of contagion focus on a variety of polluting elements as experienced in particular ways by particular people. Magic flourishes when there are no sufficient ways of solving problems and anxiety runs high (see Thomas and Malinowski). The revival of witchcraft in the late 1950s and its explosion in the 1970s can be seen as the solution for women who saw no way out of patriarchal religion and culture, which had even infiltrated the radical left. If magic is a time-specific coping mechanism revived time and again by the powerless for the generation of power, then we must question Starhawk's contention that she and other witches hold a continuous, practical, historical connection to primitive magic. Delightful as her work is artistically, it suffers when she attempts to force magic into the grand narrative mode of thinking, a control mechanism that we have already identified with the oppressor. In other words, her work is not as free as she thinks from masculine hegemonic thought.

The reason for this is Starhawk's acceptance of the fundamental division between the sacred and the profane. But other great minds, such as Durkheim and Weber, have done the same thing. Like many feminists in the women's spirituality movements, Starhawk appears unwilling to make the sacrifice that magic demands, a sacrifice Durkheim and Weber found irrational. Magic demands a sociability that goes beyond love and eros. Magical community demands of its membership complete surrender to a world that does not need the individual self.

These theorists explicitly or implicitly agree that magic is what is left when men desert communal religion for religion of the men's house. When one agrees, then one can imagine standing with the men looking back on what they call the profane. Communal primitive religion before abandonment by men is not magic: even the men did not consider it to be magic. Rather, it was something infused with erotic sociability— something akin to agape love. The Goddess, who is the "Guardian of the Threshold" (see Starhawk), is already a functionary in an inherently conflictual society. Starhawk's Goddess arises as such only after men have separated themselves from community. Starhawk's Goddess is not the divine presider over sociable life; she does not develop a social theory and practice of inclusion. Instead, she participates willingly in a dualistic society that considers and even values the masculine deity as servant.

The differences between Starhawk, Allen, and Teish are instructive. For Starhawk the Goddess accepts the life of her male protector; for Allen and Teish the Goddess gives her life for community. Starhawk begins with the conflict between the masculine and the feminine and ends up searching for the original, continuous unity. Allen and Teish begin by longing for erotic sensibility but recognize that the unity never was and may never be a reality. Both Allen and Teish represent racial groups that are currently socially marginalized. The concern for unity appears to be a middle-class, socially dominant concern. The lack of concern for the telling of secrets cuts across race, as seen in Starhawk and Teish. The question arises: Are they then not really secrets but a public mourning of what once was and may never be again? What "may never be again" also troubled Troeltsch, Weber, and Durkheim.

Interestingly, Troeltsch began his career with a search for unity and gave it up, concluding that there are only particular unities. Weber, on the other hand, began with an acceptance of many fractured life spheres and ended with a glimmer of what unity between them might be. The need for unity is their Hegelian thorn in the side.

Both Troeltsch and Weber in their own ways and with varying degrees of success attempted to remove the irritating universalistic structures that shaped their thinking. However, for most of his life Weber lost the particular in his attempt to create universalizing discourse. Weber's near-totalizing discourse resulted from his compulsive, intense need to create and maintain order. This was also the need of his contemporaries, the need of their homeland and a need emerging from the repressed consciousness that threatened to overwhelm them.

This need to protect masculine personal, social, and national identity forced theorists such as Freud, Weber, Durkheim, and Troeltsch to create a new meaning system, a new truth. But their own work on primitive life shows that this activity is not new to men—men who have managed for centuries to do this apart from and in opposition to the community of women, children, and the demilitarized and demasculinized men.

However, the historical causes for the alienation and homelessness they witnessed and experienced are rooted in ordering the world and not in supporting and maintaining a community home. Awareness of misogyny, the cause of women's alienating experiences, only helps when some action is carried out to end it. Feminists suggest that community building is the solution.

This community-building action is an action against oppression, and it is never the same throughout history, as we see in Allen's collection of ever-changing indigenous mythology. Actions must address the current oppression in its current manifestations. Monastic life, which rejected hierarchical and civil community, was created as a reaction against church corruption. However, it is not a popular modern response to the same problem. Whereas Weber wished to give the self greater power to act, some feminists, like some Buddhists, claim that there is no self to save—that is, apart from humankind. In this sense Starhawk is right on target: to save womankind one must work toward world peace.

For Starhawk, Allen, Teish, and many feminists, this action is not heroic; it is a requirement for daily living. Weber foreshadows the end of the heroic culture in a last great attempt to resurrect warrior gods and to patch up the modern political-economic meaning system. Some feminists can be seen to have paralleled his activity in the attempt to create new religions: "Since there are no established female-centered religions around, counter-cultural feminists have been engaged in trying to re-discover or create them" (Ruether 1984, 117). What Ruether describes is women's resistance to oppression. Christ, Starhawk, Teish, and others struggle to ensure the future of womankind by empowering women through religion. However, this resistance, with its focus on women, is not necessarily a sociable one. Even Ruether observes that these new religions tend to project evil and alienation onto males and often deny self-alienation and oppression of women by women. If women's religion, which is based on magic, is in such state, of what help is magic to people who favor nongendered, nondifferentiated life?

The Problem of Authority

All is not lost for magic. Our notion of it must be refined. Magic must be renamed so as to describe what the sacred/profane totality might be.

If one can envision a community that does not seek to be differentiated along power-domination lines, then one can understand why the forces that have attempted to suppress and oppress this community have attempted to limit its identity by calling its spirituality (or its "way of being") "magic" and "profane." This community, however, infrequently (if ever) uses the term "magic," and its first inclination is not to think in a dualistic way.

People who live in the dark surrender themselves to a different authority than those who live in the light and have no secrets. It is in our Western religiocultural meaning system to think that these people surrender to evil, to the devil, to darkness itself, and to think that they are voiceless. In our thought system, rooted in the sociable community of eros, we discover that these people have surrendered to an authority unknown to those who claim to live in the light. They have surrendered to a comprehensive meaning system articulated by a variety of gods in a variety of languages. Most important, they speak. What is most clear in Durkheim's description of the profane, in Hartsock's limited discussion of religion created for women, in Weber's sociology of religion, in Simmel's focus on the content of theology, and in Troeltsch's insistence on understanding worship is that those that live in the dark struggle to live there together in diverse community. Obeying a voice outside of themselves, those that call themselves sacred live in the light as individuals. This light has repressed or does not remember the light of the Shekina; it is an artificial light, a light not lit by a communal fire.

At a critical moment Simmel notices the artificiality of dominant culture, but he dismisses the thought that it may be dominance and not nature that creates culture and a religion that requires domination:

> I shall not consider the issue of whether this masculine character of the objective elements of our culture is a result of the inner nature of the

sexes or is a consequence of male dominance, a matter that really has no relation to the question of culture. (Simmel 1982, 67)

Unlike Simmel many feminists find the question of dominance to be the key to the question of objective, socially valued culture. Indeed, Durkheim's, Weber's, and Simmel's sociology of religion implicitly outlines the suppression of and hostility toward the feminine necessary for religion and culture to exist in the first place. Religion's ability to sacralize males is what makes men masculine. By defining females as not men, women and their feminine identity are created. All of those people seen as threats to masculinity are given feminine identities.

This dominance of the masculine is facilitated by a religious and political will to violence. Force has gathered objective justification to transform "might into right" (Simmel 1982, 104). The male is no longer the arbitrary exploiter but the embodiment of law. Why is this law necessary? Put in Durkheimian terms, why is the totemic religion, with its access to the strong god of action, threatened by the profane? Put in Weberian terms, why is the erotic caring for the small, personal, everyday affairs a cause for hostility? Simmel has his own answer:

> For the man, the absolute that represents sexuality or eroticism as a cosmic principle becomes nothing more than the relationship to the woman. For the woman, the relativity that this domain possesses as a relationship between the sexes becomes the absolute, the autonomous being of her nature. On the other hand, the ultimate result of this constellation is the feeling, which is frequently confirmed, that even the most complete surrender of a woman does not release a final reserve of her soul. This is because she is *intrinsically* sexual, not merely in her relationship to her man. It is as if she has a secret sense of self-possession and a self-contained completeness. . . . this secret self does not become accessible to the other person . . . although it has come to belong to him, it still always remains rooted in its own ground and inaccessibility. (Simmel 1982, 109; emphasis added)

The feminist question, "What are women protecting with their secret inaccessibility?" seeks to understand what cause would precipitate a shielding from another, when the original, natural response might be one of openness, of sociability. Perhaps in his oppressive ownership of her the man forces her to protect what his religion says she does not have: a soul. She protects the possibility of sociable community.

Simmel was wrong. Women may appear to have a continuous existence, but radical feminists have shown that they do not. There is no fundamental meaning in birthing, nurturing, caring, in any of women's traditional tasks, apart from their role in securing life for loved ones. Many women do not find meaning in their socialized and gendered roles. Nor have men, apparently, found meaning in the polis-civilization that they have created for themselves (Stoltenberg 1990). Could it be that men wanted what they thought women had: the future, a meaningful death, and knowledge of nature? From Durkheim can be derived a more complicated picture that includes the purposeful creation of an alternative masculine ideal world and its future, and its immortality rooted in science—a world built on the exclusion of the natural world.

However, it cannot be maintained that Durkheim saw men consciously understanding that their participation in the sacred is also participation in this exclusionary world. Indeed, most people are not aware of themselves "constructing" the sacred. Rather, they find the sacred actively constructing them. Young men called to the sacred society of men are not often conscious of a personal decision to leave community for society controlled by men, although they know they have become associated with a brotherhood. What they may be most aware of is that their mother, through her own required participation in sacred rituals, facilitated the leaving of the home. They may even be aware of being forced out. However, the mother does not see herself as tearing her child from herself, causing her son great emotional insecurity, leaving him to long for the continuity she appears to possess. Through sacralization processes, religion provides the way for people to interpret these events as beyond their control. Likewise, religion hides the naked horror of violence behind a sacred shield. The requirement for participation of the sacred in the act of violence suggests that if not sacralized, no one, not even men, could naturally perform acts of violence. One must be persuaded to separate from community and maintain that separation. Sacrificed in this separation is meaningful existence.

One feminist perspective finds that women's experiences are not in themselves helpful for solving the problem of meaning (particularly true if women have claimed a sacralized identity for themselves and assumed masculine identity). Rather, women as oppressed people may have access to particular knowledge and ways of knowing generated by the experience of oppression; this meaning may be available for critical praxis.

Most available is the notion of surrender. Surrender necessitates new social life. The feminist vision of redistributing power throughout the world community could do nothing other than revolutionize the way we live. It is in the unrealizability of the task that Weber found himself depressed and living in a disenchanted, demagicalized world. Similarly, it is in the frightening darkness of what this recommended sociable future could be like that Troeltsch despaired, gave up teaching, and left the university. However, it is in the potential of such a rich opportunity for creative and fulfilled living, however silent, unseen, and protected by the darkness, that Karl Marx seized the moment and insisted on nothing less than revolutionary change.

For those who live in the darkness already and have lived there all their lives, these issues and visions are less frightening and less dramatic. However, they are no less powerful. This is the life Weber wished for himself. In the end he realized that personal greatness could not establish a life that is generated by the grace found in community. Grace is a sociological reality. It is a place-holder, it generates the ability to live in the meantime between what is and what is to be. Through the establishment of grace, sociable community enables its membership to live and speak in the dark without taking refuge in the violent resources of sacred society.[3]

---

3. A sociology of grace is much needed. Theologically, grace does not require knowledge of the future, an established vision. Sociologically, grace in sociable community is the mechanism through which psychological, physical, moral, spiritual lives receive the support needed to maintain membership in community. The absence of grace helps sponsor the desire or creates the need to leave community. The lack of grace and the disappearance of sociability appear to be directly related.

Part Three

SPEAKING IN THE DARK AND HEARING THE VOICES

8

HEARING THE VOICES

IS REMEMBERING

RESISTANCE

*Western culture has placed what it calls sexuality in a more and more
distinctively privileged relation to our most prized constructs of individual
identity, truth and knowledge, it becomes truer and truer that the language of sexuality not only intersects with but transforms other languages
and relations by which we know. . . . "Clostedness" itself is a performance initiated as such by the speech act of a silence—not a particular
silence, but a silence that accrues particularity by fits and starts, in
relation to the discourse that surrounds and differentially constitutes it.*
—Eve Kosofsky Sedgwick, *Epistemology of the Closet*

The Revolutionary Folk Experience
of the Filipino Katipunan Confradias

Durkheim's and Weber's sociological disinterest in magic is most likely
related to their inability to see the everyday practical accomplishments
of the magical life. Magical communities are sheltered in secrecy; the
oppressed live in a world that Charles Long, a black American historian
of religion, describes as "opaque" (1986). The popular world of folk
magic has always been of interest to social scientists, who most frequently declare that the "popular" is impossible to define. Michel de
Certeau (1986) suggests that the impossibility of finding the oppressed
is rooted in the language of the oppressing class. Their language "represses" knowledge of the oppressed and their origin (127–28). Instead
of discovering the origin of the oppressed, the popular scientific studies
discover "*their own* origin. They pursue across the surface of texts, before

their eyes, what is actually their own condition of possibility—the elimination of a popular menace" (de Certeau 1986, 128; emphasis original).

For de Certeau it is not "surprising" that science's pursued object, the popular and its origin, is lost. Finding it missing, making it a "mythic representation," is a political action. Science, then, finds it impossible to bring "the popular" into discourse. "And, doubtless, it will never resolve its internal contradictions as long as this founding deed is 'forgotten' or 'denied'" (de Certeau 1986, 128; Sedgwick 1990) makes a similar argument about the invisibility of homosexual reality in a homophobic culture). The denial of the origin of the oppressed forces scientific disciplines to speak of the popular as "folktales, supernatural, pagan." Because our language has not allowed "the popular" to exist as its own domain, the popular become "our primitives." The "popular" is not a reflection of the historical situation but that which is excluded from it:

> [T]he shepherd—by profession a social marginal, the subject and object of nature . . . could well reveal, incidentally, the other's gaze upon a society built on silence and the exclusion of the other. (de Certeau 1986, 130)

De Certeau suggests we pursue "the shepherds'" understanding of existence, which is located in popular religiosity. He finds that Catholicism is "the religion of the poor and that the God of the almanacs is the God of the poor" (1986, 130). The poor are "a social group striving to make its truth heard . . . through its allegorical participation in the sufferings of the Gospel" (de Certeau 1986, 131). Religious language is important to the poor, who "retreat" into it as

> the only language still available for its expression after the triumph of reason, which desires to negate it. The language of religion would then be the last recourse of a culture that could no longer find expression, that was being forced to fall silent or mask itself so a different cultural order could be heard. This takes us to the root of the problem: popular culture can only be grasped in the process of vanishing because, whether we like it or not, our knowledge requires us to cease hearing it, to no longer know how to discuss it. (de Certeau 1986, 131)

When he looks at popular literature written for the average reader he discovers that children, sexuality, and violence "outline a geography of the *forgotten*" (de Certeau 1986, 131; emphasis original). The child becomes an allegorical representation of what "the writer thinks about people." The children are fatherless; therefore they no longer experience the violence of the father, because they have taken on the image of the father (de Certeau 1986, 132). "The same thing was done to the people: in the studies of popular culture 'sexual knowledge and relations' are put to sleep. They 'enter the unconscious of scholarly literature'" (de Certeau 1986, 133). In addition to sexuality, scholars also "forgot" that peasants remembered anything about revolts, uprisings, and violence. "The elimination of violence from the study of localisms and popular 'culture' is explained by a political violence. What allowed these lost paradises to be handed over to the scholars was in every instance the victory of a certain power" (de Certeau 1986, 134). To understand popular culture, then, we must turn the light on the silhouettes of children, sexuality, and violence. And we must listen to religious language, a language that is about violence.

De Certeau calls modern culture a "celibatory machine: without woman or god, a fiction." Somewhat like Freud's regression, "it is removed from time, from the body and from the woman. It is also taken out of God's reach. . . . But it is still a theology (a discourse of the male, of the unique, of the same: a henology) that excludes the mystical (an altered feminine discourse: a heterology)" (de Certeau 1986, 165). Central to the celibatory machine is difference, as it is structured by sexuality. This machine does have power, masculine power, to include and express the feminine, but it chooses not to. "Despite everything the apparatus inherited from alchemy, a central figure in that ancient tradition seems to get frayed in the new machinery: the androgyne, the perennial virile ambition to play both roles" (de Certeau 1986, 166). De Certeau claims, and feminists agree, that discourse has a sex. By placing the body-woman-subject outside of itself, it fuels itself on the energy of repression, of the eliminated. "This makes discourse antimagical, areligious, and nonsymbolic" (de Certeau 1986, 166).

Although the machine breaks down, it still keeps running. "Dominated but not vanquished, they [the repressed other, the dominated] keep alive the memory of what the Europeans [the oppressor, the dominator] have 'forgotten'—a continuous series of uprisings" that threaten the machine (de Certeau 1986, 227). The violence done to the oppressed by not remembering is a violence done to its body. But, *the body is memory.*" "It carries, in written form, the law of equality and rebelliousness that not only organizes the group's relation to itself, but also its relation to the occupiers" (de Certeau 1986, 227; emphasis added).

This "collective memory of the social body," with its tortured existence and "spilled blood," resists oppressive ideology in its desire to be self-managing. It is its own response to reality. Solidarity among people who have their own way of doing things, says de Certeau, brings revolution. He suggests that to face the complexities of the modern world, there will need to be a "federation" of these communities of solidarity that "contracts with the earth for its culturally pluralistic future."

Speaking in Native American terms, de Certeau predicts that in the federated revolution we will hear "discrete" references to the Great Spirit because the "daily recognition of the Unseen and Eternal" is "unspoken." "Each soul must meet the morning sun, the new sweet earth and the Great Silence alone" (de Certeau 1986, 232). Such silences form the "cornerstones" of community. People outside of the "popular culture" have a role in this revolution; they are attracted by their desire to assist in the work, but the inspiration must be converted; they must "rise to the same beat as the Indian awakening" (de Certeau 1986, 233). Whereas Starhawk, Durkheim, and Weber found in magic individualistic, self-centered activity, de Certeau and Allen see the possibility of meeting the Great Silence, which argues for radical notions of community. Communities of sociability differ from religious communities in that they do not require creeds and confessions, sameness and orthodoxy; they thrive on members' distinctiveness and the potential similarity that empowers solidarity.

There is no revolutionary vanguard in these "magical" sociable communities, but only the popular voices, voices that speak "magical" words. A feminist sociology of liberation open to seeing these realities, claiming its children, naming the violences, and, most important, experiencing eros and erotic silence is a sociology capable of developing a theory of spiritual life in sociable community. What we have yet to do is to convince ourselves that we do and must choose between radical solidarity with our people, ourselves, the oppressed, and moving away from them as a part of the vanguard elite whose language is the language of the repressed, masculine, celibatory machine. If we straddle the fence, will we contribute anything concrete to the transformation we seek other than saying something about it?

The Katipunans

The Katipunans are a group of oppressed Filipino people who belong to the still-subjugated nation of the Philippine Islands. A Southeast Asian archipelago, the Philippines have witnessed a thousand years of foreign economic domination, first by the Chinese and then by a variety of Muslims and Christians. Political domination has weighed heavily upon Philippine history. Most recently it was burdened with several hundred years of Spanish colonial rule that ended in 1898 with the arrival of the United States Army, which reconquered the islands as the Spanish fleet was sailing out of Manila Bay (for an extended discussion of this history see Erickson 1992d). The United States has stayed influential in Filipino politics since the islands' liberation on July 4, 1946. The Katipunans organized revolts against the Spanish forces and continued to fight against the United States; there is evidence that they still survive today.

The Katipunans were or are a network of religiopolitical associations, called *confradias*, that practice their own particular form of "folk religion." Reynaldo Clemeña Ileto, in *Pasyon and Revolution* (1979),[1] studied the revolutionary activity sponsored, housed, nourished, and protected by folk religiosity. The magical religion of the Katipunans grandparented a currently functioning religiopolitical movement. While visiting the Philippine Islands in 1980, I was informed of grandchildren and great-grandchildren of the Katipunans who still draw upon the Katipunan heritage for spiritual and political direction in their revolutionary efforts. However, to my knowledge the following critique of Ileto's discovery of Katipunan liturgical texts does not represent or disclose current religiopolitical practices.

Ileto revives a memory of the Katipunans for those who have forgotten. Aiming to understand folk reality in order to merge the excluded folk aspirations into the national development, Ileto asks: What do magioreligious beliefs do for the community that holds them? How do communities use their knowledge of their origin? Does it have something to do with sociopolitical resistance?

Ileto insists that to write history "from below" requires the proper use of documents and other sources "from below." This leaves him

---

1. Ileto is a Filipino, Cornell University-trained historian, whose history-become-social-theory model follows the Annales School of Marc Bloch, Braudel, and Lefebvre, who were, like Derrida, synchronic-thinking grandchildren of Durkheim. On resistance in the Philippines see also B. Kerkvliet 1979, R. Constantino and L. Constantino 1975.

little with which to work. However, his collection of narratives, poems, songs, prayers, and folk sayings (Ileto 1979, 13) bears fruit enough for this project. Ileto could be criticized for making a lot out of nothing; feminists have been criticized for the same thing. Often all they have are their grandmother's memories, her quilts, and if they are lucky, their mother's letters and diaries. Oppressed and socially marginalized persons often do not leave much behind. Given the Spanish friars' dislike for the Katipunans, it is amazing that any literature has survived.

Ileto has shown that the only access to Katipunan reality exists in the products of their communal life: liturgy and revolt. Until actual recordings are made of conversations, all that is extant are the officially recorded stories of revolt and the liturgies the Katipunans left behind. In a Geertzian perspective all societies interpret themselves; the problem is locating a source. Ileto's source became the Pasyon stories through which Katipunan *confradias* interpreted their reality. The Pasyon is a folk drama reenacting the Christ event. In these stories can be seen a social war of ideas. The primitive fights with the modern, the colonized with the colonizers, the sacred with the profane, the masculine with the feminine, with such intensity that the outside Western eye often saw "madness" and the "demonic." However, Katipunan magical formulas are not as irrational as they appear; they maintain a rationality of their own. Their purpose is to retain a particular form of communal life that cannot be proven to have existed, yet exists in historical memory.

In ethnomethodological terms, if for no other reason than because the Katipunan believes that it is, Katipunan origin is real in its consequences for Katipunan life. The memory of the reality and value of its historical existence has brought about the death of thousands, some say millions, of adherents. This memory has existed for at least four hundred years and shows no sign of disappearing.

The Katipunan memory houses the Katipunan soul, *loob*, which protects a hidden refugee: Katipunan national identity. I will argue first that nationalism is the expressed reason for Katipunan religiosity—the experience of Kalayaan is the religion itself; it is its soul. Yet it will become clear that another word for "nationalism" is needed. It would appear that the function of activities that keep the historical memory alive indicates that not "ethnicity" (see Fischer's suggestion in Clifford 1986) but "ethnocommunal identity" for "ethnocommunalism" would be preferable.

After three hundred years of Spanish rule the Philippines became and remain a "Catholic country." In the past one hundred years of

American Protestant leadership, the country remains 98 percent Catholic. Out of the indigenization of Catholicism grew a folk Christianity "from which is drawn much of the language of anticolonialism in the nineteenth century" (Ileto 1979, 15). Ileto discovered that this language is preserved in Holy Week (Pasyon) narratives. To understand these narratives, modern readers need a new "set of conceptual tools, a grammar" that would help us understand the world of the Kapatid, a revolutionary peasant stock. Prior to 1872 there is reference to this revolutionary group, which opposed the prosperous classes of elites (*principales*) and Western-educated (usually in Spain) Filipinos (*ilustrados*), who worked together to install and retain Spanish culture and colonial presence.

Ileto's historical study pinpoints the beginning of the Kapatid movement. In the 1890s a separatist movement, the Katipunion, spread through the mass population. The *ilustrados* and *principales*, as well as the church, whose friars favored the elites, were targets of their revolutionary anger. The Katipunans formed a "little tradition," distinct from the elites who, although they sought freedom from Spanish rule, were tied into the "grand tradition." Both groups led movements for liberation. However, the elites wanted a liberation that kept ties with the mother country (Spain) and mother church (Roman Catholicism) and that controlled the labor of the peasants. The Katipunans desired radical liberation and a return to indigenous life.

The organization and mobilization of the "little tradition" depended upon its ability to gather the people together and plan strategies under the watchful eyes of the friars and soldiers. They communicated through public recitals of the church-sponsored Pasyon story. It was the official policy of the Catholic missionaries throughout the world to "allow" such indigenous cultural forms as the Pasyon stories to be assimilated into worship. What the friars often did not know was the meaning behind words, symbols, and images, which reflected Filipino ideals, hopes, dreams, and strategies for liberation. Although the friars constantly edited the stories, through repetition the stories eventually became the property of the people, and the church could do little to prevent indigenization of the Pasyon. The Pasyon came to mirror collective consciousness.

Mother and Child: The Personal Is Political

Ileto discovers in the Pasyon narratives a countervailing force to the Spanish desire of pacification. The Pasyon speaks of social values and relationships. The critical verses appear in sections of the Pasyon describing "Jesus Christ's preparations to leave home . . . the role of *utangna loob* in defining an adult's response to his mother's care in the past" (Ileto 1979, 19).

In Filipino society leaving family is a shocking idea. Yet as Christianity grew in authority, people found that in order for the Christianized soul, now the inner self, to be allowed to grow, it must be prepared to leave family. The Katipunans found that they also certainly had to leave the status of wealth and education in their search for the true familyhood, the true self. Here they adopted the rationalized form of the oppressing body by accepting the need to leave family; and yet they resisted the goal of modern rationalized religion's affiliation with the political-economic order by denying the status it gave wealth and education. Instead the Katipunans rejected the individualist repudiation of family and sought for a way to return to "familyhood" wherein is found the true self. The Katipunans co-opt the official destruction of family for revolutionary ends.

The lowland Filipinos saw in Jesus Christ the "Tagalog peasant." Jesus' defiance was their defiance. As Christ empowered his followers to leave family and errant social life, so too did the Katipunans receive special powers to do the same. As in rationalized religion, the Katipunans replaced the broken, traditional familial bonds with a strong bonding with the holy family, Jesus and his parents Mary and Joseph. However, the bonding left open wounds that never healed. Feeling broken off from their natal mother, they also felt broken off from the holy mother, from all maternal contribution to life; they saw their trials like Joseph's trials, as necessary steps toward unification with her. Their suffering for the sake of happiness was a suffering for the reunification of family. The conceptual world underlying the struggle was a familial one. Identifying with Jesus' father—a man whose paternity was taken away, yet who willingly suffers for Mary—the Katipunans claimed the happiness Joseph must have felt when united with Mary. Saint Joseph became a guide for the adherents suffering for the new familyhood, which they thought would be achieved in this world.

Maintaining mixed worldviews, the Katipunan believed that one must be reborn into the Katipunan family, reborn to face reality with no fear and with complete control of the self. The true test of this rebirth is the ability to withstand persecution from outside, especially from the biological family (Ileto 1979, 53). Only when people are powerful is God powerful. Katipunans reversed the effect of the sacred/profane dichotomy. The powers achieved through rites are obtained by the self; eventually the powers made a rock-hard self that could face the difficult task of moving toward family to reach beyond what it was and is toward what it shall be again. The Pasyon narratives longed for an integrated life in which:

> Our women companions
> also carried rocks, like men,
> thus no matter how trying it was
> we could not complain to our companions.
> (Ileto 1979, 90)

Longing for what once was, the Katipunans bemoaned the loss of "wealth and good behavior in everyone." Before the Spanish, "young and old, women included, could read and write using their native alphabet" (Ileto 1979, 103). The Spanish conquering forces destroyed native literature societies and their libraries. They forbade the use of native languages. The loss of wholeness represented in this oppression facilitated the Katipunan folk religious struggle for wholeness.

The Katipunans often expressed wholeness in terms of mother-child relationships and nondifferentiated male-female relationships. Freedom, independence, and equality are described in rituals as "pampering treatment by parents" (Ileto 1979, 108). "Like the tendency of mothers in lowland Philippines to pamper their children and develop strong emotional ties with them . . . [the Katipunan] is none other than the extension of the experience of unity between mother and child" (Ileto 1979, 109). This vision of regaining the powerful feminine is expressed powerfully and tenderly in the Pasyon:

> Mother, at the horizon has risen
> the sun of Tagalog fury,
> three centuries we have kept it
> in the sea of woes wrought by poverty.
> (Ileto 1979, 126)

And in this memory

> the people were truly happy, free to enjoy life . . . women's stores were open all day and night. . . . But, at the first sign of fighting all the men and women straightened up and grab[bed] their weapons of war. (Ileto 1979, 135)

The "Brotherhood" and the Need for Leadership

The 1898 Katipunan revolt that liberated the islands from the Spanish was preceded by thirty-six other recorded revolts. The Katipunan resistance was not an insignificant movement. In addition to active resistance, they developed a well-thought-out social praxis. The collection of poorly written Pasyon narratives reflects a crystallization of knowledge concerning the enemy. The "darkness" that "threatened to kill the *loob*" is named as Christianity, classes, colonialism, status groups, loss of the maternal, men of war, and Western education. The Katipunans were struggling against the abstract rationality of the Spanish. They can even be said to have developed something akin to the sophistication of Max Weber. This premodern consciousness knew that the enemy of *loob* needed to be confronted with powerful charismatic leadership. It knew that followers were needed who were transformed and purified by their disassociation with the *ilustrado* classes that wanted continual contact with Spain. They went beyond the requirements of communities described by Weber and required the development of charisma in each member of the community.

Power: East versus West

Ileto evaluates the concept of power in Western political thought as "an abstraction, a way of describing relationships between individuals and groups" (Ileto 1979, 30). In the West sources of power are "wealth, social status, formal office, manpower, organization, weapons," in contrast to the Southeast Asian sources of "intangible, mysterious, divine energy which animates the universe . . . [and] is manifested in every aspect of the natural world, in stones, trees, clouds, and fire" (Ileto 1979, 30). Retained most fully in Javanese culture, this power is formless.

This formless, creative energy produces a unique Javanese politics. Ileto sees strong connections between Philippine and Javanese modes of accumulating power. First, the individual must be pure. "The idea of purity is connected not necessarily with moral questions, but with the idea of concentration of power versus diffusion. . . . [A] central concept of Javanese traditional view of life is the direct relationship between the state of a person's inner life and his capacity to control the environment" (Ileto 1979, 31). As Mary Douglas pointed out in *Purity and Danger*, the valued diffused power of Asian life was no match for the accumulation of consolidated power developed in situations of "progress."

The person who is recognized as a leader must have a pure inner self and "radiate" power. In addition to "radiance," another sign of inner purity is sexual fertility. These notions of radiance and fertility do not separate *loob* from its other concerns of leadership, power, "nationalism," and revolution as they do in Western rationalism. Ileto then describes the purification process necessary if a person is to be politically successful (1979, 32). Worked out publicly, the Katipunan purification process wipes the slate clean and confers good membership status on each *confrade*. Good membership rests on an ability to stay on the margins of life, uncontaminated by elitist desires.

Mary Douglas considers rituals of purity and impurity to be the way through which cultures create order and unity in experience. Observing spirituality and economics, she concludes that the primitives handle the economy directly and their spirituality is unpredictable. The moderns handle spirituality directly and their economy is unpredictable. The danger zones in both systems lie in the margins. The marginal person is most at risk during transitions. Fear of the margins is located in the fear of leaving traditional structures. But the margins are also sources of power: power to harm authority. The margins are not given this power; they hold it.

The Katipunans received some of their sense of power from the mere fact that they existed on the margins; they knew they were feared by authorities. According to those models that hold the body to be a symbol of society, one would expect the Katipunans to have shown through their bodies how life is lived on the margins, where life is most vulnerable. This was indeed the case. As a result of elaborate ascetic and purification rituals, the Katipunans displayed strong emotional, physical, psychological, and sexual power. As long as the inner life was kept pure, the Katipunan was strong to act. Where the body needs protection is on the level of the soul, the *loob*. In summary, human transformation from an impure state of association with the source that threatens the Katipunan way of life to a pure state of Katipunan commitments is the prerequisite for magical powers. Self-discipline prepares the *loob* to respond to these magical powers as a conscious choice of will.

It is not difficult to see how this Kalayaan worldview supported the Katipunan magical belief of *anting-anting*, which brought the adherents' unarmed bodies into the direct line of fire of Spanish guns. The adherents' belief that the magical powers they possessed would deflect the Spanish—and, later, American—bullets from their unprotected bodies left thousands of Katipunans to face death.

Charisma

The more Katipunans that died, the more charismatic the communities became. The otherworldliness of the Katipunan religion became its strength (Ileto 1979, 38). The divine plan, which is also the Katipunan plan, allowed them to reorient their being toward

> an order of reality in which the disruption of one's "normal" role in society, including death itself, was a distinct possibility. The events that culminated in the bloody revolt of 1841 was not simply a blind reaction to oppressive forces in colonial society; it was a conscious act of realizing certain possibilities of existence that the members were made conscious of through reflection upon certain mysteries and signs. . . . The connection between the events of 1840–1841 and later upheavals in the Tagalog region can be posited. . . . Certain common features of these upheavals, or the way these events were perceived, indicate that the connections do exist. These lie perhaps, not in a certain chain of events, but in the common features through time of a consciousness that constantly seeks to define the world on its own terms. (Ileto 1979, 38–39)

A legitimate opportunity to change social roles and social praxis was created under the authority of religion.

The Katipunans recognized leaders by their similarity to the previous leader. All leaders addressed the common themes, using the Kalayaan language. They knew the ancient prayers and could recite them from memory. Their leaders became either God or Jesus; in either case, they became the savior. The leader radiated light, giving the follower strength to continue to purify the *loob* and to face death on the journey toward wholeness.

The leader bridges the gap between the everyday world and the Pasyon world (Ileto 1979, 54). *Confradias* organized the *confrades'* experience so that they could withdraw from extra-*confradia* (social) pressures.

The *confrades'* experience of what they believed to be authentic charisma challenged Spanish and American notions of leadership. Charisma was judged by the *loobs'* beauty and not by wealth or education. Having a good mind had little to do with certificates and degrees and everything to do with maintaining equilibrium and "seeing" the wider context. The women's *confradias* led the way to the most beautiful *loob* by discouraging the distinction between age and classes within the Katipunan order. "Perfect unity means that the social positions that differentiate men on earth will be dissolved" (Ileto 1979, 49). Purification in the Katipunan order was meant to blur the differences between people while distinguishing the good from the bad.

> High-born or low,
> rich or poor,
> all will look alike
> this is God's vow.
> (Ileto 1979, 49)

The "seeing" of the wider context demanded constant prayer (Ileto 1979, 59). Ancient prayers were whispered from one generation to the next. Spanish colonizers noted that through self-strengthening, the leader channeled the willing *confrades* into an orderly community that, in its massive numbers and strength of intergroup affiliation, was "not common among Indios" (Ileto 1979, 60). The leader assumed the maternal role and demanded *confrade* dependence as "children upon their mothers" (Ileto 1979, 63). "Folk memories of a leader's personality [had also] been shaped in terms of the Pasyon image of Christ" (Ileto 1979, 64). The leader was God and mother as well. The group was held together by the god-mother call for *damay* or participation in another's work (Ileto 1979, 65). This could also be called erotic solidarity.

Ileto maintains that the function of leadership was "analogous to the singing of the Pasyon narrative: to evoke *damay* and the development of potentialities of *loob*" (1979, 68). The leader then was a pastor-parent, a special kind of spiritual being who prayed incomprehensible prayers sprinkled with the names of biblical prophets, and who started "fires" using the brothers and sisters, the *confrades*, as "kindling" to light a glowing fire attracting other potential *confrades* (Ileto 1979, 69). The call of the leader brought joy and music to the ears of the *confrades* who moved as one body. Removed to a retreat in the mountains, they could see that the beauty of the surroundings matched the beauty of their *loob* (Ileto 1979, 88). In touch with the communal *loob*, as many as five thousand to ten thousand persons would gather in their retreat places and prepare themselves to face the enemy army with their special *anting-anting* magical powers. Often, in a few hours thousands would lie dead. When observers thought them "mad" they thought themselves "totally regular and determined" (Ileto

1979, 83). Much to the panic of the liberal *ilustrados*, the poor became more and more uncontrollable:

> Contrary to the image of the passive and acquiescent Indio peasant, the members of the Confradia refused to pay taxes and fulfill the annual personal service. They also disavowed any connections with the priests of the Catholic Church, for their church, they claimed, was in the mountain. That is why an armed force was sent to disperse the community. . . . The invading party also cut down sacred trees and attempted to destroy the sacred rock which formed part of the cult. . . . Those which the inhabitants call temples, hermitages, and holy places, are represented only by rocks, trees, and streams. . . . Marriage ceremonies were conducted by this rock . . . the miraculous springs . . . heal all those who have faith. . . . By the time the revolution against Spain began in 1896 [thirty-six years after the armed destruction of the holy places], the cult was an established center for the Lenten pilgrimage, attracting not only Tagalogs but people from all over the archipelago. An organized priesthood of men and women existed. Branches of the society or brotherhood flourished in other areas, headed by pastors trained at the mountain. (Ileto 1979, 85–87)

The towns sponsoring such communities became retreat centers where people sold their individual properties and lived together. Leading these communities was one of its own who was granted power to lead the community in pursuit of Kalayaan goals.

Power, Leadership, and Purpose

Leaders—chosen, recognized, and followed by *confrades*—had only one mandated purpose: revolution. In fact, there is no other way to understand the Katipunan.

> A serious obstacle to contemporary understanding of the Katipunan is the established view that the rise of a nationalism culminating in the revolution of 1896–1900 was purely a consequence of heightened Westernization in the nineteenth century. . . . [Although it is true that they wanted reform and not independence, *ilustrados*] first conceived of a Filipino national community. . . . [but the fact is] revolutionary impulse had to start from "below." (Ileto 1979, 97–98)

Ileto maintains that the nationalism of Western-trained Spanish mestizos is not the same as that of the Indio *confrades*. He finds a great discontinuity between folk traditions and the liberal ideas of the nineteenth century.

"The 'poor and the ignorant' that swelled the ranks of the Katipunan had certain ideas about the world and their place in it, ideas quite different from those of the better classes" (Ileto 1979, 99). Although the Katipunans fought against colonialism and outside intervention of all kinds in favor of Filipino control, "the limit of the aspirations of the Katipunan was a communistic republic . . . [a] community of property . . . [a] . . . brilliant future . . . in an atmosphere of liberty and general happiness, based on honorable work for all" (Ileto 1979, 100).

Honor is a major Katipunan theme. The friars were seen as "blinding the natives to the true nature of religion" (Ileto 1979, 105). Joining a Kalayaan society would not bring one the material wealth of the friars but would entail one's own death.

The Kalayaan leader's sermons became an opportunity for the whole community to speak. Although the friars suppressed this ancient public-forum style of "communal preaching" (rather like the American black church experience), it survived and the spirit was heard. The story line of the sermons spoke of multiple oppressions that united women with a race of people linked in slavery to the dominant powers of Spain and official religion. The leaders spoke "with gentle, supplicating language of a woman in chains who seeks compassion from her sons" (Ileto 1979, 121). The leader represented Mother Filipinas. But there was a foster mother who raised them from birth: Mother Spain, who neglected and abused them. They plead "her forgiveness for their act of separating from her" even though she neglected them (Ileto 1979, 129). Mother Country and Virgin Mother melt into each other, allowing the repressed mother's voice to cry out and her children to hear her:

> Fear not Mother Filipinas
> Whatever fate has in store for us,
> We will not cease to struggle until
> The Kalayaan we search for is found.
> (Ileto 1979, 134)

Those who respond to her voice are the poor and the nonpoor who struggle for the cause. They have all chosen to give up what they have and become poor. Being poor is the way of being. There is no turning back.

Ileto tries not to superimpose an outside ideology on Katipunan religiosity; he recognizes that in a very real way the political aims of the *confrades* are superseded by the mystery of their faith. As the people spoke through their religious leaders, the Spanish friars realized that disembodied spirits were being spoken of. The friars moved to suppress this magical interpretation of knowledge. Such knowledge gave energy to the Katipunan claim that they could rise, that their old way of life would be resurrected, made whole, and embodied. It is no wonder, Ileto writes, that the Katipunans chose Holy Week, the time of Jesus' resurrection to new life, for their pilgrimage up the mountain.

These mountain experiences merged national and religious idioms in the reenactment of the Pasyon. Being poor became a way of being. This way of being created its own language, and familiarity with it facilitated a leader's rise and the rise of the resistance movement. It also facilitated the execution of all captured Katipunan leaders at the hands of the Spanish and, later, the American armies.

The powerful aspirations of the poor in the Philippines were not understood by the Corazon Aquino government or by the United States. The people in the mountains are there, as they have been for several hundred years. In their struggle with Cory Aquino they wanted the same things that they wanted four hundred years ago: they wished to focus not on the problems of a nation but on the communal life found in locality; instead of "citizenship" they wished the government would understand what it means to become "one in *loob*" with the people.

Buried deep in the historical memory of the Kalayaan lies an experience of harmony, equality, and happiness. Where this memory comes from becomes a secondary question to governments that wish to modernize and pursue modern rational capitalism. Understanding the traditional mind in order to manipulate it into cooperation becomes its primary task. Ileto, on the other hand, has sought to understand the voices from below in order to form a cooperative alliance between primitive and modernizing forces.

A study of the Katipunans reveals that once prompted by repression, oppression, or chaos, it is people themselves that create resistance, and no effort originating outside people's experience can create the kind of resistance that survives several hundred years. This means that the people can be their own liberators. They may not have achieved a particular kind of revolution often required by critical theorists, but they have moved toward social transformation by keeping their spirit of resistance alive. Keeping the soul alive is revolutionary activity itself.

This revolutionary spirit can be found in the experience of Hispanic and black American women as well.

The Sanctified Church and Mujerista Theology

Zora Neale Hurston was a writer who "celebrate[d] the genius of Black-south folks" (1981, 7). Having "never ever ever cut those critical ties with the 'lowly down under,'" Hurston journeyed to New York City during the Depression to "wrassle me up a future" (1981, 7). She is celebrated for launching a genre of black women's literature and social ethics frequently referred to as "womanism" (Katie Cannon, Alice Walker, Shirley Ann Williams) and for her ability to capture the strong heartbeat of black folk who lived and survived in the South three-quarters of a century ago. In her stories of black religiosity one can see—like moonlight shimmering on a lake—a liberationist interpretation of life.

Father Abraham, Mother Catherine, Uncle Monday, and Aunt Judy Bickerstaff

After working for thirty-five years as a manual laborer, Henry Abraham got tired, and as he rested and contemplated his weariness, he heard the call from the Lord. He put down his plow and "at once began his holy work" (Hurston 1981, 16). Called by God to be an herb doctor, Abraham spontaneously picked up the trade, set up shop, and became a well-known healer. His healing sessions followed more or less the same pattern. Prepayment was placed in the open Bible; he massaged the affected body part; he prayed indescribable prayers and named a few prophets; and he announced that the patient was well—or would be after a few more sessions. Many people proclaimed healing.

Hurston refers to the beliefs and remedies of the South as the "old" religions (Hurston 1981, 16). These old religions adapted to Christian culture and took from it what they needed to heal the patient, to save the soul.

The goal of the practitioner was to seek knowledge and wisdom and to feed the followers "good food" (Hurston 1981, 24). Mother Catherine always had "good food" and did not "crush the individual"; she "encouraged originality" and "did not require money for healing" (Hurston 1981, 25).

In her religious meetings there was no talk of heaven or hell: she only talked of the earth. Her religious world reversed the political order: blacks were lifted up and women given priority.

It is right that a woman should lead. A womb was what God made in the beginning, and out of the womb was born Time, and all that fills up space. So says the beautiful spirit.

Some are weak to do wisdom things, but strong to do wicked things.

He could have been born in the biggest White House in the world. But the reason He didn't is that He knowed a falling race was coming what couldn't get to no great White House, so He got born so my people could all reach.

It is not for people to know the whence.

Don't teach what the apostles and the prophets say. Go to the tree and get the pure sap and find out whether they were right. (Hurston 1981, 26)

The mother-leader, Mother Catherine, was an equal with Christ and, like Jesus, distrustful of people who claimed authority. These persons and their roles were simply edited out of the holy story:

Mother Catherine's conception of the divinity of Christ is that Joseph was his foster father as all men are foster fathers, in that all children are of God and all fathers are merely the means. (Hurston 1981, 27)

Her syncretistic form of folk Christianity was "all sympathetic magic" (Hurston 1981, 27), magic for the children. Mother Catherine mothered the "white and the colored," the "saints and the conzempts (convicts)" (Hurston 1981, 28). Her church was called a manger and "dedicated to the birth of children in or out of wedlock. Over and over she lauds the bringing forth. *There is no sinful childbirth*" (Hurston 1981, 28; emphasis original). She believed that her theology came directly from God. She had no need for intermediary figures such as Christ and the Spirit. She was Christ and the Spirit. As with the Katipunans, Hurston's characters become unified with God in order to break down divisions between people.

Zora Neale Hurston describes a religiosity that recognizes no real difference between conjuring and faith. The Blacksouth folk were able to see visions and spirits and select and create, by sheer will, voodoo practitioners. Thereupon it was agreed that no one knew this person. Ordained to voodoo status in a silent cultural process, Uncle Monday had access to "singing stones" that allowed him to walk on water, to know everything without being told, to bring life and death, and to heal. That is, Uncle Monday was chosen by his community to be like God.

The powerful singing stone could only be taken from the serpent's mouth in a weak moment of violence and chaos:

> The serpents who produce these stones live in the deep waters of Lake Maitland. . . . She comes only to nourish herself in the height of a violent thunderstorm, when she is fairly certain no human being will be present. . . . It is not necessary to kill her to take the stone. . . . It is her pilot, that warns her of danger. (Hurston 1981, 34)

When one possessed this magical singing stone, one had the power to wish death and to protect life. Hurston recognizes that it was violence and chaos that defined the religious context. Violence and chaos involved men and women, particularly women.

Voodoo doctors could be women. Aunt Judy had the power to reverse Uncle Monday's spells until, surrounded by red light, he threatened her with powers gathered deep in the dark, murky lake, with which he threatened to kill her. It seems that the people knew, much like Durkheim and Mauss, that men who were surrounded in red light (blood?) found in the deep, dark, murky lake (the womb?) were more powerful than women, even women who went to the lake to get power and to be healed.

In this folklore,

> God and the Devil are paired, and are treated no more reverently than Rockefeller and Ford. . . . The angels and the apostles walk and talk like section hands. And through it all walks Jack, the cultural hero of the South; Jack beats them all—even the Devil, who is often smarter than God. . . . The gods of physical violence reverse roles and stop at nothing to serve their followers. (Hurston 1981, 54, 57)

The people became powerful people by controlling and redirecting divine violence. They reverse the theology of the "official church."

Hurston evaluates the Sanctified church to be

> a protest against the highbrow tendency in Negro Protestant congregations as the Negroes gain more education and wealth. . . . In fact the Negro has not been civilized as extensively as generally believed. The great masses are still standing before pagan altars and calling old gods by new names. (Hurston 1981, 103)

For Hurston the Sanctified church is a revitalizing agent of "Negro religion" because it keeps its African religious roots alive and resists white religious forms. The Sanctified church is a religion of magical healing, not a "religion of the Book." Like the Katipunans it resists ethnic dissolution and builds community. It wills itself power.

Mujerista Theology

Ada María Isasi-Díaz and Yolanda Tarango's work with Hispanic women produced similar themes (1988). Across class and country of origin their interviews documented Hispanic women's conversations with and descriptions of God, the Virgin Mary, the church, and the Bible. These are set out below. Hispanic women "feel God" and "feel the church." Their feelings shape what they can say about God; feelings create their language.

God
  - is a deep force that makes me move
  - says I am special, I am not bad, I can move mountains
  - is my grandmother smiling
  - is my grandmother with her hands open
  - is like my grandmother, I pray to her, she is my favorite saint
  - is something outside of me
  - is strength and courage, only a part of which is Jesus
  - is red roses, love; not a cross; I don't understand about crosses
  - is a complete spirit, "he is prettier and more supreme than the shape I give him"
  - feels like a father, my protector, a brother, a friend, a mother
  - is a punisher
  - God and Jesus are one and the same
  - Jesus is God's pilot project
  - he is not to be prayed to
  - he and I get *cachetadas* (slaps in the face together)
  - is goodness and miracles
  - miracles make up for being stepped on and all the confusions and all the hurts and all the unanswerable questions
  - is the one who makes it up to you
  - is one who lifts up
  - is busy but can be influenced
  - is one who gives *frijoles* (daily bread)
  - is a pregnant woman
  - works in secret

The Virgin Mary
  - gives me dignity
  - is a brown woman, an Indian woman, a pregnant woman, a mother
  - comes from outside, from Italy; she did not appear to us
  - is faithfulness

Bible
- I live by feeling and example, not by the Bible
- I go straight to God and I see visions
- it demeans women, I don't like reading it

Church-Mass
- I teach my children religion of my home, not the religion of the
  church
- I take my children to Sunday School
- I often do not go to mass
- I go to mass

Isasi-Díaz and Tarango find little tension between the women, their spirituality, and the world. Hispanic women have a deep sense of being the church and one with God (Isasi-Díaz and Tarango 1988, 55). Relating most directly to God, with some reference to the Virgin Mary and little to the Bible, they create a religiosity that promotes justice and love. Their world is shaped by the struggle for survival, self-determination, and self-definition (Isasi-Díaz and Tarango 1988, 65).

"In other words, the religious dimension in their lives constitutes a 'revolutionary urge.' It is precisely the struggle for survival that defines the essence of religion for Hispanic Women" (Isasi-Díaz and Tarango 1988, 65). The everyday religious-spiritual practices of Hispanic women are pieced together from many sources, including official Christianity, unofficial Christianity, and native religions, and includes only those things that promote survival. Hispanic women creatively reinterpret their traditions to make them useful.

Popular religiosity is part of the source of Hispanic Women's Liberation Theology to the extent that, and insofar as, popular religiosity is an intrinsic part of the daily lives of Hispanic Women. Hispanic Women's Liberation Theology understands popular religiosity as a rich tradition of religious beliefs and practices that fuses Christian, Amerindian, and African religious traditions and is the most operative "system of symbols" used by Hispanic Women in establishing "powerful, pervasive, and long-lasting moods and motivations" [Geertz 1978, 90] (which) . . . offer needed correctives to some of the religious understandings of "official" Christianity. . . . Popular Christianity has always been a source of embarrassment for "official" Christianity. What the "official" church has done, therefore, is either denounce it and work actively against it or look for ways of purifying it, of "baptizing" it into Christianity—accepting only those elements that can be Christianized. (Isasi-Díaz and Tarango 1988, 67–68)

Like Katipunan folk beliefs, *mujerista* theology is social theory as well. It understands that God and Hispanic women must be companions, equals, in order for the women to survive. Yet these women do not see themselves as "sacred" or different from something "profane." They ignore the institutional, "official" church teaching whenever it does not promote justice for them and their communities. They feel they "are the church," and by feeling they guide their actions. They are guided by knowing the difference between what comes from them and what comes from outside them. Although they exist under the authority of the church, which has the power to excommunicate them and to disrupt their lives, they live by the authority that arises in their hearts as they work out a way to a just life.

The next chapter will explore this conflict between official religion and folk-indigenous-heart spirituality as it is encountered in liberation movements that have grown up from within the church.

9

RESISTING

THE

SACRED

It has been said that the calendar of the Brazilian Catholic year, which is full of pilgrimages and processions and festivals, accounts for much of the pleasure and most of the beauty in the lives of the Brazilian poor, and without it those lives would be desolate. The people here love their saints. They love the stories of the saints, the horrible sufferings of their saints. They love the color and music and holiday of a pilgrimage, and they love to put on gaiety and wear it, like a papier-mâché procession saint, hung with wishes, through the mud streets of their favelas. *They love to conspire at forgetting, and the pleasures of forgetting are hard to replace with the pleasures of a* comunidad eclesia de base *and sixteen subject areas on the way to salvation. In one sense, the Brazilian poor are as cynical as any princes of the Church. They do not really believe in a better life—certainly not in a better life of their own making— and so they prefer the distractions of saints, and Mary's indulgence, and shrines, fetishes, pilgrimages, and anything else they can think of to produce miracles. They say that in Brazil miracles are better than social justice or a living wage or a clinic that actually opens. . . . This is what their hard Brazilian life has taught them, and this is what a priest like Frei David has to answer for—and still sound like a priest of the Church who by faith and calling believes in miracles himself.*

—Jane Kramer, "Letter from the Elysian Fields,"
The New Yorker

Liberation theologians have long acknowledged the necessity of integrating social theory and theology; traces of Durkheim, Weber, and Marx are found throughout the genre. Sociologists, in their turn, are becoming interested in liberation theology's claims to have lighted a fire under the laboring and the burdened. Radical sociologists have taken a new look at radical theology, finding materialist opposition to theology no longer tenable:

> Radical theologians discover in Marxism an important way to liberate theology from its "other worldly" predilections. . . . their interpretation of Christian theology tends to decode its subversive, emancipatory content. (Aronowitz 1981, 42, 103)
>
> But Marxism's whole *raison d'être* . . . lies in worldly success. Failure is liable to be ultimately dispiriting, whereas for most religions it would serve more as a salutary (literally) warning. . . . Few would dispute that there is a better future for religion than for Marxism. (McLellan 1987, 172)

It is time for feminist social theorists of religion to make a contribution to the critique and support of profeminist liberation theology as they develop a feminist social theory of religion that adequately engages the struggles of oppressed people. Feminist theory has resisted the patriarchal interpretations of history, culture, and theology as exclusionary tools designed to tell the story of the rich and the dominant while suppressing the stories of the poor and the disempowered. Religion's suppression of magic and the erotic, its labeling of women as profane creatures responsible for the fall of "Man," its feminizing or demasculinizing of homosexual men and men who do not wish to carry a sword, and its suppression of popular experience and religiosity systematically work against liberation. A feminist sociological critique interested in the full liberation of all human beings can be brought into critical dialogue with liberation theology.

This is a particularly crucial time to begin such a conversation. The North American church is trying to adopt and adapt the liberation theology, theory, and *comunidad eclesia de base* or Base Christian Community (BCC) praxis models of Latin American liberation theology to the North American context. Academic theologians continue to create communities of discourse with Latin American liberation theologians. Both of these are occurring at a time when the response of the Latin American oppressed to these programs is declining. This latter reality is demonstrated by the work of Canadian sociologist Warren Hewitt (1988) and Brazilian sociologist Cecilia Mariz (1988), both of whom have documented the decreasing size of the BCCs. Hewitt's conversations with Clodovis Boff, brother of Leonardo Boff, shows him to be increasingly more guarded about the political future of the BCCs. Hewitt finds the BCCs to be heterogeneous and institutionally dependent. Even so, among the BCC the desire still exists, in small or large ways, to change the world. Patron-client mentality, he reported, is being replaced by enlightened self-interest. But this sense of "citizenship" is threatened by the decreasing size and more frequent membership turnover of the BCCs. Instead of the anticipated political agenda, more attention is being paid to devotional activities. All but one of the eight oldest and advanced BCCs that Hewitt intensively studied had suspended their involvement in anti-impoverishment projects. Three of the groups supported individual involvement in projects, but "dormancy" appeared to be a potential problem.

Hewitt concluded that the liberalizing atmosphere in Brazil might have diffused the sense of urgency; that some people might be disillusioned and did not bother to complain anymore; that the church is confused as to its role in sociopolitical justice; and that conservatism in the church is growing. The church is reverting to direct influence instead of organizing through the BCCs. The communities are further removed from pastoral priorities, and their lay leaders speak of being abandoned by the church. Indeed, in 1988 Hewitt found more advanced groups abandoned by the pastoral agents (priests and nuns) than he had previously.

In her analysis, which is in some ways a response to Hewitt, Cecilia Mariz found that the Pentecostal viewpoint was more easily accepted by the poor Brazilian peasants than the BCC way of life and liberation theology. The BCCs break strongly away from popular culture, whereas the Pentecostal churches do not. Noting that both Pentecostals and the BCCs see themselves as different from culture, Mariz attributes the greater attraction to Pentecostalism to the difference between what Pentecostalism and the BCCs, respectively, want to change in popular culture. Whereas the BCCs, wanting cognitive change, seek to transform people by saying that they have "the wrong knowledge," Pentecostalism, wanting normative change, declares that the people maintain "wrong values." The desire to change values does not cause Pentecostalism to break from popular culture; it sees culture as different from religion and seeks to change religiosity rather than culture. According to Mariz, the BCCs have a different goal: they want to change culture while allowing for the contextualization of the Bible. They want to break away from popular culture. The BCCs, thinking that people adopt the symbols of the dominant class, seek to reinterpret and secularize the symbols. But, finds Mariz, secularization destroys the power of the symbols. The BCCs put nothing of comparable worth in their place. The people have not accepted the BCCs' linear concept of history and transformation as a valid substitute for their symbolic life.

Most critically, Pentecostalism is very concerned with miracles and their power *in this world*. Mariz found that the BCCs do not identify with miracles and certainly do not connect miracles with God's plan of liberation and transformation. Pentecostals share with the popular culture the belief that the spiritual (supernatural) can be experienced. The BCCs do not consider spirits important. But among the poor, Mariz argues, this is a critical debate. The BCCs find that Pentecostalism does not encourage "community" to see itself as a political community. However, there is great solidarity between the popular culture and Pentecostals, a solidarity that the BCCs want to reorganize.

On this point Hewitt is in agreement: the poor opt for Pentecostalism, just as the Catholic church opts for the poor. Mariz and Hewitt agree further that the people who left the BCCs were not running to Pentecostalism. Many went to other political groups. Mariz believed that the BCCs were populated in the early stages by people who were already engaged in the political process. Whereas many priests left the BCCs under gunfire and threat to their lives, the poor stayed and found themselves abandoned by the church, which considers the BCCs an evangelization tool and not a political one.

These church-BCC dynamics are critical for understanding why BCC activity is decreasing. The current state of the BCCs contradicts the initial hope that they would liberate the poor.

Whether it is the North American feminist movement or the Latin American liberation movement, it is of utmost interest to discover the hidden biases that prevent the poor from adopting the platform or prevent the platform's creators from seeing the inappropriateness of their agenda. Building a theology around gender-blind social analysis can only facilitate the production of gender-blind and -biased theology. Simply put, a gender-biased social theory is oppressive, and no matter where this theology is transported it will remain biased if basic theoretical assumptions are maintained. Liberation theology suffers from gender bias.

This section will focus on only two theologies, those of Juan Luis Segundo, a self-identified theologian, and Leonardo Boff, a self-identified pastor-priest, both European-trained Latin American theologians who are indebted to the classic social theorists. Together their work spreads its wings broadly over the Latin American scene.

Juan Luis Segundo

Juan Luis Segundo is a theologian radically committed to the poor. He studies sociology in an effort to gain the critical tools necessary for directing the church's attention toward the poor, its "original focus," and for assisting the poor in their revolutionary role. He fears for the salvation of the poor and for the future of the gospel. His fears are based on a deep sense of ecclesiastical failure to preach the word and to reach out to the poor. The church has failed to be the church, and Segundo therefore calls for a new ecclesiology. Contemporary theology is much indebted to Segundo's endeavors to root his work in social reality and to bring to it insights from the discipline of sociology.

In *The Liberation of Theology* (1976) sociological observations form the basis of Segundo's discovery that the "masses who are fully integrated into modern culture-forms maintain relationships with their primitive past solely in and through religious practices that have no relationship whatsoever with their present roles and values in the everyday life of modern society" (201–2).

He concludes that Latin America's future lies not in preserving primitive cultures but in moving them toward "modernization that is the precondition for survival to a revolution that will thoroughly and radically humanize the social structures of the population as a whole" (Segundo 1976, 202). Segundo finds that this revolution depends on a vanguard that "is free to see what is happening, [to] discern the shape of the future, and accept a new vocation over against the system. It is with respect to this specific goal, and perhaps to no other goal of any sort, that the Church possesses a powerful instrument" (Segundo 1976, 202).

One can see in Segundo's recommendations for liberation theology's heroic leadership of the masses, who are not intellectually capable of self-determination, Karl Marx's sociological prescription for the evolutionary path to revolution, which contained a privileged role for intellectuals, and Max Weber's call for the masses to put their faith in a heroic leader. He believes that because the church is now "of the poor," it is capable of contributing this vanguard. Because this vanguard has committed itself to the masses, the vanguard is "free" to "inject" into the masses *"the crisis of an authentic evangelization process"* (Segundo 1976, 202; emphasis original). This crisis would:

1. liberate the popular Catholics from their cyclical nature;

2. integrate into social life the "original dimension of the Christian religion" of communitarian solidarity;

3. point out that protest to oppression is inherently religious;

4. point out that the masses and the minority vanguard must become one church.

In dealing with the "problem of popular religion," Segundo must find ways to reinforce the masses' value as persons while devaluing what he perceives to be their nonpoliticized and nonconscientized and often victim status (Segundo 1976, 203). He finds that the popular masses belong to one type of religion that is "shaped by physical and psychic insecurity, environmental pressures and so forth. . . . The second type of religion is . . . represented by voluntary consumers of religion. . . . This latter group of people constitute a minority . . . but they are more active and inclined to commit themselves to the overall liberation process" (Segundo 1976, 203–4). It is the task of the second group, the minority vanguard (who are apparently not shaped by environmental factors or who can rise above them), to evaluate popular religion and to discover ways "of exerting a liberating influence on it" (Segundo 1976, 205). This problem belongs not only to the church but to Marxists as well, who "have never solved this basic issue either" (Segundo 1976, 205).

Segundo appears to favor Weber's political strategy of individual, "heroic" leadership: freedom is an "intolerable burden" on the masses "and only a 'heroic' minority can bear its weight" (Segundo 1976, 208). The masses need to be relieved "from the burden" of choosing options in which they must act consistently—a behavior they fail to accomplish (Segundo 1976, 209).

Segundo's sociological observations—which deviate from both Marx and Weber, who associated Christianity with the masses (that is, the laboring and the burdened)—help him address what he believes is an essential methodological issue: "Was the original Christian message aimed at masses as such, so that it must be thought out and propagated in those terms; or was it rather aimed at minorities [Segundo's vanguard] who were destined to play an essential role in the transformation and liberation of the masses?" (Segundo 1976, 209). The picture is complicated by his model of mass education, which requires the vanguard minority to be educators of the masses, who aspire to obtain from the vanguard the learning and conscientization they require. Do the masses desire this knowledge for themselves? Segundo's frustration with the masses seems to stem from a lack of interest on their part; a question, then, might be: What *is* their interest, their desire? For Segundo this question is premature. Faith does not yet exist; it is the goal, ideology is the means.

For Segundo sociology and religion are separate realms requiring separate analytical modes. This concept prevents him from establishing a method that would assure some correlation between the discursive realms. However, he cannot give up his "two worlds" concept because for him there are two Christianities:

> [T]here is majority Christianity of very low religious caliber . . . [and] there is a minority Christianity which is characterized by a much more profound grasp of the Christian message and the commitment it demands, however much they accuse it of being class-conscious and intellectualistic. (Segundo 1976, 185)

Segundo is really describing a class system within theology in which the "critical thinkers" are the elitist theologians, a description in which one hears echoes of Lenin.

Segundo does not see the oppressed as capable of "disestablishing themselves from the system" or of "expressing and thinking their own thoughts" (Segundo 1976, 186–88). Apparently, therefore, he resists and represses familiarity with the folk experience he wants to influence. His attachment to universal and evolutionary models and to "maturation" concepts does not allow him to see folk religion and primitive experience to be as valuable, complete, authentic, and therefore as faithful as his own. Instead of incorporating its social critique, he wants the church to "keep its hands off the inflexible and relatively negligible factor of popular catholicism" and "commit itself instead to accepting and encouraging the forward movement of the overall popular masses" (Segundo 1976, 198–99). This advice is based on and informed by scripture verses that talk about the "scarcity of the laborers, the little flock, the chosen few" (Segundo 1976, 228). Elsewhere he compares this vanguard of heroic individuals to the Israelites, "God's heroic minority of strong-willed people." Yet he is aware of a potential problem and warns that liberation theology must lead to a "theology of the people" that "compares culture that is logically and conceptionally structured in a tight-knit way with the wisdom of common people, the content of their rituals and imaginative creations, and internal logic of their strangest attitudes" (Segundo 1976, 236).

Given his orientation to the poor, Segundo vastly inhibits his ability to engage them. On one level he must be as confusing to them as they are to him. What he thinks about the common people's "rituals," "imaginative creation," "internal [but not external] logic," and "strangest attitudes" is the key to his problem. On his own grounds he has not completed his hermeneutical circle because he cannot accept the world of the poor "as it is" and consequently jeopardizes his commitment to understanding that world.

In *Faith and Ideologies* Segundo attempts an even greater shift from thinking about social realities theologically to seeing these realities sociologically, because he has concluded that God and Jesus favor the profane world over the religious (Segundo 1984, 41). Jesus performs in such a way as to distinguish what is good for people from what is good for religion. Segundo declares that religion may point to God, but God points to people and to the nonreligious, the human, the secular.

In *Our Idea of God* secularization shifts from "the realm of the sacred ... to the realm of the secular or the profane"; the movement from God to the people "desacralizes" (Segundo 1974a, 74). But the intent of desacralization is to resacralize the profane:

> So we can make a statement that seems paradoxical. Secularization, far from signifying an abandonment of the profane to its profaneness, is a recognition of the sacred that it contains within its very dynamism. It is the authentic *consecration* of the profane. Why? Because everything in the little temple is supposed to be in the service of humanity and its tasks, then the latter are recognized to be sacred, to be the site of the encounter between God and human beings, to be the big temple. (Segundo 1974a, 75; emphasis original).

To live in this paradox, to meet the demands of the day, is not uncomfortable for Segundo largely because the day demands it. The capitalist, universal, grand-scheme theology needs to be matched with a universal, grand-scheme narrative. The Christian universal story, the grand story of the big temple, the Catholic church, can be a match for oppressive forces. This Christian grand-scheme narrative of the big temple necessitates excluding the local, small-temple narratives on the grounds that they are illogical, magical, and romantic. Segundo concludes that those people who defend "popular religion" "represent an established order in which the 'death of God' is already an accomplished fact" (1974a, 79). He does not believe that the "profane" encounters God apart from encountering the holy through the sacred "big temple" traditions. If there is no God, no sacred, in the profane, then there is no need for the Christian theologian to defend the popular. Segundo goes on to distinguish between the "death of God" and "secularization" and its "anthropological faith."

Segundo is attracted to Marx's "anthropological faith," an attraction facilitated by the recovery of Catholic theologies of the intellectual heritage of Saint Thomas Aquinas, a heritage claimed as the basis for anthropological faith. From this anthropological perspective he now sees that religion "greatly influences" repression and people's longing "for the security of the womb"; for these reasons Segundo is "disturbed" that people do not see these dangers in "popular religion" or in "religion of the common people" (1984, 55). Yet he himself does not see that popular religion and official religion have the same goals, or that both offer womblike security. Segundo has skirted Marx's critique of religion, in which Marx found that official religion of the grand-narrative traditions represses people's longing.

Finding that transcendent religion produces and defines values openly while sociologists of knowledge must sneak values in through the back door (1984, 184), Segundo applies his "transcendent data" to Marx's "anthropological faith," and "transforms" it into "authentic faith" (1984, 76). Even though both anthropological faith and religious faith are now transcendent, Segundo does not have the same concern about the quality of the sacred character of anthropological instruments and instrumentalities that he has about religion's sacral instruments. In asymmetrical ways religion purifies Marxism without Marxist social theory purifying religion.

In *The Humanist Christology of Paul* (1986) Segundo follows the classical theorists in distinguishing between the sacred and the magical. In believing that the magical is not transformative, he is most like Emile Durkheim. *The Sacraments Today* more clearly demonstrates an affinity with Durkheim's understanding of the role of religious rites and rituals in producing solidarity and in producing mechanisms used by the sacred to separate itself from the profane. Segundo then asks: "Is there room for the sacraments in a world that is desacralized or that is, at the very least, moving in that direction?" (Segundo 1974b, 2). He answers yes, the sacraments must be modernized (secularized); but even so, they form the "very essence of authentic Christian experience" (Segundo 1974b).

The sacraments are vital for Christianity's continuing need to distinguish itself from magic (Segundo 1974b, 13). Now "the people of God itself, as an ecclesial community, is transformed into a sacrament" (Segundo 1974b, 15). The crisis of the future of the sacraments and their regulating power is averted by the Lutheran notion of the priesthood of all believers. Marx wanted the sacred to see itself as nothing but a masquerade; what is real is the profane, the everyday, the common life. Segundo's institutional commitments require him to keep the sacred separate and distinct from the profane, claiming that God chooses to focus on profane life so that it might be sacralized—that is, brought into the church.

Segundo is not alone in questioning whether folk religion is authentically Christian. A thirty-year investigation by "religious sociologists, theologians and (most) pastoral workers (who are) united in a negative view" (Galilea 1980, 42) concluded that folk religion is incompatible with the consciousness and practice of liberation. Christian belief without liberation is only ideology. "Salvation" and "liberation" are the same word in the Hebrew language; therefore all liberation is "Christian." This universalist religiocentric worldview makes it difficult for them to see the integrity of other religions, or even of other Christian viewpoints.

In contrast to Segundo, Galilea concludes that as liberation theology matured, a voice developed that required the theological community to understand the consequences of its judgment of popular religion. It protested the end of popular culture. The protest pointed out that

> the deepest constituent of the Latin American people is its culture—popular culture or cultures. Defence of the values of this culture, threatened by ideological domination and socio-economic oppression, is a defence of the soul and the roots of the people, the sources of its freedom. Liberation, in the final analysis, must be a cultural liberation, a blanket notion embracing liberation from economic and social dominations as well as from ideologies that alienate and crush popular culture. . . . "Elitist" culture is domineering and invades popular culture in the shape of liberalism, capitalism, consumerism—and also Marxism. The peoples of Latin America, rooted in their own cultural identity, should bring about their liberation without selling their souls to *elitist*, secularizing and Northern ideologies. (Galilea 1980, 43; emphasis original)

Those who lift up popular culture are few compared to those who find popular religion in need of "politicization" and "purification" from infection by alienating tendencies.

Summary

Professor Segundo is unquestionably committed to the poor in Latin America and wants Latin America to survive in the modern economic and political world. However, the precondition of this survival is based on the systematic dismantling of popular culture. Left alone, popular culture retards modernization and the progress of civilization. He wants the poor to be less passive and more heroic; strong and not weak; less burdened by intellectual work that he believes they are not capable of doing and more dependent on the intellectual vanguard who is committed to their liberation even when the poor themselves are not; less cyclical and magical (less "feminine" and more "masculine") in their religious and cultural affairs—that is, more able to leave behind attitudes strange to modern life. Segundo requires the masses to leave their local stories, small temples, and ways of being (all of which prevent them from encountering God), and to sacralize and purify this profane life by participating in the sacraments controlled and administered by the church, which has been reshaped by the minority vanguard who have carried on the authentic faith of the grand narrative, the big temple, holy and sacred traditions. Any defense of popular religion is a defense of the death-of-God movement.

The people have successfully maintained their objective of keeping their soul from outsiders, Segundo in this case. It may be the purpose of liberation theology to understand, but it is the purpose of folk religion to confuse, to keep protected the knowledge that only the folk have of themselves. To join the grand narrative may be the goal Segundo has for them, but apparently it is not their goal.

The school that evangelizes the poor as Segundo does has the largest membership among liberation theologians and missionaries. But there is another group of evangelists more interested in the poor evangelizing the church (Barreiro 1982). Its members include Leonardo Boff.

Leonardo Boff

If there is a liberation theologian whose first instinct is to respect the concrete experiences and stories of the people, the "small temples," it is the Brazilian liberation theologian Leonardo Boff. Although he firmly plants himself within the dominant Roman Catholic tradition, he describes himself as listening patiently for grass-roots direction and, as much as possible, works to change the church toward it. Boff is a careful craftsman of liberative praxis. He is a pastor regardless of official church status. He sees in liberation theology a new emergence of a church base rather than a maturing of official traditional theology. Boff notes that through historical materialism the secular came to have theological value and argues for a greater role for social theory in liberation theology. However, Boff, in common with other liberation theologians, constructs his liberation theology upon a gender-blind sociology.

In *Church: Charism and Power* Boff presents liberation theology as an original gift and emphasizes that which comes from the "pastoral, religious, mystical practices" (1985, 12). Although he supports the institutional church, he desires to reform its structure, arguing for a more "Lutheran" relationship between priest and congregant—that is, he wants to put the control of one's "calling" under the local church. Boff insists that a new division of labor is necessary if the church is to survive. Rare among male liberation theologians, he invites women to join the priestly ranks. Ahead of his colleagues, Boff made early efforts to work at being gender-inclusive. His students testify that this struggle brought Boff to appreciate the potentialities of the inclusive worshiping community:

> Frei David . . . has learned from Boff that the Church is in its "Western-democracy phase," and mirrors a world in which emperors have been replaced by fathers—fathers superior, fathers of families, fathers of countries—and he likes to say that when Christian society becomes "authentically" socialistic there will be less talk about God the Father and more about God the community. (Jane Kramer, *The New Yorker*, "Letter from the Elysian Fields," 2 March 1987, 58)

In this decision for inclusivity, and others like it, Boff asks: Do churches have the courage to be the heart of God? (1985, 46).

Because the church as an institution appeals to divine authority through tradition to substantiate its power, it does not easily change the function and pathology of this type of power. Boff asks: Can a new church be born of the old? Here he partially accepts a Marxist critique of institutions as needing to be changed, and he encourages people to be like Sarah, who in her old age took on motherhood, a new way of life. Yet here theologians must be careful: feminist theologians have pointed out that it was this same Sarah who cast out into the wilderness Hagar and Ishmael once her legitimate heir was born to her (Tamez 1987; Trible 1984).

It is perhaps this notion of legitimacy that Boff deals with best, but always implicitly. He claims that what concretely exists is not Christianity but Catholicism. Those who defend institutional and theological knowledge, those who defend Catholicism, fear syncretism. Yet the church must in certain ways become syncretistic and then struggle for justice. It must return to its traditional focus on the poor, but it must not include impotent leaders in the priesthood. It must guard against impotency and be strong.

In a gender asymmetry of which Boff is apparently unaware, he maps out a plan for this institutional church based on the masculine experience of playing by the rules (Gilligan 1982) and of superior strength and potency (Bologh 1990). In this struggle toward freedom, he presents four levels of personal response (Boff 1985, 96–97). The table places these levels next to a synthesized feminist analysis of magic, eros, and the masculine primitive experience important to the maintenance of patriarchy.

Stages of Freedom	Feminist Analysis of Patriarchy
1. A cry for help in the face of threatening situations: the Transcendent appears as the savior.	1. The hunters' and, later, warriors' experience on the fringe of existence: a need for protection against harm.
2. A desire for fulfillment in which the Transcendent realizes the desires of the heart: happiness, eternal love, reconciliation.	2. Once separated from the feminine, the magical, and the protection of community, the masculine finds resource in the Other and the holy Other.
3. An attitude of respect in which the radical otherness is recognized; it has nothing to do with needs but with a recognition that all existence is directed toward the Transcendent.	3. Once life is created outside the community, it continues to recognize a need for the immanent and the feminine but suppresses both in favor of its own source of life: the Transcendent. Outside of community, the needs of members remain unseen.

| 4. As a gift to the Other one reaches out and surrenders to the designs of Mystery. Life is dedicated to the Transcendent, and love, the source of existence, is consecrated to it, resulting in the crystal-clear work of disinterested freedom we call love. | 4. Radically separated from the immanent, a new source of life is created that allows abstract thought and experience, which becomes a holy experience. Instead of surrendering to the community, one surrenders to the holy Other. |

Boff writes cautiously of the magical:

> One should mention now that there is always a possibility of a magical interpretation of God, one who attends to the vital needs of individuals. This danger and other deviations are present whenever the process is detained at a particular stage (Boff 1985, 96).

Boff sets out to teach the individual, "who lives with others in the world" and prefers tasks traditionally associated with feminine life, to understand experiences that are expressed through psychic, intellectual, material, social, cultural, and other realities (Boff 1985, 97). In feminist terms he attempts to channel people from a feminine to a masculine understanding of religiosity, from the profane to the sacred world.

For Boff religion is "expressed and institutionalized faith," and faith "is the core and essence of religion." Boff describes the rules of this faith in terms of abstract truth: "Faith is a fundamental experience and cannot be reduced to any other" (1985, 97). He resists the notion that faith can be shaped by elements such as intellect, psychosexual development, or culture. For him faith is elemental and all faith is valuable, including popular expressions of it:

> Popular religiosity is as valuable as other expressions of faith. . . . It was through this popular religiosity that God visited his poor people. . . . It was through their . . . feasts . . . that the people have been able to resist centuries of political and economic oppression and ecclesial marginalization. (Boff 1985, 130)

He discovers that

> community has this fine sense of the religious dimension . . . and so community gatherings are never completely profane or devoid of God's presence. . . . A people who knows how to celebrate is a people with hope. They are no longer a wholly oppressed people but a people who march toward their liberation. (Boff 1985, 130)

In order to organize this communal religious experience of faith, Boff organizes "base communities." He is concerned that these communities of faith "will be left to themselves" (Boff 1985, 125) and wishes them to be put "in touch with the grand apostolic tradition . . . and [to] reaffirm the unity of the Church" (Boff 1985, 126). The church must not forget the people, but the people must not forget the church. However, the priestly effort to "bring the people to the church" was originally not successful: "they did not surrender" (Boff 1985, 132). In order to capture the poor, the church must elevate the role that people play in the church. The church must assist the poor in overcoming fears and impotence; it must bring them "into a deepening of faith, hope, love, trust and patience lest they lose hope and turn to violence and terrorist activities. . . . The feeling of impotence must be overcome because it tears the individual apart" (Boff, 1985, 136–37). The poor can be forgiven for impotence and lack of courage.

Boff wants a new church built upon the reformation of the old one. But his genuine, deep concern for the people causes him to insist that people surrender to the grand tradition. In order to be a part of the church, the poor must give up quasi-profane religiosity.

In the end Boff is unwilling to surrender political power to community. Rather, he retains an exclusionary notion of the priestly function by insisting that the individual acts for the good of all. Boff needs to retain the role of the official charismatic individual so that the people "obey God not men." The priest thus keeps intact his ability to speak for God and he retains the right to stand over and against the experience of people.

In *Ecclesiogenesis: The Base Communities Reinvent the Church* (1986), Boff documents and supports "base Christian communities" that have sprung up all over Latin America in reaction to and rejection of the hierarchical church—an outcome prompted by the laity, who, due to the shortage of priests, performed clerical functions and became quite critical of the hierarchical institution. He sees this lay-led church representing a new "birthing the church" phenomenon that promises to allow it to renew itself.

The new movement has its own language, and in Boff's view, it warns the church to prepare for radical change. Of great future impact is the growing demand for the priesthood of women. To understand this phenomenon, Boff turns to the social sciences. Communitarian demands are deinstitutionalizing demands. Therefore community-oriented movements can revitalize the church but they cannot fundamentally change it because the church will move to protect its institutional interests. Boff wants to allow both to coexist because "the church sprung from the people is the same church sprung from the apostles" (Boff 1986, 7).

> The will to impregnate the institutional, organizational aspect of the church with the spirit of community will never die in the church, and this is the wellspring of its vitality. After all . . . these two poles abide forever. The real problem resides in the manner in which both are lived, the one as well as the other. (Boff 1986, 7)

The two poles are radically set apart. The institutional church is affluent, "an interlocutor with the powers of society. The other is centered . . . deep within the popular sectors and the poor masses, on the margin" (Boff 1986, 8). The movement toward one another represents the institution's "discovering its meaning and responsibility in the creation, support and nurture of the communities"—although in the process they sacrifice purity (Boff 1986, 8). In addition, communities have found a need to be a part of the great institution: they have found a need for Catholic identity.

"The church never lost its authenticity," states Boff, but, to be authentic, base communities need the institutional church. He warns the base Christian communities (BCCs) not to see themselves as replacing the parish but as rejuvenating the church.

However, it is not clear that the BCCs desire to be the leaven of the whole loaf; Boff neither demonstrates that the BCCs want to be the seed "impregnated" in the church nor proves that they need or want a "Catholic" identity. What he does implicitly describe are people all too willing to live in communities without priests. What does not allow them to share fully in the "historic community" is the absence of "celebrating and offering the same sacred Victim [Holy Communion]" (Boff 1986, 13). There is no guilty party here; the church was held back from sending priests to consecrate the bread because the people lived in "wild territories" (1986, 13). The "wild" often prevented the church from reaching the people.

A Durkheimian analysis of rites and rituals suggests that the absence of priest-led Holy Communion would greatly facilitate lay leadership and direct the community away from the Catholic Church. The controlled dispensing of the sacred elements keeps the balance of power in the hands of the dispenser. The absence of the dispensing agent changes the social dynamic.

Much like the struggle recognized by Durkheim and Weber between the sacred and the profane and between the religious and the magical, Boff understands the struggle between the universal church and the particular, local expressions of church to be a struggle over the local tendency to define the church by what the universal church says it is not. Against the local expression, the universal church says it is not a geographical, statistical, sociological, historical concept. Its "identity resides in the unity, singleness, of its faith in God, who has sent the Son in order to save, in the power of the Holy Spirit, all men and women—this faith being mediated by the church, the universal sacrament of salvation" (Boff 1986, 17).

Because the church "possesses the nature of mystery, of divine transcendence, of universality, the first and the last *prima novissima*," it must determine who may speak on its behalf. Although the church "manifests herself" in the "local churches," the particular church is not "a part of the whole"; the whole is the universal church *prima novissima*. The local, particular church is a "sacramental presentation" of the universal church (Boff 1986, 17–20).

The BCCs have questioned "the prevailing manner of being a church" (Boff 1986, 23). In addition to operating without the Eucharist, they also operate under "community coordination, organization of liturgy, caring for the sick, teaching people to read and write, looking after the poor. All this is done in a deep spirit of communion" (Boff 1986, 23).

Boff finds these actions ones of "reinventing the church." Since this is a new phenomenon, he finds it to be a birth event: the church is "beginning to be born at the heart of God's People" (Boff 1986, 23).

It is disturbing that Boff apparently has not recognized that such activities existed earlier. Since the first century, women of the church have fed the hungry, healed the sick, and cared for the poor (Thurston 1989). The Bible frequently tells that when the great prophets were starving and near physical and spiritual death, God often sent them to a woman to be fed and cared for. Boff indirectly shows that the BCCs are challenging the church to recognize that what has been traditionally called "feminine labor" has been devalued and never made "official." Commitment to this "feminine behavior" has radically separated the masses from the church, and seeing this way of attracting the poor, the church moves to incorporate it! In all sincerity Boff sees these communities as helping the church, after these long centuries, to become truly the church. The hierarchical church, existing for itself, suppressed community and was always in confrontation with it. Although he finds that the church "inverted the natural order" in which the flock (the community) comes first, he does not wish to give the community full control. "The hierarchical function is essential in the church—but it does not subsist in and for itself" (Boff 1986, 24). The sheep need a shepherd.

The goal of the new church is to include all human persons. Boff suggests that in order to accomplish this, we need not a linear, hierarchical church, but a circular, concentric church with the divine trinitarian relationship on top of the circle pointing to the circular ministries of unity. This model replaces the pope-bishop-pastor-faithful model that has proven inadequate for modern life. The linear model is replaced by tiny bishop-priest-faithful triangles set inside the circles. Apparently the pope's role is to sit in the center, ensuring the unity of the entire project.

To the feminist eye Boff is clearly attempting to combine the masculine, triangular, hierarchical church with the feminine, circular, community-building church, a struggle old as the church itself (Schillebeeckx 1987). He claims that he is not describing a "new church" but a "reinvented one." So there is no "new birth" after all. Rather than claiming that the reinvented church is a "global option," Boff and his colleagues at the Centro de Estistica Religiosa e Investigacões Sociais (CERIS) have a Weberian prediction, that the BCCs will institutionalize and specialize in revitalization.

One may be rightly concerned about this ecclesiogenesis (the church born of the people through the Spirit) midwifed by "official" members of the institutional church. It could be predicted that the offspring will not be a nurtured church. Since the church, by Boff's own admission, does not know how to nurture, this new babe might die in infancy. Boff understands that the quasi-maternal role the church has constructed for itself has not been helpful historically. It might not be inappropriate to predict that if this new voice survived into its teenage years, the church would act like its mother Sarah, who, when she realized that the "illegitimate" son would inherit the promises of God, enlisted the support of her husband to cast him out into the wild country.

As Hagar, Ishmael, and the Katipunans have taught us, the poor know better than anyone how to survive in the wild country. Boff comes close to understanding this in telling a story of a planned encounter between three hundred poor people and several bishops. The bishops had to wait their turn to speak and were asked to listen first to everyone who had something to say. When the people found no words, they frequently, spontaneously, created playlets and dramatized their concerns. At the end they sang a song about the Xoco Indios who encountered the police. Armed with their bodies and their slingshots, they faced machine guns and fought fearlessly. And when it was all over they sang a victory song:

> Saint Peter, you're not alone,
> There are Xocos all around!
> (Boff 1986, 36)

Here a poor people equate themselves with the saints and with God. They were telling the bishops that as far as they knew, God is political and fair, much like "myself."

Boff, however, does not equate the poor with God. Under the heading "The New Barbarians" Boff describes the new Christian church of the poor as giving birth to a new language. The new "barbarians" are the poor who, in their struggle to form a new society, are "rocking the empire to its foundations" (Boff 1986, 44). Perhaps the reason Boff wishes to draw these "barbarians" into the institution that they seek to rock to its very foundations is to attempt one last time to save the institutional church, and implicitly to deny the future existence the poor have claimed for themselves.

Are Boff's interest in women and his interest in the poor connected? By proclaiming Jesus Christ a feminist, Boff reveals a hidden thread that runs through his tapestry: his desire for the church to keep pace with civil society (Boff 1986, 95). In *When Theology Listens to the Poor* (1988), he states that if the church does not radically change its identity, it will not survive. Predicting the loss of institutional power, Boff seeks to widen the church base. The place to start is with the poor and women, who make up 80 percent of the Latin American church (Boff 1988, 23). Even so, Boff is not clearly committed to having the church take on feminine, feminist, and mass identities.

> The essays appearing in this book represent an effort to develop theological thought from a point of departure in the place of the poor. We shall never be as the poor. (Boff 1988, x)
>
> The Church had belonged to the hegemonical historic bloc that conducted society in Latin America in the most elitist manner imaginable. Then, with the mobilization of the popular classes beginning in the 1930s, the Church, through engaged pastoral approach on the part of a significant cross section of its leaders, began to be *with* the poor. (Boff 1988, 23–24)

Boff shows that liberation theology pushes the church to be "of the poor." But if, as Boff proclaims, the church shall "never be poor," then liberation theology can never be expected adequately to understand or gain the trust of the people. Further, if it devalues and wants to capture in order to reconstruct for its own purposes what has traditionally been women's reality, the church might never gain the full trust and participation of women.

Boff claims that the poor will purify Christianity. However, it is possible that what the poor will lose in purifying the church is their own physical and intellectual power, power rooted in the "profane" realities that the church wishes to regulate. Liberation theology assumes a militant intellectual role on behalf of the poor, while they themselves are made to be foot soldiers:

> Suddenly a theologian is more than just a teacher, a professor. Theologians are militants, Christian intellectuals organically involved with the historical movement of the poor. . . . Then gladly will they [the theologians] spend their lives and intellectual energies on behalf of those [the poor] who actualize for us the passion of the Suffering Servant, as we share with them their journey through history toward the Reign of God. (Boff 1988, 31)

When Boff asks what poor, innocent victims of injustice and torture must do, and then limits their response to three choices, "revolt, resignation, or acceptance," and when he then chooses for them "acceptance," Boff chooses, even if implicitly, against liberation. This type of action is not new; the ancient memory of the poor must remember that it has heard the church proclaim "acceptance" before.

It is one thing to die because one is poor; it is another to prescribe, celebrate, encourage, or even suggest death or ways of dying from the perspective of one who chooses not to be, or never will be, poor. To describe the death of the poor as a "welcomed expression of love" (Boff 1988, 117) speaks to a deeper agenda. In *When Theology Listens to the Poor*, Boff learns from the poor that loving and forgiving the enemy is what will bring harmony. He suggests that when we love the "crucified poor," we embrace and love those who "perpetrated" the "horrible crimes." To love the poor is to love the conditions that create the poor. In defense of Boff, who does not in practice love evil or applaud the results of evil, his larger theological agenda appears to be related to maintaining social institutions, particularly the church, through forgiveness and ritualistic purification of the profane poor.

Boff wants to "invest death and the cross with meaning" for the poor, who frequently die on crosses. For Boff, death on a cross is a sacrificial expression of historical "solidarity with the crucified of history" (Boff 1988, 119). Describing what Marxists call class suicide, Boff realizes that the nonpoor have to choose to become poor in order to suffer the lot of the poor and gain the glories of the cross. However, he also recognizes that the nonpoor will probably never be poor.

In offering resurrection as eternal justice, Boff fails to expand liberation theology to include those Christians who do not believe in a life hereafter. The problem is that those who suffer on crosses (such as Jesus Christ) often do not want a reward; they most often want to be relieved of the burden of dying. (My skepticism is rooted in my experience as a woman in a patriarchal culture and in a patriarchal church. I have yet to see the institutional church choose to stand with those who threaten its institutional existence. It has not stood with the poor or with women. It certainly did not stand with Leonardo Boff. Even liberation theologies require the poor to give up their own local, small stories for the grand apostolic narrative that does not need their stories.)

Although his attempt was risky and made from the heart, even Boff fails to stand with real women. In *The Maternal Face of God* (1987) he declares that we live in a dying patriarchal culture. This is most certainly true. But in his vision of the future the Virgin Mary remains a privileged woman who suffers in love, for she is God's mother. In his vision there is no "God-as-Woman." At the end of the book Boff devalues the life experience of real women by lifting up the Virgin Mary as the ideal role model for women: "We believe that 'the authentic, pure feminine is par excellence a luminous, chaste energy, the vessel of the ideal, and of goodness—the Blessed Virgin Mary'" (Boff 1987, 257).

This early work of Boff shows that, although conscious of its repressive nature, patriarchy has a hard time resisting itself and its own interests. However, through it Boff has performed a service on behalf of womankind and the poor by significantly challenging the church the come to terms with some feminine and feminist realities.

Boff's fundamental commitment to reshaping the church in the image of the poor stops short of demanding radical changes in the sociopolitical status of the nonpoor church. Although he moves closer than other theologians to accepting the poor as moral agents, he still associates them with profane life that, because it is not authentic in its own right, very much needs sacralization.

Liberation theology attempts to bring the church to the poor and the poor into the church. For Boff it is a return to original nature by benefit of an original divine gift, not the self-conscious social and theological construction of the poor. While recognizing that folk religiosity refuses to surrender to the grand narrative of the apostolic tradition, Boff retains the grand narrative as a supreme value, and seeks to preserve the institutional church through reformation. The goals of preserving the institutional church are antithetical to the critical sociology used in constructing this theology. The radical project is to abolish the social conditions that created oppression and thereby to abolish oppressive institutions. Boff wishes to exempt "the church" on grounds that it has now become "of the poor."

But how much "of the poor" has it become if its liberation message is that the poor are immature, illogical, strange (e.g., see Segundo 1976), and in need of potency, courage, and forgiveness (Boff 1986). Is it "of the poor" who show no sign of believing themselves to be illogical or in need of forgiveness for their material-spiritual state?

Through liberation theology the church recognizes its sinfulness and yet also wishes to reform rather than repent and be radically transformed; it wishes to regain its own potency through the energy of the poor.

At stake here is the sacred. Boff finds communal life to be profane life. It becomes sacred only to the extent that it chooses the sacred tradition. In the final analysis, it is not the communal life of the poor that is sacred but the apostolic tradition and the institutional hierarchy that embodies it.

Just as Boff's liberation theology will have problems becoming radically committed to ending oppression within the church, so also will it have difficulties being feminist. Radical materialist praxis takes as its starting point the experience of the proletariat and not of institutional life. Feminist praxis takes women as its starting point. Antiracist praxis takes as its starting point people of color. Boff's liberation theology implicitly and explicitly seeks to retain the hierarchical patriarchy of the institutional church, which continues to stand over and against communal life, women, and the poor.

Both "Weber's masculine dualistic theory of social life and Marx's masculine dialectical theory of social change" require the heroic masculine actor (Bologh 1987a, 149, 152). For Boff this role is assumed by the "church" and its vanguard. The masculine actor can be seen as a creation of rational bureaucratic life. It is easy to see why Boff, himself captured by a religious bureaucracy, predicts the bureaucratization and institutionalization of the BCCs. The poor disappear from Boff, who does not realize that Weber's paradigm is not the option of the poor, who for centuries chose another option—they disappeared into the wild country.

Oppressed women fundamentally understand a different Jesus than the one remembered by the patriarchal church. Ada María Isasi-Díaz and Yolanda Tarango have shown that for some Hispanic women he is a friend who pals around and takes *cachetadas* (slaps in the face) with them. They understand that Jesus was born in a borrowed bed; he borrowed a theology from the rabbis, a home from Mary and Martha, and, finally, a grave (1988).

The profane borrows to desacralize. In the stories of those considered "profane" Jesus is often seen as ultimately inviting believers to give up the sacred, including himself as sacred object. For the oppressed Jesus points to God. In Scripture, when he is executed outside both Roman and Jewish sacred spaces, in the land of the profane, the tent of the Holy of Holies is rent in two: symbolically, the theological and sociological boundaries between the sacred and the profane are put to death when Jesus dies.

These oppressed Hispanic women recognize in Jesus the Messiah: he is one of them. According to one Hispanic woman, God is Jesus when the community recognized that he had a good relationship with his mother, as evidenced by Jesus' first miracle, in which he turned water into wine at his mother's request (Isasi-Díaz and Tarango 1988, 37). A Jesus who points away from himself to the community is also found in black American womanist theology (Grant 1989). Yet there are critical differences between black and Hispanic women. For Hispanics the saints and not Jesus are central to spirituality. Jesus belongs to the hierarchical church and is more easily controlled by official religion, whereas the saints, who need no historical reality, are socially constructed by communities (Isasi-Díaz and Tarango 1988).

Liberation theology remains trapped in contradiction as long as it fails to embrace folk religion and points to Jesus Christ theologically without understanding him sociologically, especially his identification with the poor, the lowly, the folk. The folk hear a Jesus who says that the way to the holy is through common experience. From this perspective Western rationalized culture's theological emphasis on Jesus Christ as center can be seen to violate the New Testament understanding of Jesus as humble servant. God is at the center. Sociologically, to point to the grand narrative, to the "big temple," or even to Jesus rather than to people's encounter with the God (which may be facilitated by an encounter with Jesus, the Holy Spirit, the Virgin, or the saints) is to keep the door open to patriarchy and oppression.

Summary

Boff's work confirms de Certeau's observation that our capacity to study anything depends upon whether or not our language has developed the ability to talk about the subject matter. In the case of popular religion and magic the Westerner is at a serious disadvantage because the forces of domination have denied the very existence of the oppressed; therefore the Westerner has difficulty even speaking about them or hearing them speak. The nonoppressed must create a language and hear it into being. This language of hearing the oppressed is not the same language that the oppressed speak. More important, those who are oppressed and live magical lives must realize that what we know about ourselves is valuable to the oppressor and does not need to be shared, but can and perhaps should be kept in silence. The poor and the oppressed do not have to address the "crisis in Christendom." It is not their crisis. Neither will the end of Christendom be their crisis.

Liberation theology's response to the poor might be correctly identified as a major source of its decreasing attractiveness to them. To be feminist, a liberation theology and social theory transplanted to the United States will need to respect the authentic experiences of the poor. It must value the poor as the social agents they are, understanding their moral agency from their perspective. That means that folk, popular, and magical religion will have to be reexamined from the positive perspective of its life-giving ability. Folk religion shelters and empowers. Sociologists, like the church and its theologians, might continue to learn more about this experience from the poor themselves. This does not mean that folk experience should not be critiqued; but now is not the time for critique. Until the nonpoor intimately know the poor, until they are poor themselves, they will have no adequate resource with which to critique the poor. While the nonpoor raise constructive questions the poor might wish to engage, critique is best saved for the nonpoor who have the resources and inclination to exclude and impoverish the Other.

10

THE EVERYDAY
IS WHERE
SILENCE SPEAKS

*Many elements conspire to render unlikely any serious possibility of a
new congregational religion borne by intellectuals. This constellation of
factors includes the interest of the privileged strata in maintaining the
existing religion as an instrument for controlling the masses, their need
for social distance, their abhorrence of mass enlightenment as tending
to destroy the prestige of elite groups, and their well-founded rejection
of any faith in the possibility that some new creed acceptable to large
segments of the population could supplant the traditional creeds. . . .
Finally, and above all, there is the scornful indifference of the privileged
strata to religious problems and to the church. . . . The need of literary,
academic, or café-society intellectuals to include "religious" feelings in
the inventory of their sources of impressions and sensations, and among
their topics for discussion, has never yet given rise to a new religion.
Nor can a religious renascence be generated by the need of authors to
compose books on such interesting topics or by the far more effective need
of clever publishers to sell such books. No matter how much the ap-
pearance of a widespread religious interest may be simulated, no new
religion has ever resulted from such needs of intellectuals or from their
chatter.*

—Max Weber, *Economy and Society*

Durkheim and Weber were not so very different from the intellectuals
of their time who worked to create new forms of religiosity. A century
ago these forms were rooted in science. Their sociology and theory of
religion were never divorced from their aim to make the world a better

place, that is, from political action. Like feminists trying to create "woman church," Durkheim and Weber were aware that their political visions rested on their ability to re-create the holy. In the end, at least, Weber realized that intellectuals are not capable of producing a religiosity that is appealing to the average person.

This book has a political aim as well. It is not about creating new religions or spiritualities but about finding a way to move feminism, beginning with feminist students of religion, closer to the people it claims to have at the center of its labors: women and their communities.

In searching for a starting point from which to build a feminist social theory of religion, I have gone back to the basics. The classics are the bases upon which much of contemporary theory is built. For example, French postmodernism could not have assumed its specific form without Durkheim; contemporary German sociology owes much to Weber; and American social theory could not exist without both of them. Rethinking the elemental building blocks of sociological understanding of religion seemed to be a good place to start; others might have started in another place.

My interpretation of Durkheim attempted to show that implicit in his sociology of religion is a theory of gender. Men are associated with religion and the sacred, women with magic and the profane. Through religious will to domination, through coercion and spiritual, psychological, and physical violence, men and their societies came to control "their" women and the communities in which they live. Buried deeper in this sociology than a theory of gender are nascent theories of racism and heterosexism. Durkheim documents the social production of "the sacred." The sacred is a socially constructed mechanism used to establish a particular identity that enables the adherent to dominate and exclude others.

According to Durkheim religion gives rise to language and hence to culture. Durkheimian work must then be reinterpreted in the light of his gendered understanding of religion and its shaping of knowledge. Religion is at the center of Durkheim's sociology and the key to his practical understanding of everyday life. Although his sociology of religion is gender-blind and therefore limits what he is able to "see" in the rest of social interaction, Durkheim produces a brilliant ethnographic account of religion as a gendered social construction made possible by the creation of a particular kind of person who is able to grasp the importance of gender and to protect this constructed difference through violent action.

Durkheim's work shows that the sacred order presupposes violence and requires violence to maintain its identity and power over the subjugated. Stressing the difference between the two worlds, the sacred finds itself contaminated by contact with the profane. Through an exploration of what the sacred claims not to be, it appears that the profane exists in magical communities empowered by the "sociability of the excluded"—some feminists would say empowered by eros. Sociable life secures its identity by encouraging the surrender of "any possibility of an individual self" to community. In this sense sociable life is larger than erotic life and its focus on the individual in community.

The prospects of such a life have been so far removed from us that it is difficult, save for the very romantic, to envision what sociable community might be like. "Sensible" people see into the realities of a sociable world that will not privilege them over others and promote individualism. Nonetheless, we are not happy with avoiding sociable life. People's desire is not first and foremost conflictual, but sociable. To live in the conflictual world of individuals is to live ambiguously with a knowledge that the social world is not yet complete.

Drawing on Weber I have summarized Western religion's ability to sustain itself via its roots in asceticism, particularly Protestant asceticism. By denying the body, Western religion rationalized its understanding of the world; rationalized religion became one of the brightest stars in the constellation that forms rational capitalism. Rational capitalism, like rationalized religion, had to remain hostile to magic, sexuality, and art in order to maintain its identity. Demagicalized life, thought Weber, was the fate of the times. Through Troeltsch and Freud it is possible to see that at the center of the fate of the times is a masculine identity that creates a kind of pathological psychospiritual asceticism requiring a social pathology to support and encourage its repression and suppression of sociable life. Also created is a form of sexual identity capable of repressing knowledge of itself. Weber's personal life could be said to exemplify the ultimate tragedy of the combination of psychosocial energies shaping modern, rational, masculine asceticism.

Weber's understanding of religion, like Durkheim's, is central to his sociology. For example, Weber associated magic with the masses of demilitarized persons. For him the magical religions prevent progress. He is not alone in this belief. People who wish to modernize and "be progressive" must first deal with popular and primitive religion (see, for example, Loomis [1969] on Weber and India's development efforts).

In contrast, I believe that in responding to oppression, suppression, and repression, the popular (nonsacred) culture moves to protect itself in the darkness of sociable (not limited to magical) life. Socially constructed as belonging to an excluded people, popular culture becomes, in the eyes of the sacred, the conquered other. Taking refuge in (magical) sociability allows the excluded, the conquered other, to protect its soul.

"Profane" spirituality must also fall under the critical eye of feminism. Given the feminist values of cooperation, mutuality, equality, democratic use of communal power, and erotic enjoyment of body and work, we must ask: What in folk spirituality can be useful in the ongoing struggle for liberation of all people, and what will detract from it?

Furthermore, social theory is not enough to address liberation; a praxis is necessary. In order to move toward community we must transform sacred space into community space. This space will not be "profane" space, carrying with it the limitations set by the sacred. We do not know yet what it will be. Developing ways for the fractured and often isolated categories of sociable (profane) life to speak to one another is the first step in promoting a solidarity necessary for common community-building action.

The possibilities of "profane" life suggested in "folk religions" are so real and so threatening to modern bureaucratic (masculine) asceticism that black American theorists of religion such as W. E. B. DuBois and Charles Long have suggested that these possibilities are protected through opacity—through lives lived in the dark.

In the same way that Long (1986) describes the opacity of the repressed and remembered past in the African signs, symbols, movement, and message being found in the black church experience, so, too, Simmel can talk about the "secret inaccessibility of women" and recognize that it is this eternal quality of unreachableness that irritates men.

Protecting the secret place of inaccessibility is a crucial skill for feminist practitioners. In this regard I disagree with those who suggest that it is the profane who could lead the oppressing forces to the "real sacred." This move would be unfortunate. First, it is not the profane who have named or produced the dichotomy. To claim one's force or ground of being as "the sacred" is to assume the sacred position that caused the misery for the "profane" in the first place. Second, to bare the soul, that is, to reveal and make vulnerable the ways in which the oppressed manage to survive and overcome, places the oppressed at great risk of violence and death, a risk that hardly seems a reward for the everyday struggle to maintain an already fragile life. To argue that "the profane" can teach what "the real sacred" is is a mistake. In reality, that which calls itself "the sacred" simply does not want to be reminded of the values it abandoned when it left community. It needs to repress those values in order to maintain its hegemonic control and its social distance from the oppressed. Perhaps the real gift the profane offer to the world is surviving to tell the story.

In music, poetry, and art the sociable world creates a safe space for people considered profane, a place to keep alive souls that the sacred seeks to stamp out. The very language of sacred society, of the great traditions, has embedded in it mechanisms that make it impossible even to talk about the profane and the popular (de Certeau 1986). How much harder it is for the sacred society and those indebted to it to hear the voices and the music, or to see the dance and feel the art. The origins and language of the profane, the popular, are "lost" in mythic representations ensuring that they cannot be spoken of; they are replaced by the origins and language of the sacred. Excluded from social speech and history, the profane, the popular, and the poor "retreat" into a language of their own.

In de Certeau's terms, repressing the popular from memory creates masculine patriarchal life in the image of a celibatory machine: a fiction removed from the body and from woman and out of God's reach (1986, 165). But the body is memory. It may be dominated but not vanquished. The collective memory of the social body with its tortured existence and spilled blood is self-managing and has its "own way of doing things." It vindicates the dead as it speaks their names into the dark.

The tools for understanding the reality of the oppressed will become increasingly sophisticated as the connections among the multiple oppressions people suffer are made evident. Since to name them all would take forever, I will simply refer generally to communities of people excluded from the sacred centers who suffer tremendously yet exclude and cause people within their communities to suffer as well. What do misogyny, racism, and heterosexism have in common? Whether intragroup or extragroup, I have suggested that they share a certain type of effective domination allowing for forcible exclusion of and acts of violence toward the subjugated. This type of domination (misnamed as "power") is created and sustained in several key religious ritual experiences held together by notions of sacredness. Here Orlando Patterson's model of the enslavement of persons worldwide is invaluable (1982). In the following, I have taken his four basic rituals and added references to the oppressor. In other contexts additional rituals might be found as well.

(1) Rituals of naming. To enslave, the oppressor must first name or create a notion of that which it wishes to subjugate (see also Riley 1988). These naming ceremonies are ritualized, for example, on the auction block, in the temple, and in board and locker rooms. In Western culture those enslaved are frequently referred to as "feminine" and are infantilized. They are profane and untouchable. Also named is the oppressor. In this case he is named "the sacred," the master-owner, "the masculine."

(2) Rituals of natal origin. In classical social theory and history of religions we find that sacred societies replenish the ranks through the boy-child who is made a man through ritual acts that forcibly remove him from his natal community. This natal community is then denigrated and memories of it forced into repression and memory. The same is true in the history of slavery, in which the key to successful enslavement is to sever ties with the slave's origin of birth. The social and psychological destruction of personal and national maternal ties necessary in domination was graphically described for us in the poetry of the Katipunans.

Girls are taught that, like their mothers, they were not born with free agency, but rather that "they belong to their father," and later "to their husband." Western religions frequently teach girls that they are without birthrights, like one having never been born. Like enslaved people of color, women in Western culture have been "dead to society."

(3) Ritual marks of servitude. In the case of Western culture, gender, homosexuality, and race are constructions enabling subjugation of female persons, homosexual persons, and people of color. Gender, sexual orientation, and color are distinguishing marks.

Marked also are the initiates into enslaving societies. As often said by those who have "made it" into the fast-track world of high finance and real estate: "I know this sounds awful, but I am glad I am not a woman or a black."

(4) Ritual assumption of new status. Western marriage ceremonies focusing on the bride and "her day" are perhaps the most vivid example of the subjugated ritually participating in captivity. Patterson documents similar rituals for slaves brought into new families.

Also subjugated through psychic and social forces are the foot soldiers of the masculine celibatory machine. A choice not to enter the sacred masculine space once invited carries with it the knowledge that one will be tortured like the feminine body that the initiated male gains the right to torture.

Theorists of liberation continually need to look critically at the ritual life of oppressors. We have redefined the realities we see; we have rewritten biased theories of religion. Needed in every generation is a systematic review of both the form and content of ritual. In itself ritual is not "bad." It brings people together and empowers them to act as a collectivity. The ritual life of the excluded and oppressed must be carefully examined for its life-giving functions and for the points of possible contact between communities that might facilitate federation.

In addition to knowing how ritual keeps the "feminine" and oppressed community alive, it would be instructive to know how a mother about to lose her son to the male machine ritualistically separates from him so that he can find his way back to her (which he frequently does) when expelled from the sacred society because he is discovered incapable of carrying a spear, inflicting violence, or living in heterosexual relationships. Through what rituals are these expelled men taken back into the natal community? What rituals do people called "women" create and use to protect their souls held captive in religion? How is it that mothers and daughters become "resurrection" for each other?

Everyday Sociable Community

Like many feminists I have frequently mentioned "community." Community only exists through relationships constructed by language. A century ago Durkheim and Weber realized that their attempts to create a new language were connected to a reshaping of French and German culture. Languages are systems of exclusion that enable particular speech. The feminist language of erotic inclusivity creates a notion of cooperative life valuing shared power across particularity. As seen in various collectivities across time, the desire for sociability seeks to exclude domination and violence. I demonstrated that sacred societies are created through religion's language of sacralization. This language system, which excludes the feminine, is backed up materially by force and violence, which ensures compliance with its orders. The sacred is a source of a mighty force that represses from memory the process by which people acquire the sexual identities of male and female. Further repressed is knowledge of how these sexual identities acquire the gender identities of masculinity and femininity; males and females may achieve either gendered identity but are expected to acquire the one assigned to "their sex." Sacred rituals contain elements that discourage us from thinking about a time when people had no sex or gender. The sacred temple begins to tremble when people realize that they are more alike than different.

From my viewpoint too much feminist energy has been lost in efforts to "sacralize" women, to show that they too are "sacred," to create women's "sacred rituals," and to move women "from the margin to the center." Not only does the continual reference to "women as sacred," followed by "therefore she has a right to the sacred center," reveal a linguistic handicap—our inability to talk about people assigned female and feminine gender identities by sacred society in anything other than sacred language—it also reveals our desire to capture for the people gendered feminine the sacred identity of dominant society, along with its ability to dominate and control.

In a society that rewards those who form alliances with sacred, masculine life and tortures those who do not, it is understandable that people known as women (as well as the other feminine) would want to be sacred. It is also understandable, when language offers no other memory of existence than that "women are the profane," that some people gendered feminine would pursue and celebrate the profane, pagan world. It is further understandable that those people born with vaginas would seek a liberation motif that lifted up their socially con-structed identities as equal to that which is considered its opposite and superior and would name this liberation thought "feminist." People are not "more alike than different" in that they share one half of the sacred/profane dualism with others like them; people are "more alike than different" in that deep down inside they protest sacralized differ-ences. Just what is it about genitals, race, or sexual orientation that allows one set to be considered the opposite of the other? Here Durkheim is tremendously instructive: when left alone, people have this tendency to confuse themselves with one another.

Using the sacred/profane, masculine/feminine, male/female, black/white, heterosexual/homosexual linguistic frame is to speak the lan-guage of patriarchy. Feminism itself has become dependent on the existence of the masculine, patriarchal opposition. What is the feminine without the masculine? If there were more than one sex, if there were as many sexes as there are people (Stoltenberg 1990), feminism would lose its theoretical ground. The reason we see two sexes is that sacralized language prevents us from seeing more than two. Within the Durkheim-Weber observation continuum we can carve out at least three genders: masculine-male; feminine-female, and feminine-male.

One sign that feminist theory has yielded too much to patriarchy's demands that we live a life acceptable to the sacred is its desire to establish for "woman" the possibility of being an "individual self." Feminism is frequently trapped in the self/no-self dualism that is constructed by a language that needs an individuated self in order to operate the rational capitalist machine. The task, then, is to enable this newly discovered self "to speak," to find "her voice." "Enabling a voice" often masquerades as liberation, when in fact it disempowers and prevents the speech already found in the everyday world of the oppressed. The assumption that voices need to speak must be made by those who are not speaking. People without speech are those people, including the oppressed, who seek to speak to the masculine sacred machine in a language it recognizes. Inside this machine are held captive others who resist being captured; they form what the machine hears as silence. But they can hear themselves. They sing Pentecostal songs and dance ecstatically in conversation. The oppressed with voices tell stories about their resistance and pass along strategies for survival. They write their own poetry and maintain literary societies. They do not need to be helped into speech by those people, past or present, who have been admitted to the masculine world and who therefore cannot hear the speech of the oppressed.

If we wish to hear the voices that so threaten the fragility of modern bureaucratic masculine capitalist asceticism that they must protect themselves by living in the dark, then we must seek to change not the voices we cannot hear, but ourselves. We need to understand why we do not want to hear them, why these voices are repressed and suppressed within us. We need to appreciate the nonvoluntary membership responsibilities in community. Idealist and artificial women's collectives created in the academy rarely require the total surrender required of sociable community made up of people who come together because they must.

Academic feminists developing a theory of religion and spirituality might consider adopting a methodology that secures access to or even membership in sociable communities and collectivities that many of us avoid engaging: for example, "women's" associations in churches, Pentecostal storefronts, shelters for the homeless, park benches in the South Bronx, and prisons. It is here, in the everyday spaces that shelter the poor and the nonsacred, that one learns how people resist or yield to the atomizing, destructive actions of sacred society. It is here that we learn how actors live as members of a body held together by continual surrender of any desire to answer the call to sacred status as an individual with a voice detachable from the sociable community. A feminist theory of sociable spirituality will not get very far if it cannot find its way to the very mechanisms used by the nonsacred to establish indigenous theories of social life that organize and hold actors accountable to it. In search of the indigenous and the local, some American feminists have joined the French postmodern movement. Although I enjoy the ride, ultimately one cannot take this vehicle onto everyday terrain. It is too much a tool of the academy. To go into the South Bronx we are going to need something much more practical and something very American. Outlining a methodology and theory of the everyday from a perspective that values voices that speak in the dark will have to be another project.

Feminist sociology and theory must also discover under what conditions people's voices, valuing sociability, become unliberative, misogynistic, and exclusive; and then it will have a few preliminary tools for the construction of a feminist social theory of religion.

In the end I believe that it will be a postfeminist theory of religion and spirituality that adequately addresses the multiple layers of oppression felt by racially and sexually marginalized persons. The feminist focus on "women and their experiences" has too often ignored the other "feminized" members of the "feminine" collectivity. Because of the debt owed to sacred society, feminist theory and its focus on women's lives has too often been narrowed to white, middle-class women's lives, thereby keeping the focus most important to sacred society. However, there will be no liberation for people called "women" without a simultaneous liberation for people called "colored" and people called "homosexual." Our oppressions, like our liberations, are woven tightly together. Unraveling them threatens the very foundation of Western culture. A social theory that insists on the liberation of all oppressed persons takes feminist goals along with it as it moves to meet the critical realities facing us at the close of the modern age.

BIBLIOGRAPHY

Adler, Ruth. 1982. "The Shekina." Jeannette Picard public lecture, Macalester College, St. Paul, Minnesota.

Alexander, Jeffrey C. 1987. "The Dialectic of Individualism and Domination: Weber's Rationalization Theory and Beyond." In *Max Weber: Rationality and Modernity*, ed. Sam Whimster and Scott Lash. Boston: Allen and Unwin.

Allen, Paula Gunn. 1986. *The Sacred Hoop: Recovering the Feminine in American Indian Traditions*. Boston: Beacon Press.

Andreas, Carol. 1985. *When Women Rebel: The Rise of Popular Feminism in Peru*. Westport, Conn.: Lawrence Hill and Company.

Andreski, Stanislav. 1984. *Max Weber's Insights and Errors*. Boston: Routledge and Kegan Paul.

Aronowitz, Stanley. 1981. *The Crisis in Historical Materialism: Class, Politics, and Culture in Marxist Theory*. Boston: Bergin Publishers.

Avis, Paul. 1989. *Eros and the Sacred*. Harrisburg: Morehouse Publishing.

Baer, Hans A. 1984. *The Black Spiritual Movement: A Religious Response to Racism*. Knoxville: University of Tennessee Press.

Banks, Olive. 1986. *Faces of Feminism: A Study of Feminism as a Social Movement*. Oxford: Basil Blackwell.

Barreiro, Alvaro. 1982. *Base Ecclesial Communities: The Evangelization of the Poor*. Trans. Barbara Campbell. Maryknoll, N.Y.: Orbis Books.

Barreiro, Julio. 1978. "Rejection of Christianity by Indigenous Peoples of Latin America." In *Separation Without Hope?* 127–36. Geneva: World Council of Churches.

Bellah, Robert N., ed. 1973. Introduction to *On Morality and Society: Selected Writings* by Emile Durkheim. Chicago: University of Chicago Press.

———. 1976. *The Broken Covenant: American Civil Religion in a Time of Trial*. New York: Seabury Press.

————. et al. 1986. *Habits of the Heart: Individualism and Commitment in American Life.* Berkeley: University of California Press.

Bendix, Reinhart. 1977. *Max Weber: An Intellectual Portrait.* Berkeley: University of California Press.

Benhabib, Seyla, and Drucilla Conell. 1987. *Feminism as Critique: On the Politics of Gender.* Minneapolis: University of Minnesota Press.

Benjamin, Jessica. 1987. "Bonds of Love: Rational Violence and Erotic Domination." In *Future of Difference,* ed. Eisenstein and Jardine. New Brunswick: Rutgers University Press.

Berger, Peter. 1963. "Charisma and Religious Innovation: The Social Location of Israelite Prophecy." *American Sociological Review* 28, no. 6:940–50.

Bernard, Jessie Shirley. 1971. *Women and the Public Interest: An Essay on Policy and Protest.* New York: Atherton.

Berryman, Philip. 1984. *Religious Roots of Rebellion: Christians in Central American Revolution.* Maryknoll, N.Y.: Orbis Books.

Bittner, Econ. 1963. "Rationalism and the Organization of Radical Movements." *American Sociological Review* 28, no. 6:928ff.

Bleicher, Josef. 1982. *The Hermeneutic Imagination: Outline of a Positive Critique of Scienticism and Sociology.* London: Routledge and Kegan Paul.

Boff, Leonardo. 1985. *Church: Charism and Power: Liberation Theology and the Institutional Church.* Trans. John W. Diercksmeier. New York: Crossroad.

————. 1986. *Ecclesiogenesis: The Base Communities Reinvent the Church.* Trans. Robert Barr. Maryknoll, N.Y.: Orbis Books.

————. 1987. *The Maternal Face of God: The Feminine and Its Religious Expressions.* Trans. Robert Barr and John W. Diercksmeier. New York: Harper and Row.

————. 1988. *When Theology Listens to the Poor.* Trans. Robert Barr. Maryknoll, N.Y.: Orbis Books.

Bologh, Roslyn Wallach. 1987a. "Marx, Weber, and Masculine Theorizing: A Feminist Analysis." In *The Marx-Weber Debate,* ed. Norbert Wiley. Newbury Park: Sage Publications.

————. 1987b. "Max Weber on Erotic Love: A Feminist Inquiry." In *Max Weber: Rationality and Modernity,* ed. Sam Whimster and Scott Lash. Boston: Allen and Unwin.

————. 1990. *Love or Greatness: Max Weber and Masculine Thinking—A Feminist Inquiry.* Boston: Unwin Hayman.

Bottomore, Tom. 1981. "A Marxist Consideration of Durkheim." *Social Forces* 59, no. 4:902–17.

Bourdieu, Pierre. 1987. "Legitimization and Structured Interests in Weber's Sociology of Religion." In *Max Weber: Rationality and Modernity,* ed. Sam Whimster and Scott Lash. Boston: Allen and Unwin.

Bourdieu, Pierre, and Jean-Claude Passeron. 1977. *Reproduction in Education, Society, and Culture.* London: Sage Publications, Studies in Social and Educational Change, vol. 5.

Bourguignon, Erika, ed. 1980. *A World of Women: Anthropological Studies of Women in the Societies of the World.* New York: Praeger.

Braudel, Fernand. 1980. *On History.* Chicago: University of Chicago Press.

Brod, Harry, ed. 1987. *The Making of Masculinity: The New Men's Studies.* Boston: Allen and Unwin.

Brown, Robert McAfee. 1987. *Religion and Violence: A Primer for White Americans.* Philadelphia: Westminster Press.

Brubaker, Roger. 1984. *The Limits of Rationality: An Essay on the Social and Moral Thought of Max Weber.* Boston: Allen and Unwin.

Burridge, Kenelm. 1980. *New Heaven, New Earth: A Study of Millenarian Activities.* Oxford: Basil Blackwell.

Cakenaka, Masao. 1986. *God Is Rice.* The Risk Book Series. Geneva: World Council of Churches.

Cannon, Katie. 1988. *Black Womanist Ethics.* Atlanta: Scholars Press.

Cardenal, Ernesto. 1978. *The Gospel in Solentiname.* Vol 2. Maryknoll, N.Y.: Orbis Books.

Carmody, Denise Lardner. 1979. *Women and World Religions.* New York: Pantheon Books.

Cavendish, Richard. 1984. *A History of Magic.* Boston: Allen and Unwin.

CCA-URM. 1981. *Struggling to Survive: Women Workers in Asia.* Hong Kong: Christian Conference of Asia–Urban-Rural Mission.

Chafetz, Janet Saltman, and Anthony Gary Dworkin. 1986. *Female Revolt: Women's Movements in World and Historical Perspective.* Totowa, N. J.: Rowman and Allanheld.

Chodorow, Nancy. 1978. *The Reproduction of Mothering: Psychoanalysis and the Sociology of Gender.* Berkeley: University of California Press.

Christ, Carol P. 1987. *Laughter of Aphrodite: Reflections on a Journey to the Goddess.* New York: Harper and Row.

Christ, Carol P., and Judith Plaskow. 1979. *Womanspirit Rising: A Feminist Reader in Religion.* New York: Harper and Row.

Clifford, James. 1986. *Writing Culture: The Poetics and Politics of Ethnography.* Berkeley: University of California Press.

Collins, Patricia. 1990. *Black Feminist Thought: Knowledge, Consciousness, and the Politics of Empowerment.* Boston: Unwin Hyman.

Collins, Randall. 1982. *Sociological Insight: An Introduction to Non-Obvious Sociology.* New York: Oxford University Press.

———. 1986. *Weberian Sociological Theory.* Cambridge: Cambridge University Press.

Constantino, Renato, and Letizia R. Constantino. 1975. *The Philippines: A Past Revisited.* Manila: privately published.

———. 1978. *The Philippines: The Continuing Past.* Quezon City: Foundation for Nationalist Studies.

Coser, Rose Laub. 1989. "Reflections on Feminist Theory." In Wallace, Ruth, *Feminism and Sociological Theory.* Newbury Park: Sage Publications.

Cuddihy, John Murray. 1987. *The Ordeal of Civility: Freud, Marx, Lévi-Strauss, and the Jewish Struggle with Modernity.* Boston: Beacon Press.

Daly, Mary. 1968. *The Church and the Second Sex.* New York: Harper and Row.

———. 1978. *Gyn/Ecology: The Metaethics of Radical Feminism.* Boston: Beacon Press.

Davies, Stevan L. 1980. *The Revolt of the Widows: The Social World of the Apocryphal Acts*. Carbondale: Southern University Press.

Dawson, Christopher Henry. 1950. *Religion and the Rise of Western Culture*. London: Sheed & Ward Publishers.

de Certeau, Michel. 1986. *Heterologies: Discourse on the Other*. Minneapolis: University of Minnesota Press.

Delphy, Christine. 1984. *Close to Home: A Materialist Analysis of Women's Oppression*. Amherst: University of Massachusetts Press.

Donovan, Josephine. 1985. *Feminist Theory: The Intellectual Traditions of American Feminism*. New York: Frederick Unger.

Douglas, Mary. 1984. *Purity and Danger: An Analysis of Concepts of Pollution and Taboo*. London: Ark Paperbacks.

Douglas, Mary, and Aaron Wildavsky. 1982. *Risk and Culture: An Essay on the Selection of Technological and Environmental Dangers*. Berkeley: University of California Press.

DuBois, W. E. B. 1987. *On Sociology and the Black Community*. Chicago: University of Chicago Press.

Dupré, Louis. 1983. *Marx's Social Critique of Culture*. New Haven: Yale University Press.

Durkheim, Emile. 1951. *Suicide: A Study in Sociology*. Trans. John A. Spaulding and George Simpson; ed. George Simpson. New York: Free Press.

———. 1953. *Sociology and Philosophy*. Trans. D. F. Peacock. New York: The Free Press.

———. 1965. *The Elementary Forms of Religious Life*. Trans. Joseph Ward Swain. New York: Free Press.

———. 1966. *The Rules of Sociological Method*. Trans. Sarah A. Solovay and John Mueller; ed. George E. G. Catlin. New York: Free Press.

———. 1973a. *Moral Education: A Study in the Theory and Application of the Sociology of Education*. Trans. Everett K. Wilson and Herman Schnurer; ed. Everett K. Wilson. New York: Free Press.

———. 1973b. *On Morality and Society: Selected Writings*. Ed. Robert N. Bellah. Chicago: University of Chicago Press.

———. 1984. *The Division of Labor in Society*. Trans. W. D. Wells. New York: Free Press.

Eames, Edwin, and Judith Goode. 1973. *Urban Poverty in a Cross-Cultural Context*. New York: Free Press.

Eden, Robert. 1983. *Political Leadership and Nihilism: A Study of Weber and Nietzsche*. Tampa: University Presses of Florida.

Eisenstadt, S. N. 1968. *Max Weber on Charisma and Institution Building: Selected Papers*. Chicago: University of Chicago Press.

Eisenstein, Hester, and Alice Jardine. 1983. *Contemporary Feminist Thought*. Boston: G. K. Hall and Company.

Eliade, Mircea, 1958. *Birth and Rebirth: The Religious Meanings of Initiation in Human Culture*. Trans. Willard R. Trask. New York: Harper and Brothers.

———. 1959a. *The History of Religions: Essays in Methodology*. Chicago: University of Chicago Press.

————. 1959b. *The Sacred and the Profane: The Nature of Religion*. New York: Harvest/HBJ Books.

————. 1973. *Australian Religions: An Introduction*. Ithaca: Cornell University Press.

Elizondo, Virgilio. 1983. *Galilean Journey: The Mexican American Experience*. Maryknoll, N.Y.: Orbis Books.

English, Jane, ed. 1977. *Sex Equality*. New Jersey: Prentice Hall.

Erickson, Victoria, ed. 1981. *Delaware Valley Land-Use Planning Resource Guide to Citizen Participation*. Washington, D.C.: H.E.W., Office of Education, Bureau of Higher Education.

Erickson, Victoria Lee. 1989. Book review of Michael Levin's *Feminism and Freedom* in *Contemporary Sociology and International Journal of Reviews* 18, no. 1:18.

————. 1991. "Enter, A New Student Breed." *In Trust* 3:1.

————. 1992a. "Back to the Basics: Feminist Social Theory, Durkheim, and Religion." *Journal of Feminist Studies in Religion*, no. 8:35–46.

————. 1992b. "Christians, Marxists, and the Economy." *Christianity and Crisis* 52, no. 90:205–7.

————. 1992c. "Men's Lives: A New Paradigm." *Christianity and Crisis* 52, no. 8:178–80.

————. 1992d. "Remembering the Whole Story: A Sociological Analysis of Public Opinion and the Decision of the United States to Retain the Philippine Islands (1898–1903)." *Asia Journal of Theology* 6, no. 3.

Erickson, Victoria, and Marc Greenberg. 1992. "Homelessness and Education for Ministry." *Human Development* 13, no. 2.

Etienne, Eleanor. 1975. *Women and Colonization: Anthropological Perspectives*. New York: Praeger.

Fenton, Steve. 1984. *Durkheim and Modern Sociology*. Cambridge: Cambridge University Press.

Ferrarotti, Franco. 1977. *Toward the Social Production of the Sacred: Durkheim, Weber, and Freud*. La Jolla: Essay Press.

Fiorenza, Elisabeth Schüssler. 1983. *In Memory of Her: A Feminist Theological Reconstruction of Christian Origins*. New York: Crossroad.

————. 1984. *Bread Not Stone: The Challenge of Feminist Biblical Interpretation*. Boston: Beacon Press.

Firestone, Shulamith. 1980. *The Dialectic of Sex: The Case for Feminist Revolution*. New York: William Morrow and Company.

Foreman, Ann. 1977. *Femininity as Alienation: Women and the Family in Marxism and Psychoanalysis*. New York: Pluto.

Foucault, Michel. 1972a. *The Archaeology of Knowledge*. Trans. A. M. Sheridan Smith. New York: Pantheon Books.

————. 1972b. *Discourse on Knowledge*. Trans. A. M. Sheridan Smith. New York: Pantheon Books.

————. 1977. *Language, Counter-Memory, Practice: Selected Essays and Interviews*. Ed. and trans. D. F. Bouchard. New York: Cornell University Press.

————. 1977. *Power/Knowledge: Selected Interviews and Other Writings*. Ed. Colin Gordon. New York: Pantheon Books.

――――. 1980. *The History of Sexuality, Vol 1: Introduction*. New York: Vintage Books.

Fox-Keller, Evelyn. 1985. *Reflections on Gender and Science*. New Haven: Yale University Press.

Frazer, Sir J. G. 1918. *The Golden Bough: A Study in Magic and Religion*. 3rd ed. London: Macmillan & Co.

Frend, W. H. C. 1984. *The Rise of Christianity*. Philadelphia: Fortress Press.

Freud, Sigmund. 1929. *Future of an Illusion*. Trans. W. D. Robson-Scott. New York: Horace Liveright Publisher.

――――. 1939. *Moses and Monotheism*. Trans. Katherine Jones. New York: Vintage.

――――. 1950. *Totem and Taboo: Some Points of Agreement between the Mental Lives of Savages and Neurotics*. New York: W. W. Norton.

――――. 1958. *On Creativity and the Unconscious: Papers on the Psychology of Art, Literature, Love, Religion*. New York: Harper Torchbooks.

――――. 1961. *Civilization and Its Discontents*. Trans. James Strachey. New York: W. W. Norton.

Freud, Sigmund, and D. E. Oppenheim. 1958. *Dreams in Folklore*. New York: International University Press.

Freund, Julian. 1968. *The Sociology of Max Weber*. New York: Pantheon Books.

Friedan, Betty. 1976. *It Changed My Life: Writings on the Women's Movement*. New York: Dell Publishers.

Galilea, Segundo. 1980. "The Theology of Liberation and the Place of Folk-Religion" in Mircea Eliade and David Tracy, eds., *What Is Religion? An Inquiry for Christian Theology*. New York: Seabury Press.

Garfinkle, Harold. 1984. *Studies in Ethnomethodology*. New York: Polity Press.

Gaskell, George Arthur. 1960. *Dictionary of All Sacred Scriptures and Myths*. New York: Julian Press.

Geertz, Clifford. 1973. *The Interpretation of Cultures: Selected Essays*. New York: Basic Books.

――――. 1983. *Local Knowledge: Further Essays in Interpretive Anthropology*. New York: Basic Books.

Gerth, H. H., and C. Wright Mills. 1946. *From Max Weber: Essays in Sociology*. New York: Oxford University Press.

Giddens, Anthony. 1972. *Emile Durkheim: Selected Writings*. Cambridge: Cambridge University Press.

――――. 1983. *A Contemporary Critique of Historical Materialism*. Berkeley: University of California Press.

Giddings, Paula. 1974. *When and Where I Enter: The Impact of Black Women on Race and Sex in America*. New York: Bantam.

Gilkes, Cheryl. 1985. "Together in Harness: Women's Traditions in the Sanctified Church." *Signs* 10, no. 4:678–99.

――――. 1986. "The Role of Women in the Sanctified Church." *Journal of Religious Thought* (Spring 1986): 24–41.

Gilligan, Carol. 1982. *In a Different Voice: Psychological Theory and Women's Development*. Cambridge, Mass.: Harvard University Press.

Girard, René. 1986. *Violence and the Sacred.* Trans. Patrick Gregory. Baltimore: Johns Hopkins University Press.

Glennon, Lynda. 1979. *Women and Dualism: A Sociology of Knowledge.* New York: Longman.

Godlove, Terry. 1986. "Epistemology in Durkheim's *Elementary Forms of Religious Life.*" *Journal of the History of Philosophy* 24, no. 3:385–401.

Goldenberg, Naomi. 1979. *The Changing of the Gods: Feminism and the End of Traditional Religions.* Boston: Beacon Press.

Gould, Carol C. 1983. *Beyond Domination: New Perspectives on Women and Philosophy.* Totowa, N.J.: Rowman and Allanheld.

Gould, Carol C., and Marx W. Wartofsky. 1976. *Women and Philosophy: Toward a Theory of Liberation.* New York: Putnam and Sons.

Gramsci, Antonio. 1983. *Prison Notebooks.* New York: International Publishers.

Grant, Jacquelyn. 1989. *White Women's Christ and Black Women's Jesus: Feminist Christology and Womanist Response.* Atlanta: Scholars Press.

Green, Martin. 1974. *The von Richthofen Sisters.* New York: Basic Books.

Griffin, Susan. 1978. *Women and Nature: The Roaring Inside Her.* New York: Harper and Row.

Hammond, Phillip E. 1985. *The Sacred in a Secular Age: Toward Revision in the Scientific Study of Religion.* Berkeley: University of California Press.

Harding, Sandra, ed. 1987. *Feminism and Methodology: Social Science Issues.* Bloomington: Indiana University Press.

Harjo, Joy. 1989. *Secrets from the Center of the World.* Steven Strom, photographer. Tucson: University of Arizona Press.

Harrison, Beverly. 1983. *Our Right to Choose: Toward a New Ethic of Abortion.* Boston: Beacon Press.

———. 1986. *Making the Connections: Essays in Feminist Social Ethics.* Boston: Beacon Press.

Hartsock, Nancy C. M. 1983. *Money, Sex, and Power: Towards a Feminist Historical Materialism.* Boston: Boston University Press.

Heschel, Abraham J. 1962. *The Prophets.* Vols. 1 and 2. New York: Harper and Row.

Heschel, Susannah, ed. 1983. *On Being a Jewish Feminist: A Reader.* New York: Schocken Books.

Hewitt, Warren E. 1988. "Base Christian Communities (CEBs) and Democracy in Brazil." Paper presented at the Annual Meeting of the Society for the Scientific Study of Religion, October 1988.

———. 1989a. "Liberation Theology as Social Science: Contributions and Limitations." In *Sociological Studies in Roman Catholicism: Historical and Contemporary Perspectives,* ed. Roger O'Toole. Lewiston, N.Y.: Mellen.

———. 1989b. "Origins and Prospects of the Option for the Poor in Brazilian Catholicism." *Journal for the Scientific Study of Religion* 28, no. 2:120–35.

———. 1990. "Religion and the Consolidation of Democracy in Brazil: The Role of the *Communidades Eclesia de Base* (CEBs)." *Sociological Analysis* 51, no. 2:139–52.

———. 1991. *Base Christian Communities and Social Change in Brazil.* Lincoln, Neb.: University of Nebraska Press.

Heyward, Carter. 1984. *Our Passion for Justice: Images of Power, Sexuality, and Liberation*. New York: Pilgrim Press.

Hock-Smith, Judith, and Anita Spring. 1978. *Women in Ritual and Symbolic Roles*. New York: Plenum Press.

Howitt, A. W. 1904. *Native Tribes of South-East Australia*. London: Macmillan & Co.

Hughey, Michael W. 1983. *Civil Religion and Moral Order: Theoretical and Historical Dimensions*. Westport, Conn.: Greenwood Press.

Hull, Gloria. 1982. *Some of Us Are Brave*. New York: The Feminist Press.

Hume, David. 1956. *The Natural History of Religion*. Stanford: Stanford University Press.

Hurston, Zora Neale. 1981. *The Sanctified Church*. Berkeley: Turtle Island Foundation.

Ileto, Reynaldo Clemeña. 1979. *Pasyon and Revolution: Popular Movements in the Philippines, 1840–1910*. Quezon City: Ateneo de Manila University Press.

Isasi-Díaz, Ada María, and Yolanda Tarango. 1988. *Hispanic Women: Prophetic Voice in the Church*. New York: Harper and Row.

Jaggar, Alison M. 1983. *Feminist Politics and Human Nature*. Totowa, N.J.: Rowman and Allanheld.

Jay, Nancy. 1981. "Gender and Dichotomy." *Feminist Studies* 7, no. 1:38–55.

———. 1992. *Throughout Your Generations Forever: Sacrifice, Religion, and Patriarchy*. Chicago: University of Chicago Press.

Kautsky, Karl. 1925. *Foundations of Christianity: A Study in Christian Origins*. New York: International Publishers.

Keller, Evelyn Fox. 1985. *Reflections on Gender and Science*. New Haven: Yale University Press.

Kerkvliet, Benedict J. 1979. *The Huk Rebellion: A Study of Peasant Revolt in the Philippines*. Quezon City: New Day Publications.

Kermode, Frank. 1979. *The Genesis of Secrecy: On the Interpretation of Narrative*. Cambridge, Mass.: Harvard University Press.

Kim, Yung-Chung. 1979. *Women of Korea: History from Ancient Times to 1945*. Seoul, Korea: Ewha Women's University Press.

Koehane, Nanneral O., Michelle Z. Rosaldo, and Barbara C. Gelpi. 1981. *Feminist Theory: A Critique of Ideology*. Chicago: University of Chicago Press.

Koltun, Elizabeth, ed. 1976. *The Jewish Woman: New Perspectives*. New York: Schoken Books.

Kornblum, William. 1974. *Blue Collar Community*. Chicago: University of Chicago Press.

LaCapra, Dominick. 1985. *Emile Durkheim: Sociologist and Philosopher*. Chicago: University of Chicago Press.

Lanternari, Vittorio. 1963. *The Religions of the Oppressed: A Study of Modern Messianic Cults*. New York: Knopf.

Lee, Bernard J., and Michael A. Cowan. 1986. *Dangerous Memories: Invasion and Resistance since 1492*. Kansas City: Sheed and Ward.

Lerman, Hannah. 1986. *A Mote in Freud's Eye: From Psychoanalysis to the Psychology of Women*. New York: Springer.

Lever, Janet. 1976. "Sex Differences and the Games Children Play." *Social Problems* 23:478–87.

Levine, Lawrence. 1977. *Black Culture and Black Consciousness: Afro-American Folk Thought from Slavery to Freedom.* New York: Oxford University Press.

Loewenberg, Bert James, and Ruth Bogin. 1976. *Black Women in Nineteenth-Century American Life: Their Words, Their Thoughts, Their Feelings.* University Park, Penn.: Penn State University Press.

Long, Charles. 1986. *Significations: Signs, Symbols, and Images in the Interpretation of Religion.* Philadelphia: Fortress Press.

Loomis, Charles P., and Zona K. Loomis. 1969. *Socio-Economic Change and the Religious Factor in India: An Indian Symposium on Max Weber.* New York: Van Nostrand.

Lorber, Judith, and Susan A. Farrell. 1991. *The Social Construction of Gender.* Berkeley: Sage Publications.

Lorde, Audre. 1978. *Uses of the Erotic: The Erotic as Power.* Trumansburg, N.Y.: Out & Out Books.

———. 1979. "The Erotic as Power." *Chrysalis* 9 (Fall): 29.

Lukes, Steven. 1972. *Emile Durkheim: His Life and Works.* New York: Harper and Row.

Lyotard, Jean-François. 1974. *Just Gaming.* Minneapolis: University of Minnesota Press.

———. 1984. *The Postmodern Condition: A Report on Knowledge.* Minneapolis: University of Minnesota Press.

Madan, G. R. 1979. *Western Sociologists on Indian Society: Marx, Spencer, Weber, Durkheim, Pareto.* London: Routledge and Kegan Paul.

Malinowski, Bronislaw. 1925. "Magic, Science and Religion." In *Science, Religion and Reality.* Ed. Arthur J. Needham. London: Sheldon Press.

———. 1948. *Magic, Science, and Religion and Other Essays.* Boston: Beacon Press.

Mariz, Cecilia. 1988. "Popular Culture, Base Communities, and Pentecostal Churches in Brazil." Paper presented at the Annual Meeting of the Society for the Scientific Study of Religion, October 1988.

Marx, Karl. 1967. *Capital.* Vols. 1 and 3. New York: International Publishers.

———. 1973. *The Grundrisse.* New York: Vintage Books.

———. 1975. *Early Writings.* Ed. Lucio Colletti; trans. Rodney Livingstone and Gregor Benton. New York: Vintage Books.

Marx, Karl, and Friedrich Engels. 1964. *Karl Marx and Friedrich Engels on Religion.* Ed. Reinhold Niebuhr. New York: Schocken Books.

Masters, R. E. L. 1974. *Eros and Evil: Psychopathology and Witchcraft.* Baltimore: Penguin Books.

Mauss, Marcel. 1972. *A General Theory of Economic History.* London: Routledge and Kegan Paul.

McLellan, David. 1987. *Marxism and Religion: A Description and Assessment of the Marxist Critique of Christianity.* New York: Harper and Row.

McMillan, Carol. 1982. *Women, Reason, and Nature: Some Philosophical Problems with Feminism.* London: Basil Blackwell.

Mill, John Stuart. 1868. *The Social and Political Dependence of Women*. Boston: William S. Spencer.

Mitzman, Arthur. 1969. *The Iron Cage: An Historical Interpretation of Max Weber*. New York: Knopf.

Mol, Hans. 1976. *Identity and the Sacred: A Sketch for a New Social-Scientific Theory of Religion*. Oxford: Basil Blackwell.

Mollencott, Virginia Ramey. 1983. *The Divine Feminine: The Biblical Imagery of God as Female*. New York: Crossroad.

Morgan, Robert, and Michael Pye, eds. 1977. *Ernst Troeltsch: Writings on Theology and Religion*. Atlanta: John Knox Press.

Morris, Brian. 1987. *Anthropological Studies of Religion: An Introductory Text*. Cambridge: Cambridge University Press.

Mudflower Collective. 1985. *God's Fierce Whimsy: Christian Feminism and Theological Education*. New York: Pilgrim Press.

Mumford, Lewis. 1961. *The City in History: Its Origins, Its Transformation, and Its Prospects*. New York: Harvest/HBJ Books.

New Bible Dictionary. 1982. Wheaton: Tyndale Press.

New English Bible. 1983. Oxford Study Edition. New York: Oxford University Press.

Newell, William Lloyd. 1986. *The Secular Magi: Marx, Freud, Nietzsche*. New York: Pilgrim Press.

Newton, Judith, and Deborah Rosenfelt, eds. 1985. *Feminist Criticism and Social Change: Sex, Class, and Race in Literature and Culture*. New York: Methuen.

Noble, Mattie Wilcox. 1927. *Victorious Lives of Early Christians in Korea*. Seoul: Christian Literature Society.

O'Keefe, Daniel Lawrence. 1982. *Stolen Lightning: A Social Theory of Magic*. New York: Continuum Books.

Otto, Rudolf. 1952. *The Idea of the Holy: An Inquiry into the Non-rational Factor in the Idea of the Divine and Its Relation to the Rational*. Trans. John W. Harvey. New York: Oxford University Press.

Pagels, Elaine. 1981. *The Gnostic Gospels*. New York: Vintage.

Park, Robert E., and Ernest W. Burgess. 1967. *The City*. Chicago: University of Chicago Press.

Patterson, Orlando. 1982. *Slavery and Social Death: A Comparative Study*. Cambridge: Harvard University Press.

Pickering, W. S. F. 1975. *Durkheim on Religion: A Selection of Readings with Bibliographies*. Boston: Routledge and Kegan Paul.

———. 1984. *Durkheim's Sociology of Religion: Themes and Theories*. Boston: Routledge and Kegan Paul.

Portis, Edward Bryan. 1986. *Max Weber and Political Commitment: Science, Politics, and Personality*. Philadelphia: Temple University Press.

Puckett, Newbell Niles. 1969. *The Magic and Folk Beliefs of the Southern Negro*. New York: Dover Publications.

Raboteau, Albert S. 1978. *Slave Religion: The "Invisible Institution" in the Antebellum South*. Oxford: Oxford University Press.

Rabuzzi, Kathryn A. 1982. *The Sacred and the Feminine: Toward a Theology of Housework*. New York: Seabury Press.

Rahner, Karl. 1979. *Volksreligion—Religion des Volkes*. Stuttgart: Kohlhammer.

Ricoeur, Paul. 1984. *Time and Narrative*. Chicago: University of Chicago Press.

Riley, Denise. 1988. *Am I That Name? Feminism and the Category of "Women" in History*. Minneapolis: University of Minnesota Press.

Roith, Estelle. 1987. *The Riddle of Freud: Jewish Influences on His Theory of Female Sexuality*. London: Tavistock Publications.

Rolston, Holmes. 1987. *Science and Religion: A Critical Survey*. New York: Random House.

Roth, Guenter, and Wolfgang Schluchter. 1979. *Max Weber's Vision of History*. Berkeley: University of California Press.

Rowan, John. 1987. *The Horned God: Feminism and Men as Wounding and Healing*. New York: Routledge and Kegan Paul.

Rubin, Lillian. 1976. *Worlds of Pain: Life in the Working-Class Family*. New York: Basic Books.

Ruether, Rosemary Radford. 1975. *New Woman, New Earth: Sexist Ideologies and Human Liberation*. New York: Seabury Press.

———. 1977. *Mary: The Feminine Face of the Church*. Philadelphia: Westminster Press.

———. 1979. *Faith and Fratricide: The Theological Roots of Anti-Semitism*. New York: Seabury Press.

———. 1983. *Sexism and God-Talk: Toward a Feminist Theology*. Boston: Beacon Press.

———. 1984. "Sexism, Religion and the Social and Spiritual Liberation of Women Today." In Gould, Carol, *Beyond Domination*. Totowa, N.J.: Rowman and Allanheld.

———. 1985. *Women-Church: Theology and Practice of Feminist Liturgical Communities*. San Francisco: Harper and Row.

Ryan, Michael. 1982. *Marxism and Deconstruction: A Critical Articulation*. Baltimore: Johns Hopkins University Press.

Sabrosky, Judith A. 1978. *From Rationality to Liberation: The Evolution of Feminist Ideology*. Westport, Conn.: Greenwood Press.

Sargent, Lydia. 1981. *Women and Revolution: A Discussion of the Unhappy Marriage of Marxism and Feminism*. Boston: South End Press.

Sayers, Janet. 1986. *Sexual Contradictions: Psychology, Psychoanalysis, and Feminism*. New York: Tavistock Publications.

Sayers, Janet, Mary Evans, and Naneke Redclift. 1987. *Engels Revisited: New Feminist Essays*. New York: Tavistock Press.

Scharfenberg, Joachim. 1988. *Sigmund Freud and His Critique of Religion*. Trans. O. C. Dean, Jr. Philadelphia: Fortress Press.

Scharper, Philip, and Sally Scharper. 1984. *The Gospel in Art by the Peasants of Solentiname*. Maryknoll, N.Y.: Orbis Books.

Schillebeeckx, Edward. 1987. *The Church with a Human Face: A New and Expanded Theology of Ministry*. New York: Crossroad.

Schluchter, Wolfgang. 1981. *The Rise of Western Rationalism: Max Weber's Developmental History*. Trans. Guenther Roth. Berkeley: University of California Press.

————. 1987. "Weber's Sociology of Rationalism and Typology of Religious Rejections of the World." Trans. Ralph Schroeder. In *Max Weber: Rationality and Modernity*, ed. Sam Whimster and Scott Lash. Boston: Allen and Unwin.

————. 1989. *Rationalism, Religion, and Domination: A Weberian Perspective*. Trans. Neil Solomon. Berkeley: University of California Press.

Schoffeleers, Matthew, and Daniel Meijers. 1978. *Religion, Nationalism, and Economic Action: Critical Questions on Durkheim and Weber*. Assen, The Netherlands: Van Gorcum.

Scully, Diana. 1990. *Understanding Sexual Violence: A Study of Convicted Rapists*. Boston: Unwin Hyman.

Sedgwick, Eve Kosofsky. 1990. *Epistemology of the Closet*. Berkeley: University of California Press.

Seger, Imogen. 1957. *Durkheim and His Critics on the Sociology of Religion*. New York: Columbia University Bureau of Applied Social Research.

Segundo, Juan Luis. 1974a. *Our Idea of God*. Trans. John Drury. Maryknoll, N.Y.: Orbis Books.

————. 1974b. *The Sacraments Today*. Trans. John Drury. Maryknoll, N.Y.: Orbis Books.

————. 1976. *The Liberation of Theology*. Trans. John Drury. Maryknoll, N.Y.: Orbis Books.

————. 1984. *Faith and Ideologies*. Trans. John Drury. Maryknoll, N.Y.: Orbis Books.

————. 1986. *The Humanist Christology of Paul*. Trans. John Drury. Maryknoll, N.Y.: Orbis Books.

Seidman, Steven. 1983. *Liberalism and the Origins of European Social Theory*. Berkeley: University of California Press.

Shorter, Aylward. 1985. *Jesus the Witchdoctor: An Approach to Healing and Wholeness*. London: Geoffrey Chapman.

Simmel, Georg. 1955. *Conflict and the Web of Group-Affiliations*. Trans. Kurt H. Wolff and Reinhold Bendix. New York: Free Press.

————. 1959. *Sociology of Religion*. Trans. Curt Rosenthal. New York: The Wisdom Library.

————. 1982. *On Women, Sexuality, and Love*. Trans. Guy Oakes. New Haven, Conn.: Yale University Press.

Sjoo, Monica, and Barbara Mor. 1987. *The Greek Cosmic Mother*. San Francisco: Harper and Row.

Smith, Morton. 1978. *Jesus the Magician*. San Francisco: Harper and Row.

Stanton, Elizabeth Cady. 1899. *The Woman's Bible*. Seattle: Seattle Taskforce on Religion.

Starhawk. 1979. *The Spiral Dance: Rebirth of the Ancient Religion of the Great Goddess*. New York: Harper and Row.

————. 1982. *Dreaming the Dark: Magic, Sex, and Politics*. Boston: Beacon Press.

Stoltenberg, John. 1990. *Refusing to Be a Man: Essays on Sex and Justice*. New York: New American Library/Dutton.

Takla, Tendzin N., and Whitney Pope. 1985. "Force Imagery in Durkheim." *Sociological Theory* 3 (Spring): 74–88.

Tamez, Elsa. 1986. "The Woman Who Complicated the History of Salvation." In *New Eyes for Reading*, ed. Pobee and Wartenberg-Potter. Geneva: World Council of Churches.

———. 1987. *Against Machismo: Rubem Alves, Leonardo Boff, Gustavo Gutierrez, José Míguez Bonino, Juan Luis Segundo . . . and Others Talk About the Struggle of Women*. Trans. John Eagleson. Oak Park: Meyerstone Books.

Teish, Luisah. 1985. *Jambalaya: The Natural Woman's Book of Charms and Rituals*. New York: Harper and Row.

Theissen, Gerd. 1978. *Sociology of Early Palestinian Christianity*. Trans. John Bowden. Philadelphia: Fortress Press.

Thomas, Keith. 1971. *Religion and the Decline of Magic: Studies in Popular Beliefs in Sixteenth and Seventeenth Century Church*. New York: Scribner's Sons.

Thompson, John B. 1984. *Studies in the Theory of Ideology*. Berkeley: University of California Press.

Thurston, Bonnie Bowman. 1989. *The Widows: A Women's Ministry in the Early Church*. Minneapolis: Fortress Press.

Tonnies, Ferdinand. 1957. *Community and Society*. New York: Harper and Row.

Torres, Sergio, and John Eagleson, eds. 1982. *The Challenge of Liberation Theology*. Maryknoll, N.Y.: Orbis Books.

Trask, Haunani-Kay. 1986. *Eros and Power: The Promise of Feminist Theory*. Philadelphia: University of Pennsylvania Press.

Trible, Phyllis. 1978. *God and the Rhetoric of Sexuality*. Philadelphia: Fortress Press.

———. 1984. *Texts of Terror: Literary-Feminist Readings of Biblical Narratives*. Philadelphia: Fortress Press.

Troeltsch, Ernst. 1960. *The Social Teaching of the Christian Churches*. Vols. 1 and 2. Chicago: University of Chicago Press.

———. 1991. *The Christian Faith: Based on Lectures Delivered at the University of Heidelberg in 1912 and 1913*. Original lectures 1912–13. Trans. Garrett E. Paul; ed. Gertrud von le Fort. Minneapolis: Fortress Press.

Tucker, Robert C. 1978. *The Marx-Engels Reader*. New York: W. W. Norton.

Turner, Jonathan H., ed. 1989. *Theory Building in Sociology: Assessing Theoretical Comulation*. Newbury Park: Sage Publications.

Van Herik, Judith. 1982. *Freud on Femininity and Faith*. Berkeley: University of California Press.

van Leeuwen, Arend. 1972. *Critique of Heaven: The First Series of the Gifford Lectures Entitled "Critique of Heaven and Earth."* London: Lutterworth Press.

Vidich, Arthur, Joseph Bensman, and Maurice R. Smith. 1965. *Reflections on Community Studies*. New York: John Wiley and Sons.

Walker, Barbara. 1983. *Women's Encyclopedia of Myths and Secrets*. New York: Harper and Row.

Wallace, Ruth. 1989. *Feminism and Sociological Theory*. Newbury Park: Sage Publications.

Warner, R. Stephen. 1970. "The Role of Religious Ideas and the Use of Models in Max Weber's Comparative Studies of Non-Capitalist Societies." *Journal of Economic History* xxx, no. 1:74–99.

Weber, Marianne. 1975. *Max Weber: A Biography*. New York: John Wiley and Sons.

Weber, Max. 1947. *The Theory of Social and Economic Organization*. New York: Oxford University Press.

———. 1949. *Max Weber on the Methodology of the Social Sciences*. Tran. and ed. Edward A. Shils and Henry A. Shils. New York: Free Press.

———. 1958. *The Protestant Ethic and the Spirit of Capitalism*. New York: Scribner's Sons.

———. 1963. *Sociology of Religion*. Boston: Beacon Press.

———. 1966. *The City*. New York: Free Press.

———. 1978. *Economy and Society: An Outline of Interpretive Sociology*. Vols. 1 and 2. Ed. G. Roth and C. Wittich. Berkeley: University of California Press.

———. 1984. *General Economic History*. Trans. Ira Cohen. New Brunswick: Transaction Books.

Weingartner, Paul. 1960. *Experience and Culture: The Philosophy of Georg Simmel*. Middletown, Conn.: Wesleyan University Press.

West, Cornel. 1982. *Prophesy Deliverance! An Afro-American Revolutionary Christianity*. Philadelphia: Westminster Press.

———. 1988. *Prophetic Fragments*. Grand Rapids: Eerdmans.

Whimster, Sam, and Scott Lash, eds. 1987. *Max Weber: Rationality and Modernity*. Boston: Allen and Unwin.

Wilmore, Gayraud S. 1983. *Black Religion and Black Radicalism: An Interpretation of the Religious History of Afro-American People*. Maryknoll, N.Y.: Orbis Books.

Winquist, Charles E. 1986. *Epiphanies of Darkness: Deconstruction in Theology*. Philadelphia: Fortress Press.

Wirth, Louis. 1961. *The History of Cities*. San Diego: Harvest/HBJ Books.

Wolff, Kurt H. 1950. *The Sociology of Georg Simmel*. New York: Free Press.

———. 1959. *George Simmel 1858–1918*. Columbus: Ohio State University Press.

Worsley, Peter. 1968. *The Trumpet Shall Sound: A Study of "Cargo" Cults in Melanesia*. New York: Schocken Books.

Wuthnow, Peter. 1979. *The Religious Dimension: New Directions in Quantitative Research*. New York: Academic Press.

———. 1985. "Science and the Sacred." In *The Sacred in a Secular Age*, ed. Philip E. Hammond. Berkeley: University of California Press.

NAMES INDEX

SUBJECT INDEX